Praise for
TO SAVE AN ELEPHANT

'Allan Thornton and Dave Currey's story is a savage indictment of an obscene trade . . . A real-life adventure yarn, it is laced with chilling encounters'

BBC Wildlife Magazine

'In a flurry of moral courage, the world agreed to shut down the international ivory trade . . . Without Thornton's sleuthing, the poachers could still be doing business'

Country Living

'It's thanks to Allan Thornton and his team that future generations will know what African elephants look like . . . A daring investigation'

Options

'*To Save An Elephant* is a blend of intrigue and comedy, low politics and high adventure'

Toronto Star

'The best of this spring's conservation-based books'

Time Out

TO SAVE AN ELEPHANT

The Undercover Investigation into the Illegal Ivory Trade

Allan Thornton
and
Dave Currey

BANTAM BOOKS

TORONTO · NEW YORK · LONDON · SYDNEY · AUCKLAND

ACKNOWLEDGEMENTS

Our heartfelt thanks to Pam Cockerill for her great patience in working on the manuscript. Without Pam's dedication we would not have been able to produce the book.

We would like to pay tribute to Christine Stevens for her support and encouragement. None of our investigations would have happened without Christine's inspired dedication to saving the elephants.

We cannot thank in name many of the people who assisted us or who provided invaluable information, documents, tapes and copies of interviews without endangering their lives or positions. But we acknowledge their vital contribution to our investigations.

We especially wish to thank those researchers and interviewers who provided us with vital evidence in the form of taped interviews.

We have been particularly lucky to have worked with a devoted team of caring people at EIA: Jenny and Clive Lonsdale, Charmian Gooch, Susie Watts, Dr Ros Reeve, L.A. 'Nick' Carter, Maureen Plantagenet, Lorna Mac-Kinnon, Paula Whiting, Steve Trent, Peter Knights and Tina Harper.

Grateful acknowledgement is due to the Wildlife Conservation Society of Tanzania (WCST) which led the successful effort to persuade Tanzania to propose the

Appendix One listing. Thanks must go to Liz and Neil Baker, Sidney, Costa Mlay, and Ned Kitomari. Thanks are also due to Martin Lumbanga, Paul Sarakikya, Gerald Bigarubi and to President Mwinyi, the Patron of the WCST.

We would like to give very special thanks to Jorgen Thomsen and also to:

Jim Ackhurst, Nathan Adams, Brigitte Albrecht, George Alexiou, Sue Allen, Tor Allen, Carrie Baird, John Ballard, Alex Barbour, Jon Barzdo, Duncan Baxter, Ray Bolze, Richard Bonham, Peter and Jane Bouquet, Stephen Broad, John Caldwell, Jeff Canin, Juanita Carberry, Philip Cayford, J.F. Chavrier, Bill Clark, Steve Cobb, Genevieve Cooper, Tim Corfield, Joseph L. Cullman 3rd, Paul Davies, Mohinder Dhillon, Anne Dingwall, Iain and Oria Douglas-Hamilton, Dave Drummond, Maggie Eales, Steve Ellis, Brian Emmerson, Jo Fletcher, Kathryn Fuller, Polly Ghazi, Nick Gordon, Mark Graham, Desmond Hamill, Patrick Hamilton, Gary Hodges, Clive Hollands, Brian Jackman, Katia Kanas, Mickey Kaufman, Roz Kidman Cox, Peter Knight, Ron Lambertson, Sandy Laming, Richard Leakey, Geoffrey Lean, John Ledger, Gerd Leipold, Sue Lieberman, Cathy Liss, Sue Llewellyn, John Lovell, Quentin Luke, Simon Lyster, Jeanne Marchig, Elke Martin, Esmond Bradley Martin, Mike McCarthy, Isabel McCrea, Kassie McIlvaine, Steve McIlvaine, Diane McMeekin, Ian MacPhail, John Merritt, Cynthia Moss, Simon Muchiru, Jack Murray, Greg Neale, Craig van Note, Perez Olindo, Bill and Lydia Pace, Pierre Pfeiffer, Joyce Poole, Peter Pueschel, Tricia Pye, Ian Redmond, Jo Revill, Holly Reynolds, Mstislav Rostropovich, Nehemiah Arap Rotich, Lissa Ruben, Marcus Russell, Sean Ryan, Paul Schindler, Virginia Schwein, Daphne Sheldrick, Tsang Shuk Wa, Roger Stevens, Gary Streiker, Mike Sutton, Aileen B. Train, Will Travers, Simon Trevor, Iain Walker, Jill Woodly, Bill and Ruth Woodly, Heathcote Williams, Roger Wilson.

Greenpeace Germany and Emmerson Press of Coventry deserve special thanks for their vital assistance and support, as do the following groups and companies:

African Wildlife Foundation, American Humane Association, Amnesty for Elephants, Animal Welfare Institute, The Bellerive Foundation, Elefriends, Environmental Investigation Agency Ltd, Greenpeace UK, Greenpeace US, East African Wildlife Society, Humane Society of the US, Independent Television News, Monitor Consortium, St Andrews Animal Fund, The David Shepherd Conservation Foundation, Society for Animal Protective Legislation, Traffic International, Traffic USA, Wildlife Trade Monitoring Unit, World Wide Fund for Nature (UK), World Wildlife Fund (US).

However, we do not wish to suggest in any way that the contents or material contained in this book are endorsed by the above named people or organizations.

INTRODUCTION

NOVEMBER 1988,
KENYA

The sunrise was disappointing. You feel cheated when you get up really early and the sun doesn't even bother. But the reason was obvious as soon as we stepped out on to the veranda. It had been raining hard for most of the night, and dark clouds were still hanging in the sky away to the east. The rust-coloured soil of the Tsavo national park looked several shades darker than on the previous day, with pools of water lingering in ruts and hollows. There'd obviously been quite a downpour, which meant there was a chance that some of the river-crossings we planned to use might be impassable. It would be ironic after all the build-up to this trip if nature had sabotaged it at the last minute.

It had been almost a year since the Environmental Investigation Agency had started its enquiry into ivory poaching. During that year the EIA team had been to Dubai, to Hong Kong and to America. In our pursuit of the illegal ivory trail we had talked to the smugglers who, under cover of darkness, carried tusks out to dhows and sailed back to the Middle East with them; we had interviewed the carvers who fashioned the ivory into grotesque ornaments; we had even spoken to the big Chinese dealers whose BMWs and Paris apartments were paid for by that same illegal ivory. In the course of these enquiries we had seen many thousands of poached tusks – laid out on warehouse floors, spilling out of sacks, being sliced like logs by band-saws, and carved into unnatural shapes by dentist's drills. Today at last we hoped to see tusks where they belonged: on the African elephant, in the wild. We were looking forward to it.

Following the rest of the party, we climbed into the Toyota Land Cruiser and, sliding back the roof, scrambled on to the top of the vehicle. The journey was a rough one. Every now and then, as we bounced into a gully, the vehicle's wheels spun ominously in the mud. 'Sacrebleu! Shit!' our French-born driver cursed, struggling with the gears. But on each occasion we regained traction and lurched on to the next hazard.

Jill, one of our volunteer guides, whose eyesight had been honed by a lifetime in the bush, spotted our quarry before we did. 'Over there!' Unsteadily she stood up inside the vehicle and pointed over the top of the roof. 'Elephant!'

Following her gaze, we could just make out a small herd in the distance. Eight animals: three adults and five young of various ages, their grey hides stained rusty red from dust-baths in the Tsavo soil. There seemed a disproportionate number of young in the group. 'You see herds like this all over Tsavo these days,' Jill told us. 'The poachers shoot cows whether they've got young with them or not. There are a lot of orphans. Most of them die, but sometimes another cow will foster them. That's probably what's happened here.'

Our driver took the Toyota as close as he dared, but the elephants were nervous and swung round to watch us before we could approach within a hundred metres. Then in unison they started to move away, heads up and trunks raised in alarm. There is something primevally magnificent about an elephant as it moves at speed through the savannah. We watched spellbound.

But Lissa, our other guide, had been studying the largest cow intently through her binoculars. 'I think she's wounded,' she announced suddenly. She passed her glasses to us. Something dark and pendulous was hanging down from the cow's belly in front of one of her hind legs. Instantly our pleasure at the sighting evaporated. It looked as though the poachers had got here before us.

'I think it's part of her gut,' said Lissa. 'We'd better get on and report it. It doesn't look good.'

'Who'll you report it to?'

'We have a friend who's a warden and lives inside the park. I'll tell him to look out for her.'

'What can they do?'

Lissa shrugged. 'Shoot her if she goes down. Maybe take the orphans into the sanctuary. There's nothing else you can do in a situation like this.'

We made a slight diversion to reach the park warden's office where Lissa left details of the location of the herd.

Half an hour later, as we headed towards the Galana river, we spotted another elephant herd a mile or so from the track. Like the first group, when they sighted us their trunks rose up like periscopes as they tested the air for our scent. Jill shook her head. 'They never used to be so jumpy. These days it's as if they all know about the poaching.'

We moved on, pausing occasionally, diverted by herds of impala and gazelle. Once we came unexpectedly on a troupe of baboons sitting in our path and spent several minutes watching as they carried on imperturbably grooming each other.

Eventually we reached the river and turned on to the rough track that ran along its bank. The Galana was not in flood as we had feared and, though storm-clouds still brewed on the horizon, the midday sun had broken through and was now drying out the greasy red clay making the going easier. Every now and then we passed great heaps of bleached bones near the edge of the water. 'They're all elephant,' Jill said, confirming our suspicions. 'This is an area that's taken a real hammering from the poachers.'

Soon after crossing a rickety bridge we rounded a bend in the road to find ourselves face to face with a solitary bull elephant. It was hard to say who was more taken aback. He was only about thirty feet away, and at our sudden appearance he shook his head and raised his trunk defensively. Our driver kept the engine ticking over in case the elephant charged, while we dived for cameras and video equipment to record the moment. We wanted all the pictures of elephants we could get for our ivory ban campaign, particularly if they had large tusks as this one did. After allowing us a few good shots the bull decided against standing his ground and backed nervously away into the scrub.

Setting off again down-river, we had driven perhaps ten more miles when suddenly, unmistakably the pungent odour of decay hit our nostrils. We turned off the road and drove through the bush looking for the source of the smell, but we could see nothing. The surrounding land, though pancake flat for miles, was dotted with sparsely leafed bushes and acacia trees. To wildlife they acted as a useful screen from predators, but now for us they were a maddening obstruction. The dust the Toyota's tyres were stirring up didn't help, either. Abruptly, as quickly as it came, the scent of death disappeared, and for twenty minutes we drove in fruitless circles.

Then, all at once, we caught the stench again. Turning the Toyota around, our driver headed determinedly in the opposite direction. Moments later, he braked sharply. 'Over there.' He pointed.

In a clearing in front of us, twenty feet apart, lay the bodies of two adult elephants. They had not been dead very long. Pools of blackish liquid still lay on the sun-baked soil around their bellies. But most of their flesh had already been devoured from the inside by scavengers, leaving their tough hides shrunkenly clinging to the bones beneath. Vulture droppings covered the carcasses like trailing splashes of whitewash, while from each huge head the empty eye-sockets stared out blindly. Below each socket was the explanation for their deaths. Where the long curved ivory tusks should have emerged there was nothing. Just hacked and mutilated holes.

We got out of the Toyota and walked towards the bodies. No-one spoke. The shocked silence was broken only by the constant buzzing of blow-flies. The overwhelming feeling of anger which each of us was experiencing was not something we had anticipated. This, after all, is what we had driven out here hoping to find. Statistically speaking, we knew already that killings like these happened a hundred thousand times across Africa each year. That discovery was what had prompted us to set up EIA's investigation into the illegal ivory trade in the first place. But until today our knowledge of ivory poaching had been theoretical. What we saw now, decaying hideously before our eyes, was the reality.

We set up the video equipment and moved around the bodies with our cameras, each of us thinking professionally now: light, angle, frame. We wanted to show this to millions of people. To force them to look, to smell the rotting flesh, to feel as nauseous as we did at the cruelty and waste involved in killing elephants for their ivory.

This was what buying ivory ornaments and jewellery meant. This was what it was all about. The image in the viewfinder of two dead elephants set against a background of brewing storm-clouds portrayed the threat to the African elephant better than words or statistics could ever do. These two lives had been squandered, not for food, not for clothing, but for trinkets for rich European and American tourists. In the last ten years a million elephants had died hideously like these, mown down with AK47 automatic rifles, their faces hacked off with machetes. Over half of the entire African elephant population.

Somehow we had to make people everywhere feel

as incensed as we did about what was happening. If we failed, if this slaughter continued unabated, the consequences were unthinkable. Before the end of the twentieth century the African elephant could become extinct.

I

FEBRUARY 1987,
LONDON

ALLAN

It had all started one winter's day when the phone rang in the dingy room in Farringdon Road, north London, which then served as the Environmental Investigation Agency's office.

The telephone call was from Peter Bouquet, a former skipper of *Rainbow Warrior*, with whom I'd worked many times. Peter knew what kinds of issue we dealt with at EIA. Our territory was anything that threatened wildlife; particularly if there was a possibility of a species becoming extinct.

'Allan, there's someone I think you should meet,' Peter announced. 'He's got a story to tell about ivory poaching that I think might interest you.'

'Ivory poaching? What exactly does he know about it?' I said hesitantly. My reticence had two origins: I knew little about elephants, ivory or poaching at that time, and EIA was already committed to an investigation into the export of monkeys for vivisection laboratories. I really didn't think we could cope with another project.

'Believe me,' said Peter. 'I think this could be important. Meet the guy.'

I pondered for a moment. But I'd known Peter for a long time and trusted his judgement.

'OK,' I agreed. 'See if you can fix something up.'

EIA had only been in existence for two and a half years. To

say we were a small organization is to exaggerate. *Minuscule* would be more accurate. There were just three of us. Myself, Dave Currey and Jennifer Lonsdale; all committed conservationists. We had formed the group after years of involvement with Greenpeace and other environmental groups. I had been executive director of Greenpeace UK, Jenny had been a director of Greenpeace in California, while Dave had worked as official photographer on various conservation campaigns including several for Greenpeace. In the early eighties we had all begun to feel hampered by the bureaucracy creeping into Greenpeace. I found it particularly frustrating. We loved Greenpeace, but all three of us felt a niche existed for a smaller, independent group, one which could react quickly and investigate problems involving wildlife wherever they arose. We knew that there were dozens of issues waiting to be dealt with.

In 1984 we registered EIA as a company. We had no money, and our only assets apart from our combined experience were two ancient typewriters and unbounded, perhaps unrealistic enthusiasm.

At first EIA had survived on virtually no income. We, its directors, earned a living from freelance work – Jenny as a caterer, Dave as a photographer and photography lecturer, while I, having retired from Greenpeace UK, worked as an environmental consultant for various groups. All our savings went into EIA.

Since its inception, with the aid of those savings and various grants and loans, we had conducted several successful investigations and had also grown practised at waging our own campaigns. Probably our most successful one to date had been directed at the annual slaughter of thousands of pilot whales in the Danish Faroe Islands north of Scotland. Our report on this barbaric hunt had received widespread television coverage and had provoked a public outcry. We had followed that up with a report on the illegal pirate whalers who hunted protected species of great whales. After that came an exposé of the horrific

2

conditions under which wild birds were exported from Senegal to supply pet shop cages around the world. All our work had been well received by other conservation groups. It seemed we had been right. There was room in the environmental movement for an independent investigation team.

We were never short of cases to follow up. Tales of horrors, particularly concerning trade in wild animals, flooded in. Frequently the question was not what to investigate next, but what to ignore or postpone looking into because of lack of funds and lack of personnel. In 1987 at the time of Peter Bouquet's crucial phone call, the full-time staff consisted only of Dave and a secretary. Both Jenny and I had been forced to cut down on the amount of time we spent working for EIA: Jenny because she had just had a baby, I because I had just been asked to return as executive director of Greenpeace UK. The group had been overwhelmed by public support following the bombing of *Rainbow Warrior* in New Zealand, and I went back to help with the administration and campaign problems. Consequently EIA was stretched to the limit, both in terms of manpower and of finance, which meant at that time we were really not looking for another issue to investigate.

Although my knowledge of the African elephant was limited, I had heard rumours that the species was in serious trouble. In 1981 on a visit to South Africa I had been told by Anthony Hall-Martin, a government scientist, that he expected Africa's current population of 1.3 million elephants to be reduced to a mere 100,000 'in the long term'. 'It's inevitable,' he had shrugged. 'Their habitat is shrinking because the human population in Africa is growing.'

Although, even then, I'd been concerned about the elephants' plight, I had largely accepted what I had been told. It was the way of the world, I thought. Loss of habitat. No-one could do anything about that.

3

I wasn't ignorant of the existence of the ivory trade, but other groups told us it was strictly controlled. There was a quota system governing the number of elephant tusks that could be legally traded each year, and a government export permit was required for each tusk exported from Africa. The issue of permits was supervised by CITES, the Convention on International Trade in Endangered Species. With all this control, to the layman it seemed unlikely that the demand for ivory could have played much part in the dramatic decline in elephant numbers. However, I was aware that CITES control systems had not always been as effective in practice as they appeared on paper.

So Peter's mention of ivory poaching aroused my curiosity. How could there be poaching when tusks could not be traded without permits? Where did poachers find a market for the ivory? I was intrigued.

A few days later, Dave and I found ourselves sitting at a table in a crowded London pub opposite an apprehensive-looking Scotsman of about sixty.

'If anyone finds out I've talked to you, I'll be dead,' he announced by way of introduction.

'OK. It's in confidence. You don't even have to give us your name if you don't want to,' I assured him. 'All we're interested in is what you've got to tell us. Not who you are.'

The man glanced furtively around the smoky bar. 'The thing is . . .' he started hesitantly. 'I'm a seaman. That's my living; it always has been. But I'm fond of animals, too. That's why I'm telling you this. Because I think what's going on is wrong.' He took a gulp of beer and cleared his throat.

'Just tell us what you think *is* going on.' Like me, Dave was well practised by now at encouraging nervous informants.

The man nodded. 'Right. This is what I know. A few months ago I was in port in Saudi and I ran into an old

4

friend I hadn't seen for years. We got together one night over a few drinks to talk about old times. I told him what I was doing. Then I asked him what he was up to now. He said he was working on a ship called *Fadhil Allah*. "What do you carry?" I asked him. "Ivory. Poached ivory." ' The man looked from me to Dave, assessing the effect of his words.

'You need certificates to take ivory out of Africa now. How do they get it through Customs?' asked Dave.

'They don't go through Customs, do they?' the man responded. 'Listen.' Gesturing to us to move closer, he lowered his voice. 'This mate of mine told me exactly how it was done. He says they've been smuggling ivory for years. *Fadhil Allah* is a small coastal vessel. It's owned by a Yemeni sheikh. The ship's based in Mombasa in Kenya. When the sheikh has a shipment to collect he phones his local agent to arrange the pick-up. The crew tell the port authorities that they are sailing to Dubai, but after a few hours heading north they double back to Tanzania. Then they moor near a reef offshore, and after dark the tusks are brought out to them in dug-out canoes. They load up and then they sail to Dubai.'

'They won't need permits to get into Dubai, of course,' Dave murmured to me.

'Dubai isn't a member of CITES,' I explained to the man. 'That's the organization which is supposed to control trade in endangered species. But if a country doesn't belong to CITES it doesn't have to abide by its regulations.'

'I don't know anything about that, but I do know that in Dubai the sheikh sells the ivory to a Chinese man who has a factory there where he carves it.'

I was suddenly alert. 'A factory! What sort of quantity of tusks are we talking about?'

He shook his head.'Who knows? Tonnes of it. Hundreds of tonnes maybe. My mate said *Fadhil Allah* sailed every month, and he told me there are other ships, too.'

We needed to know more. 'What names or dates do you have to back this up?' I asked.

The man pulled a scrap of crumpled paper from his pocket. 'My mate told me details of one particular trip, and I memorized what he said and wrote it down later.' He grinned. 'The booze might have affected my writing a bit, but most of what he told me is here.'

I took the paper from him. There was a date – in January 1986; and a figure – nine tonnes of ivory. In addition the paper revealed the name of the Yemeni sheikh who owned the ship: Abdullah Ali Bamakramah. His ship, *Fadhil Allah*, was registered as the property of a company called Al Redha. The name of the agent in Mombasa was Said Faraj. These were just the sort of specific details we needed to check the authenticity of his story.

I felt a prickle of excitement. I had a gut feeling this man was telling the truth. And if he was, then what he had stumbled on was not small-time smuggling at all but a smoothly co-ordinated organization which was smuggling tonnes of ivory without permits out of East Africa to the Middle East. Nine tonnes sounded a lot. I tried to calculate how many dead elephants that might represent. Several hundred at least. And they shipped that amount each month!

Dave shot me a meaningful look. I knew his adrenalin was flowing, too. If the CITES control system really was being flouted in well-organized fashion – if what we had details of was a recognized route by which poached ivory was leaving Africa in large quantities – it meant that the CITES permits were not worth the paper they were written on. In reality there was no control of the ivory trade at all. Peter Bouquet had been right. I was interested. Very interested. This sounded like our kind of issue.

We thanked our informant. He finished his drink hastily and prepared to leave.

'Tell me. Do you really fear for your life if anyone finds out what you've told us?' I asked as he stood up.

He gave a slow grin. 'Come on!' he said. 'Ivory is big business. Syndicates. Big money. When you threaten an organization like that . . .' His sentence trailed off, and he drew his hand graphically across his throat. 'I hope you can do something to save the elephants. But be careful. Thanks for the drink.' And he was gone.

Over the next few days we checked the recent arrival dates of *Fadhil Allah* in Dubai with shipping contacts. They matched the dates we had been given. A company search confirmed the existence of a company called Al Redha in Dubai. Everything tied up.

We had been given a lead into a major ivory smuggling operation. The implications were shocking. If there was a ready illegal market for poached tusks – probably cash-in-hand – what future did elephants have in a continent of poverty-stricken people like Africa? 'Habitat loss' was a red herring. On this evidence it seemed likely that it was ivory poaching which was wiping out the elephants. We were on to something big. The question was what were we going to do with our information.

We found ourselves in a familiar dilemma. We were always having to back away from worthwhile projects because we hadn't got the money and we hadn't got the time. We felt very strongly about the issue of wild monkeys being trapped for vivisection, and since no-one else in Europe was doing very much on it we felt we could not back out. For several months after our pub meeting we sat uneasily on our new-found knowledge about ivory poaching. But the memory of what we had heard in the pub that night was playing on our minds. Every now and then we'd look at each other and one of us would say: 'Well? Are we going to get involved in elephants or what?'

The deciding moment came at the CITES meeting in Ottawa that year. The meeting entailed the usual vitriolic debates between conservationists, who were genuinely seeking to protect wildlife, and government representatives and wildlife traders who, though paying lip-service to the concept of conservation, were primarily committed to protecting their own interests.

Both Dave and I spoke in support of a ban on the parrot trade. Afterwards we were invited to dinner by Christine Stevens, who was president of the American-based Animal Welfare Institute. Articulate and forthright, Christine had for many years frequented the most élite Washington political and social circles and rarely missed a chance to express her views on wildlife issues to people who had the power to get things done. Christine had always been a tremendous supporter of EIA and her group had given us a grant to help with our bird-trade investigation. We had mentioned our interest in the ivory trade to her, and it was probably no coincidence that amongst our fellow guests that night was the celebrated Kenyan scientist and conservationist Iain Douglas-Hamilton. A dapper well-groomed man, easily identified by his impeccably tied cravat, Iain had devoted his life to the study of the African elephant. He had just completed a report on elephant numbers in thirty-four African countries, and over dinner he told us about its depressing conclusions.

'Every year we're finding more and more carcasses. Sometimes we find more dead elephants than live ones. There are some areas – more and more areas – where elephants have disappeared completely.' Iain made a despairing gesture. 'They're simply being wiped out. It's an elephant holocaust.'

His report had confirmed that across the whole of Africa elephant numbers had dropped by 36 per cent in just five years between 1981 and 1986. We were staggered; neither Dave nor I had appreciated that the problem was on this scale.

'What do you think is to blame?' I asked.

Iain didn't hesitate. 'It's the bloody ivory trade that's doing it. No question of it. But no-one here wants to

8

be told that, do they?' Dismissively he waved his arm towards the CITES delegates seated at other tables in the restaurant. Obviously, Iain shared our scepticism over the motivation of some CITES members.

'We heard a story the other day that ivory was being smuggled from Tanzania into Dubai,' I said carefully. 'Have you heard anything about that?'

Iain raised an eyebrow. 'Well, let's say it doesn't surprise me.'

Another of Christine's guests that evening was Kenya's Director of Wildlife, Perez Olindo. So far he had been quietly listening to our conversation, but now he intervened. 'I know that the United Arab Emirates are involved. Lots of people know about it. We've been talking about it this week. It makes me very angry. As we see it, the UAE is waging economic warfare against Kenya by allowing poached ivory to come in. If we lose our elephants, we lose our tourist industry. They know that.' His voice was bitter. 'They will bear the responsibility if it happens.'

'Do you know where the ivory goes after Dubai?' I asked.

'No. I don't think anyone knows that,' Perez replied. Dubai is being used as an entrepôt. It's not illegal to bring tusks without permits into Dubai, you see. Somehow, once it's in Dubai, it's being laundered into the system. We don't know how it's done or where it goes from there.'

'Why don't they just ban the ivory trade altogether?' Christine demanded. 'It sounds as though that's the only way to stop poaching. If selling the stuff was illegal, surely there'd be no market for the tusks?'

Iain nodded. 'Yes, but the trouble is ivory is big business. It's worth up to a billion dollars a year, and some of that money – for the legal ivory – goes to poor African countries who desperately need it. So there's a lot of resistance to a ban in all quarters. Even the World Wildlife Fund don't support a ban. They're in favour of what they call "the commercial use of elephants on a sustainable

9

basis". They say it's the only way that African countries will be persuaded to maintain their elephant populations. If they see them as a commercial asset, they'll look after them.' He shrugged. 'That's the theory anyway.'

'So WWF are banking on the CITES system of ivory controls working at some point in the future?' said Dave.

'But surely, Iain, your report proves that the policy isn't working,' Christine interrupted. 'If elephants are being wiped out by the ivory poachers as you say, they'll go extinct if something isn't done.'

Iain smiled ruefully. 'Christine, you've put it in a nutshell.'

For a moment no-one spoke. Then decisively Christine turned to me. Her thirty years of campaigning for animal welfare had made her adept at seeing her way straight to a solution for most problems.

'Allan, you and Dave are investigators. That report you've just presented on the wild bird trade in Senegal was excellent. Why doesn't EIA do something to stop the illegal ivory trade? How about your organization doing an investigation and exposé. It might make all the difference.'

As Christine had astutely guessed, after what we had just learned there was never any chance that we would say no.

2

WINTER 1987–8, LONDON

DAVE

Our first move on returning to London was to consult Jenny about the proposed elephant investigation since, as one of EIA's co-founders, she was always involved in policy decisions. She supported us wholeheartedly. 'I want there to be live elephants in Africa when my daughter grows up,' she said. 'I don't want her to have to go to a museum to see what they looked like.'

Inevitably it would mean we would spend less time looking into the wild bird trade and the trade in wild monkeys for laboratories. The pilot-whale campaign would probably suffer, too. We were just too small and understaffed to undertake more than one on-site investigation at a time. It was a tough decision. How do you choose which species of animal it is most important to protect? But ultimately the imminent threat of extinction meant we had to give priority to the African elephant.

Because of Allan and Jenny's other commitments we decided I had to have help. We hired a young history graduate, Charmian Gooch, to collate all the existing data on elephants and the ivory trade held in files around the world. Christine Stevens's group, the Animal Welfare Institute, generously gave us a grant to pay for this.

Charmian's comprehensive study, submitted four months later, was illuminating, outlining both the origins of the ivory trade and current developments. Ivory, we learned, had been a popular material with carvers for hundreds of years because it was so easy to work with; it wasn't brittle and it didn't crumble, though its qualities could vary depending on the region from which the elephant came and on its diet. Ivory was an extremely hard-wearing substance, which explained its popularity in Europe for such items as billiard balls and piano keys. In Japan netsuke carvers had developed ivory carving to a fine art, one carver often working on a single tusk for a whole year. But the netsuke carvers had never been a threat to the survival of the African elephant as a species. That threat had only arisen in the last couple of decades with the introduction of mechanized carving, and in particular with the popularity among the Japanese of something called the *hanko*.

The *hanko* is a personal seal; each one is uniquely carved. It is used in Japan both by individuals and by companies in place of a signature to endorse cheques and other documents. In the past only the face of the seal was made of ivory, which absorbs ink and transfers it well to paper. Usually the handle had been made of wood or some other material. However, it had recently become a status symbol among the Japanese to have one's *hanko* made of solid ivory. It was an easy mass market for the traders to move into. Modern machines could punch out seals with phenomenal speed. Just by making these seals, one factory in Japan claimed to get through a tonne of ivory – that meant the tusks from at least a hundred elephants – every day.

Charmian's report revealed a total world trade of approximately 800 tonnes of ivory a year. Some of this resulted from authorized culling and from the killing of rogue elephants – the 'utilization of wildlife resources' that Iain Douglas-Hamilton had mentioned to us. But an almost unbelievable 80 per cent of traded ivory was estimated to be taken from illegally killed elephants and was smuggled out without certification. Occasionally Customs officers intercepted shipments. In recent years statistics showed the average weight of confiscated tusks had fallen drastically because most of the big adult bulls had already been killed. Now the poachers were turning to younger animals. The most recent survey showed the average weight of traded tusks had reached an all-time low of four kilograms.

As long ago as 1976, CITES had recognized that there was a problem and had tried to regulate the ivory trade, but none of its 'control' systems so far had met with much success. Ivory traders always seemed to find ways around them. The current system, in which CITES officials had so much confidence, was introduced in 1986. The idea was that before leaving Africa each tusk was to be punch-stamped or marked with indelible ink with a unique code and issued with a certificate to match. Tusks were not to be allowed into CITES member countries without these certificates.

To us there was one glaringly obvious loophole in this system: CITES did not impose any control system over worked or carved ivory. So poached tusks could be fairly easily smuggled out of Africa and taken into a non-CITES country such as Dubai which had no entry restrictions even on whole uncertificated tusks. From there, once they were chopped up and even roughly carved, it would be possible to export the tusks legally to many of the big ivory trading countries in the Far East. Even at this early stage of our investigation, it seemed to us highly likely that this flaw in the CITES system was the reason behind the tusk-smuggling operations of ships like *Fadhil Allah*. Our suspicions were strengthened by a report of 'secret Middle Eastern ivory factories' which was published in *New Scientist* at about this time.

ALLAN

Over the next few weeks we challenged several officials over the CITES policy, and time and again were given the same complacent answers. The stance of Jorgen

13

Thomsen of WWF USA was typical. 'We have to give the CITES quota system time to work,' he argued.

I respected Jorgen as an intelligent and dedicated conservationist, but this time I was convinced he was wrong. 'And are we supposed to sacrifice tens of thousands of elephants for the next eighteen months while we wait to see if the WWF plan works or not?' I demanded.

Jorgen nodded. 'Yes. I'm afraid so. I know it sounds callous, but I'm sure it's the best way to save the elephants. Regulations can help if they are strictly implemented. We've seen it with other species. We have to give it a chance. WWF have invested a lot of time and effort in getting this CITES ivory quota system into operation. Our credibility is on the line here.'

'That's why you're ignoring its complete failure to stop ivory poaching, is it?' I demanded sarcastically. From where I was standing it looked suspiciously as though the WWF was more concerned with its own image than with the future of the African elephant.

Jenny, Dave and I met at EIA's office to discuss Charmian's findings. 'What we need to do is expose the illegal ivory trade from start to finish. From the killing of the elephants right down to the selling of ivory carvings in shops,' I said. 'Our best chance of making an impact is to show people that every time they buy ivory they're helping to push the elephant further towards extinction.'

But where should we begin? I took down our dog-eared atlas from the bookshelf and opened it at the map of the world. Obviously we needed to follow the route taken by the poached ivory. That would mean visits to Africa, to Dubai and to the Far East where the biggest retail outlets for ivory were to be found.

'The logical place to start would be Africa,' Dave suggested. But Jenny, who had grown up in Uganda, disagreed.

'You'd be like a fish out of water in Africa without more to go on. There are so many countries involved.

14

Where would you start? It would take far too long. And cost far too much. What about the Far East?'

'I think somewhere like Hong Kong or Singapore would be just as difficult as Africa,' I reflected. 'I know we've got lots of names of traders from Charmian, but we've no idea which of them are legitimate and which aren't. And we haven't time or money to go chasing up lots of false starts.'

It seemed that the starting-point would have to be Dubai, the bridging country which linked poachers and merchants. It would be much easier to find a focus there. We had very specific information about illicit trading within Dubai: the name of a ship, the name of a company. We knew how the ivory entered the country. What we needed to find out now was where it had come from, how it left again and what happened to it while it was in Dubai. If we were able to discover all that, we should also have leads which we could follow back to Africa and on to the Far East.

In particular we wanted to find out if the poached ivory was being carved somewhere in the United Arab Emirates. If we could get some hard documented facts on those rumoured ivory carving factories in the Middle East, it would establish our credibility. No outsiders had ever seen these factories, though the *New Scientist* article had said they were believed to be in the Jebel Ali Free Zone. But so far their existence was unsubstantiated. We needed to locate them and, better still, film inside them.

Over the next few weeks Christine Stevens and the Animal Welfare Institute raised the money to pay for our flights to Dubai. I applied for two weeks' holiday from my job at Greenpeace, and Jenny's husband, Clive Lonsdale, a freelance film cameraman, agreed to accompany us. He had been involved in many similar previous campaigns. Jenny, who was expecting their second baby very soon, would stay at home and mind the office.

In April 1988 we set out on EIA's first on-site

investigation into the ivory trade. We had no idea what we would find. Neither Dave nor I had visited the Middle East before, and we had not chosen the best moment to sample its delights. The Gulf War had recently flared up in new violence. Every week there were bombings, assassinations or hijackings; and Dubai, which was right at the edge of the trouble zone, was currently one of the world's hotspots. The handful of people that knew of our trip told us to be careful. And not just because of the Gulf War. This illegal ivory industry was big business, they warned. Three snooping environmentalists would be regarded as small fry by the illegal ivory traders. In their world violence was a way of life, with both poachers and anti-poaching officers frequently being shot and killed 'in action'.

We left from Gatwick airport. Just before we checked in Dave took a photograph of Clive and me and asked Clive to take one of him. Then he took the film out of the camera and gave it to Jenny with a smile. 'I don't suppose you'll need this, but it'll be a record if anything should go wrong. You can tell the papers what we were trying to do.'

Without comment Jenny put the film in her bag. Then she gave us all a quick smile. 'You guys keep your wits about you and your heads down,' she said. 'OK?'

3

April 1988,
United Arab Emirates

Allan

The cool night air of Dubai blew through the open window of our hired car. There was no moon and, now that we'd left the city centre behind, no street lights, either. Occasionally the car's headlights picked out the scrawny shape of a wild camel looming up out of the desert darkness.

Our destination was the Jebel Ali Free Zone, the centre of free trade where the secret ivory carving factories were rumoured to be located. We had arrived at Dubai airport earlier that day, and after finding ourselves a cheap flat to rent and dropping our bags there we had decided to take a trip to Jebel Ali to check out the area. Our aim at this stage was just to see the lie of the land, though if it looked feasible we hoped to drive around the factory sites. Although it was dark, it was only just after seven o'clock and our presence shouldn't arouse any suspicion.

We knew little about the Free Zone other than that it had been set up in a barren area roughly the size of Greater London, fifteen miles outside Dubai, with the intention of attracting trade by offering financial incentives. We had assumed it would be comparable to an oversized industrial estate in Britain. But we were wrong.

We'd been driving for twenty minutes and I guessed that we must be getting close to our destination. I leaned forward. Dave was driving, with Clive in the front passenger seat, their faces illuminated by the faint light from the dashboard. Suddenly Dave grimaced. 'Bloody hell,' he said. His foot moved to the brake pedal.

In front of us the dual carriageway broadened dramatically into a four-lane motorway. Half a mile ahead, lit up like a neon oasis, was an imposing-looking official checkpoint. Each road-lane passed beside a small office occupied by a uniformed guard. On either side of the barrier a high chain-link fence topped with barbed wire stretched away as far as the eye could see. We stared at each other aghast. 'They've got their own police force!' Clive groaned.

We had realized we might have to pass through some sort of perfunctory check before being allowed into the Free Zone, but not a fortress-style security barrier. My heart sank. Most likely this maximum security approach was to protect the businesses inside from unwelcome attention. We would have to tread carefully. We had no idea what influence the owners of the ivory factories had with the officialdom here and, for all we knew, these border police might be primed to be on the lookout for 'spies' like us.

Dave pulled up at the side of the road. 'We've got to get it right.' He switched the ignition off. 'When we drive up to that gate we have to convince those guys on duty that we're legitimate. I don't think we've got enough papers and stuff with us to do that now. If we make a cock-up of it, they'll remember us next time.'

'We're going to have to think about this,' Clive said. 'I've got a nasty feeling our story is going to make them suspicious.' Our plan had been to say that we were making a film on art objects and jewellery in UAE. But now I, too, thought this sounded naïve. It was far too close to the truth and, as Dave had just pointed out, we had very little documentation to substantiate our claim.

'I think we should go back and ring some people in the media in London,' I suggested. 'Get ourselves as many bits of paper as we can. Filming permits. References from

TV stations and newspapers. Anything that'll back up our cover-story.'

Whatever happened, we mustn't fall at the first hurdle. If we were refused entry now, that would be it. We would be unlikely to get a second chance. Dave started up the car, pulled the wheel hard over, and headed back towards Dubai.

We had rented a cheap and basic apartment which belonged to a local civil servant who was taking a month's leave in Europe. Although we hadn't met him, we already felt we knew quite a lot about 'Jock'. It appeared that he didn't drink tea or coffee, because he had no kettle. Nor did he cook, since his only cooking facility was a small pristine microwave. And apparently he had a penchant for young Arab boys: during our first two hours there we answered the phone half a dozen times to hear youthful male voices ask 'Is Jock there?' When told he was away the response was always the same: 'Never mind. What's *your* name?'

We had called at an Indian takeaway down the road and now sat on the floor of the apartment with a curry and a cold drink to discuss our plans. By the time we turned in for the night we had decided on a new and less specific cover-story. We would say that we were making a general film about trade in the United Arab Emirates. That should give us sufficient reason to want to get into the Free Zone without arousing the same suspicion that the mention of jewellery might. Next morning we were on the phone to media contacts in London organizing references. Both the *Sunday Times* and Independent Television News (ITN) came up trumps. We had told them of our trip beforehand, and within twenty-four hours they sent letters confirming that we were preparing stories on their behalf, but discreetly omitting any mention of either ivory or EIA. The day after our first abortive attempt to enter the Free Zone we took these references to the Ministry

19

of Information in Dubai and applied for a permit to film there.

'I regret it will take at least two days,' the Ministry official informed us. 'Also, if you wish to film in the port or airport in Dubai, you will have to apply for separate permits for each location as these are high-security areas. Do you wish to do that?'

There was no question about it. After the Free Zone, the port and airport were the two main places we wanted to film. With a bit of luck we hoped to find the smugglers' ship, *Fadhil Allah*, in the port, and we also intended to look in the port area for Al Redha Trading, the company of the Yemeni sheikh who owned *Fadhil Allah*.

'Well, I suppose we might as well apply for permits,' replied Clive airily.

It seemed quite on the cards that we would fall foul of Dubai officialdom during our stay, so prudently we made ourselves known to the staff of the British embassy. We were given a warm welcome in our guise as a film crew researching trade in the Middle East. On learning that there was an embassy party that night to celebrate the Queen's birthday I suggested, rather blatantly, that we would like to be invited, realizing that our cover-story would be much more credible if we'd been seen as an official film crew among Dubai society.

The Queen's birthday party in Dubai had about it an aura of old colonial days. It was held in the embassy compound, on a green tree-shaded lawn whose contrived English atmosphere was only slightly diminished by the barbed-wire fence which surrounded it. To entertain us there was an Indian military band (in scarlet uniforms with gold braid, and painfully out of tune), while for nourishment starched waiters proffered trays of drinks and fancy canapés. Guests were announced by name and greeted by a formal reception line. Not quite the sort of party we were used to, but nevertheless we enjoyed it all

20

hugely. Dave and I spent a pleasant few hours interviewing and photographing various attractive young women in cocktail dresses, supposedly for the gossip column of the *Sunday Times*, while on the other side of the lawn Clive filmed the arrival of the Sheikh of Dubai and his retinue of jewel-laden fellow guests.

It was a relief to get Clive behind a camera again. He always gets twitchy if he hasn't filmed something within twenty-four hours of arriving in a foreign country, and since our return from the Jebel Ali checkpoint he had been obsessively checking and rechecking his camera, sound-recorder, lights and so on, and growing steadily grumpier. We had now been in Dubai for nearly three days and he was almost desperate, but filming at the embassy restored him to his usual good-natured self.

Two days later our film permits, displaying our photographs and endorsed with an official stamp, were at last ready for us to pick up. We decided against going straight to the Jebel Ali Free Zone. It seemed sensible to follow up as many of our other leads as possible first. If our identity was discovered at the checkpoint, we might well have to leave the country, but provided that was our final venture we should at least have something to show for our trip.

Accordingly we drove to Dubai's thriving Port Rashid, which we thought might be where *Fadhil Allah* delivered its poached-ivory cargo. So far we had been unable to find an address for Al Redha Trading, but we were hopeful that *Fadhil Allah* might be in port. The young Englishman in charge of the port's public-relations office gave us an enthusiastic welcome, obviously glad of a break in his routine. He arranged for us to film ships loading and unloading, containers being moved and Customs paperwork being completed. Through his office window I could see a huge oil-tanker berthed across the harbour, its port side smashed open in a tangle of wreckage. 'Another ship bombed by the Iranians,' he explained, following my gaze. 'If they belong to the US or a Western nation, they come straight in here for repair. But it's done discreetly. Don't point your camera at them or you could find your way home in a hell of a hurry.' We were obviously going to have to step warily to avoid treading on anyone's toes, even accidentally, in Dubai.

We looked through the list of ships in port but we were out of luck: *Fadhil Allah* was not among them. Finding her might have to wait until another trip. We decided to get as much material as possible anyway, and with our guide's co-operation we filmed from the port control-tower. Rows and rows of containers lined the dock area, with strange vehicles like mechanical spiders moving between the rows to pick up the long metal boxes and deliver them to the ship-side where they were loaded by gantry.

'You'd never know if there was ivory in there, would you?' Dave muttered. He was right. The widespread use of these containers had made the task both of Customs officer and of wildlife investigators much harder. One container might take Customs officers twenty-four hours to unload and search. The chance of uncovering a cache of poached ivory in a mass of containers like this was negligible. Not that anyone would bother even to look here in Dubai where trading in ivory was perfectly legal.

Shuffling along a narrow walkway on top of a hundred-foot crane, we filmed it unloading containers far below us. I was never too keen on heights and was struggling to fight off vertigo as I recorded sound for Clive. Unsympathetically Dave pointed his camera at us to record the moment. 'Fall now and the elephants have had it,' he grinned.

Climbing back down the crane, we were temporarily diverted as from somewhere far below the breeze wafted up an unwholesome scent. We traced it to a boat with a dozen open decks stacked one on top of the other. As we watched, a living stream of sheep came flooding down a gangway out of the vessel, falling over each other in a dusty stampede. At the bottom of the ramps, teams of men drove the animals into waiting trucks.

We learned that the boat had brought some 60,000 sheep from Australia, a 12,000-mile voyage. They were to be trucked all over the Middle East before being ritually slaughtered at the start of Ramadan. On the dockside a port worker came up to us. 'Two thousand of those sheep died on the way from Australia,' he confided. 'When they get sick and fall down, the crew just throw them over the side.'

We forced ourselves to put it out of our minds, conscious that we had to concentrate on the ivory story. It was unbearably hot, with the temperature in the high nineties, and it was a relief when Clive finally declared himself satisfied with the material he had accumulated. The PR man seemed delighted with the prospect of free publicity for the port, and Dave decided to try to capitalize on his goodwill.

'We'd like to get over to the Jebel Ali Free Zone,' he said casually as we bade our farewells. 'Is there any chance you could arrange that for us?'

'No problem. I know my counterpart there.' Obligingly the PR man picked up the phone and moments later was fixing an interview with the chairman of Jebel Ali Free Zone, who went by the name of Sultan bin Sulayem. Things seemed to be going our way.

The chairman was away on business, but an appointment was made for us to meet him in four days' time and the PR man relayed our address to his office so that an official invitation could be sent to us. Pleased with our day's work, we returned to our apartment for another uncomfortable night on the collections of lumpy cushions that passed for beds. For the third night in succession my sleep was disturbed by the telephone ringing. 'Is Jock there?' asked a boyish voice.

I groaned. 'Try again in a month,' I said and took the phone off the hook.

The plan for the next day was to visit the Dubai Customs statistics department. Our hope, though it seemed a pretty forlorn one, was that their import and export records might itemize movements of ivory in and out of the country. Even more forlornly, we thought we would try to obtain copies of any such records.

We fed the chief statistician the story of our film on trade, praising his work and enthusing on its importance. I explained that a copy of the import–export figures would help reduce our own workload considerably. He was an elderly man and seemed overwhelmed by our compliments. He instantly reached into his desk and to our astonishment produced a thick computer printout.

'These are all the imports and exports of Dubai for 1987,' he smiled, handing them over to us.

While Dave and Clive plied the statistician with specious questions about import trends, I searched feverishly through the index to commodity categories. Suddenly, unbelievably I found it. 'Ivory, unworked or simply prepared. Category 291–01.' Quickly I thumbed through the printout to the relevant page, and my eyes feasted on the information in front of me.

Listed in a long neat column were all the countries from which the ivory had been imported: Burundi, North Yemen, Zaïre, Kenya, Tanzania, Indonesia, Zambia, Spain . . . In another column were the exact amounts received from each country in tonnes and kilos.

I nudged Dave's arm. Realizing I must have discovered something significant, he launched once more into a stream of non-stop chatter, giving me time to scribble the figures into my notebook. Almost 150 tonnes of ivory had passed through Dubai in 1987. A rough-and-ready conversion told me that approximately 15,000 elephants had been killed to supply that ivory. Since, according to our information, Dubai's role in the ivory trade was simply to launder poached ivory, then almost certainly most of those 15,000 elephants had been shot illegally.

I turned to the next page. Maintaining a poker-face was becoming an effort. I was confronted by a list of the countries to which the illicit ivory had been exported: Hong Kong, Taiwan, Singapore, South Korea, India, China and – I did a double take – the United States of America!

My notebook was filling up. Dave gave me a sideways glance and said to the statistician: 'Would it be possible to have a copy of this printout, do you think?'

The old man was apologetic. 'We don't have any spare printouts. We just have two copies, and the Dubai government requires them both for its own records.'

Dave adopted his best cajoling manner. 'Wouldn't it be possible to give us one of them, and you could print out another copy to replace it? It would save us so much work.'

The statistician hesitated, then shrugged. 'Yes, I suppose we could print out another copy; but I would have to charge you for the computer time, I'm afraid.'

We didn't give him a chance for second thoughts. We handed over the required fee of 1,000 dhiran (about £140) to replace the printout, and his assistant duly brought us the second copy of the statistics.

As soon as we got back to Jock's apartment we spread the printout on the floor. As we pored over the statistics in that tiny room the significance of our acquisition sank in. These figures confirmed the existence of a major international ivory trading network with Dubai serving as the crucial link between Africa and Asia. It was no longer 'just a rumour'. Now we had evidence.

That night, for the first time since we'd arrived in Dubai, sleep evaded me. It was not only the uncomfortable bed. My mind was having trouble coming to terms with the sheer scale of the operation we were starting to uncover. The 150 tonnes of ivory that we now knew had passed through Dubai in 1987 was worth as much as $22½ million in its raw state – much more when it was carved. This was big business indeed.

Dubai airport was our next target. I had telephoned the air-cargo department the day before to make an appointment. What we were after was air waybills. All air freight has to be accompanied by these documents which declare not only the identity of the sender but also that of the consignee. If we could get access to the air waybills for ivory, we would not only establish the routes used but would also discover the addresses of the companies that ivory was being sent to in Asia. That would give us a starting-point for an investigation in the Far East. That was the theory.

Unfortunately the Iran/Iraq War threatened to interfere with our plans. The sky was swarming with military helicopters when we arrived at the airport, and soldiers were everywhere, both inside and outside the terminal, their automatic weapons poised ready for action. Something dramatic was obviously happening.

'What's going on?' Clive asked a man wearing an American press badge.

'The US navy has just bombed an Iranian oil-rig,' he answered. 'And, as if that's not enough, some nut has hijacked a Kuwaiti jet with half their royal family on board and they're threatening to land it here.' He smiled mirthlessly. 'It looks like being a heavy day.'

'So they're on Red Alert,' said Dave as the pressman rejoined his colleagues in front of the terminal-building. 'What a day to choose!'

To our surprise, despite all the extracurricular activity, the PR man who had been assigned to deal with the 'Film London' team, as we called ourselves, was waiting for us and greeted us with a jovial smile.

'Hi. My name's Larry. You're making a film about trade in UAE, is that right?' He led us through the checkpoints, showed our official filming permits to the airport security officers and arranged our clearance to film. From his relaxed manner you'd have thought his airport was invaded by armed forces every day of the week. We spent the morning in the cargo area, shooting film we knew we were unlikely to use, but wanting to convince them of the authenticity of our cover-story.

By midday we were ready to drop. The flaming sun was growing hotter by the minute, and we all had parched throats. Unfortunately for us, the previous evening had seen the appearance of the new moon, which signalled the start of the Muslim holy festival of Ramadan, and Muslims and non-Muslims alike were not now allowed to eat, drink or smoke during daylight hours. The combination of raging thirst, the constant noise of helicopters and the suspicious scrutiny of the soldiers was building up the tension. I felt certain that something was about to go badly wrong.

Larry, our friendly PR man, disappeared inside the cargo-building to fetch something, and almost immediately a soldier approached us. His hand hovered threateningly, over his rifle as he gestured to us to follow him. With our hearts in our mouths we walked obediently to an army vehicle where two other armed soldiers were sitting. We were motioned curtly into the back. Were we about to be unmasked? I speculated on the likely penalty for environmental investigators in Dubai and didn't like what my imagination came up with.

The jeep drove us over to another part of the airport building where we were told to get out and our captor led us indoors. Inside the building we watched apprehensively as he opened a door and disappeared. Moments later he came out and walked back towards us. He was carrying a bottle of water. Without expression he held it out to us. 'Drink!' he said.

When we had drunk our fill he drove us back to the area where we had been filming, brusquely dismissed our over-effusive thanks, and drove away. We looked at each other, and the corner of Clive's mouth twitched. 'No comment,' he said.

Larry had obtained permission for us to visit the cargo-office area and now he reappeared to take us over there. 'I'll introduce you to the senior cargo officer,' he offered as we walked past the offices of various shipping agents. 'He works just down here. I'm afraid I've another appointment, so I'll have to hand you over to him now.'

We followed Larry through a door at the end of the row of shipping agents. Inside was a small modern office with computer screens, desks and filing cabinets. The senior cargo officer, a dark man in a smart military-style uniform, shook hands with us and led us to an office worker seated in front of a computer screen. 'These people are making a film. Help them as much as you can, please,' he instructed before returning to his own desk.

The computer operator sat back in his chair and looked at us expectantly. 'How can I help you? What is your film about?' I decided not to beat about the bush. We had wasted enough time already that day. 'Our film is concentrating on the new trade markets for Dubai,' I said carefully. 'Perhaps in Asia. Is it possible for you to call up shipments by countries on your computer so we can see what exactly is being sent to them? Let's say Hong Kong, for example.'

It turned out that it wasn't possible; but, eager to help, the operator took us over to a shelf stacked with box files. 'These are all the air waybills for the different airlines for the past six months,' he said. 'I'll have to leave you to look through it yourselves, but you should find what you need in here.'

It was hard to know where to start. For nearly an hour we shuffled unproductively through pages of records, while around us the office workers went unsuspectingly about their business. Then we hit the jackpot. Out of the British Airways and British Caledonian files spilled document after document recording ivory shipments to Hong

Kong and Taiwan. It appeared that every two or three days a consignment of hundreds of kilos of carved ivory was being sent to Hong Kong on the British Caledonian flight. This was obviously one of the main routes by which the ivory smugglers were getting their 'laundered' tusks out of Dubai. The ivory was destined for various addresses in Hong Kong and the New Territories.

Clive and I followed Dave as he walked over to the senior cargo administrator, who was deep in conversation with an employee at the other side of the office. 'Do you have a photocopier we could use to copy these?' Dave asked.

The administrator studied the air waybills in Dave's hand, and apprehension clouded his face.

'These documents are for ivory!' he exclaimed nervously. 'That could make a big problem for us.'

Clive and I exchanged glances. I felt adrenalin flooding through my body.

Fortunately Dave kept cool. 'It's not illegal here, though, is it?' he responded innocently.

The man's eyes searched our faces suspiciously. 'No. It isn't,' he said irresolutely. He hesitated. 'OK. You can photocopy.'

We resumed our inspection of the files, while Dave photocopied the sheaf of ivory air waybills. Just to be on the safe side, Clive also recorded some of them in close-up on film. But we all felt we were on borrowed time now. They were suddenly edgy about us working here, and that edginess was catching.

As we worked, a crowd of office and warehouse workers had gathered round us. I felt increasingly uneasy. The presence of a film team was obviously a rare occurrence and might be the sole reason for their interest, but we couldn't be sure.

'Have you seen the shipping agents on these ivory waybills?' I demanded of Clive in a low voice. He looked.

'Gulf Express.' His brow furrowed. 'Wasn't their office just around the corner from here?'

I'd noted that, too. That did it. 'Let's call it a day,' I said. 'We don't want to get found out before we get to the Free Zone.'

Clive nodded. 'No, you're right. Just this last batch and we'll go as soon as Dave's got his photocopies.'

Reluctantly I held out more documents in front of Clive's camera and as I did so I noticed two of the workers conferring. Suddenly they turned on their heel and walked out of the building. They seemed in a hurry.

It would be foolhardy to push our luck any further. We had already copied enough to provide us with damning evidence to link the Dubai ivory factories with addresses in Hong Kong, Korea and Taiwan. I walked briskly over to Dave. 'I think they might be on to us. Let's get out of here.'

Outside, the army of press and soldiers had thinned out. Hastily we loaded Clive's heavy film equipment into our hired car and climbed in. Clive and Dave looked the way I felt: exhausted. Three hours of high tension inside the cargo office in this scorching heat had taken their toll. All at once we were weak with relief and anticlimax. And hunger, too, I realized suddenly. Apart from that one bottle of water, none of us had eaten or drunk all day. The same thought had obviously struck Clive. 'Come on. The drama's over. Let's get an Indian takeaway,' he said as Dave switched on the ignition and put the car in gear.

During the past three years it had become almost routine during our investigations to check to see if we were being followed. As I scanned the street behind us I noticed a white van pull out from the kerb seconds after we left. Circumspectly I watched it through the back window. There were two Asian men in the front seat. We took a right turn. So did the van. Another right turn. It followed.

'Maybe we shouldn't go straight home,' I suggested. 'I think we might have uninvited guests.'

A quick glance in the driving-mirror informed Dave of the situation. 'OK. We'd better see if we can lose them.' He drove a circuitous way back to the flat but, however often we doubled back on ourselves, the van kept reappearing in our rear-view mirror.

'They obviously know the backstreets of Dubai better than we do,' Clive said drily.

'Let's try down here.' Dave swung the steering-wheel abruptly around and shot down a side-street. This time the van didn't follow us. It seemed we had thrown them off.

We were on the wrong side of town by now, and it took us quite some time to find the way back to our apartment block. While we were struggling to unload the film equipment Dave nudged me. 'Don't look now. I think our friends are back.' As he spoke the white van drove slowly to the end of the street and parked there. We had to climb two flights of stairs to get to our flat. At the bottom of the stairs, I told Clive and Dave to go ahead and hung back in the shadows. After a minute the two Asians from the van appeared and started stealthily up the stairs. I gave them a few moments' start before following them cautiously. I wasn't anxious to confront them, but I did want to see what they were up to. However, when I reached the second floor, the men were nowhere to be seen.

Inside the flat we locked the door firmly behind us and with a cold drink apiece from the fridge sat down to take stock of the situation. Our discussion had barely begun when the telephone rang. Dave answered it and listened for a few seconds before beckoning silently to me. I took the receiver from him. On the other end of the phone a woman with a Chinese accent was firing questions in rapid pidgin English. I could understand little of what she was saying. The only phrase I could make out with certainty was 'English mens? Do you have English mens there?' Abruptly, after a minute or two, the woman hung up.

I sat down again, and we regarded each other contemplatively. Someone was obviously very suspicious of our activities, and since the ivory operations were known to be run by Hong Kong Chinese it seemed highly probable that the Chinese woman on the phone had been representing them.

It was not the first time we had faced opposition to the EIA's activities. All of our previous investigations – into pilot-whale killing in the Faroes, wildlife smuggling in West Africa, and dolphin killing in Turkey – had proved hazardous. On occasion, each one of us had been assaulted physically, but somehow those confrontations had felt manageable. We had been facing individuals whose livelihood was threatened, and the disputes were usually resolved on a person-to-person basis.

Now in contrast we were dealing with an organization. There were only three of us. I couldn't help wondering just how much value this organization, which derived its income from killing thousands of elephants, placed on three human lives . . .

4

ALLAN

The following morning, after an unappetizing breakfast brew of tea boiled in Jock's microwave, we set out once more on the fifteen-mile journey to the Jebel Ali Free Zone. After the events of the previous night we weren't relishing the prospect of being interrogated at the entry point. What if someone had tipped off the border guards about our activities? But our worries were unfounded. On production of our official film permits and the invitation from the chairman of the Free Zone the gateway of Jebel Ali opened before us like the door to Aladdin's cave.

We drove first to the Free Zone's administration offices where a young American woman ushered us into the office of Sultan bin Sulayem. It was one of those offices designed chiefly to impress, with no trace of any paperwork on the imposing desk from behind which the chairman, a young, impeccably dressed Arab, rose smiling to greet us. 'Good morning, gentlemen.' He spoke with a well-educated English accent.

We told him about our 'film'. He seemed delighted at the chance of publicizing the Free Zone, which was looking more and more like an expensive flop. Very few businesses had so far relocated there in spite of enormous investment. Its port, the largest man-made harbour in the world, was virtually empty of shipping. Those in charge were very anxious that the project should not fail, though probably to save face rather than money since the Dubai government with its vast income from oil was hardly short of cash.

'Do you have copies of the Jebel Ali handbook?' the chairman asked, holding out some glossy booklets.

I flipped through the handbook while the others explained our filming requirements. The guide listed more than a hundred companies. I had been afraid that the ivory factories might be registered under a false guise and be difficult to identify, but among the company names were two which openly declared their activities: Dubai Ivory and MK Jewellery. Both were owned by a Mr Poon.

The Dubai Ivory and MK Jewellery factories were situated in shed 65A. I folded the book open at that page and passed it to Clive with a meaningful look. While Dave and I kept the chairman engaged in conversation, Clive set up his lights and camera. On the wall was a huge aerial photograph of the Free Zone in which every shed was numbered. 'I'd like to film the office before we do the interview with you if that's all right – just to get some background.' Clive smiled disarmingly. He panned his camera slowly around the office walls, pausing when he came to the aerial photograph. The chairman looked on benignly, unaware that Clive's camera lens was zooming in on shed 65A.

The formal filmed interview took only a few minutes. Sultan bin Sulayem was clearly unused to being filmed and was surprisingly nervous. I asked the questions, feeding him lines which would let him extol the virtues of the Free Zone.

'We have very little red tape here because all the services are in one agency,' he said proudly. 'Everything. That means importing, exporting and Customs clearance. It makes it extremely easy for people to operate in our area.'

'Oh really?' I said, thinking that maybe we could use some of this interview in our real film after all.

When the filming was over, the chairman put a call through to the offices downstairs, and shortly afterwards a sullen-looking youth shuffled in. 'Mohammed will accompany you and show you where to go,' the chairman said. 'You can film anywhere you want to outside the factories. But if you want to film inside any company premises you'll have to get the permission of the company-owner.'

We followed Mohammed outside. He looked distinctly displeased with his assignment as chaperon. The feeling was mutual. We spent two frustrating hours filming engineering and electrical businesses until, to our relief, Mohammed got bored and left us to our own devices.

The moment he had disappeared we leaped into the car and drove to shed 65A. The home of Mr Poon's ivory factories was a long brick warehouse building which housed twelve other work-units besides his, each with huge sliding doors. Slowly circling the building in the car, we discovered that all the doors bar two on one side were wide open, allowing us to see the warehouses inside. The two that were closed were separated by three other units and were the only unlabelled units in the shed. As we passed one of these unlabelled units we noticed its doors had been left a couple of inches ajar – just enough for us to hear a strange high-pitched whining noise coming from inside. The noise was curiously reminiscent of a dentist's surgery. Intermingled with it was the unmistakable discordant sound of Chinese music.

'They've got to be carving tusks in there,' said Dave. 'How are we going to get in?'

All the windows through which we might have viewed the units were covered over. Possibly it was to keep the hot sunlight out, but it seemed more likely that it was to guard against prying eyes.

Dave stopped the car close to the gap in the door. Through it we could just see Chinese workers standing near a portable office unit. Now that we knew what we were up against, it seemed judicious to retreat and discuss our strategy rather than to risk all with a hasty approach.

Back at the flat we rejected one suggestion after another

35

as to how we could get our film. 'After that phone call last night I don't think we stand much chance if we just knock politely on the door and ask for permission,' said Clive. 'They'll almost certainly be expecting us to turn up now.'

'We could always burst in through the open door and take them by surprise,' Dave suggested whimsically. In fact the idea was not quite as ridiculous as it sounded. The door was not padlocked, and taking the workers by surprise might allow us to shoot a few feet of film. But quite possibly it would not show any poached ivory. And there was also the question of whether we would be allowed out again in one piece.

'Even if we did get out of the factory, the chances are the security police at the Free Zone gate would stop us,' Dave pointed out.

'I think our only hope is to try to approach them through the other units,' I said at last. 'We'll have to see if there's access from one of the other factories in shed 65A.'

Half-past six the next morning found us again at the Free Zone. This time we parked the car inconspicuously on an access-road some 200 metres from the ivory factories and waited. We knew from the Jebel Ali handbook that the workforce for most of the factories was brought in from Dubai. For an hour we sat, cramped and uncomfortable, watching buses and cars drive past Poon's factories. At 7.30 precisely two large vans passed us and stopped outside shed 65A. Clive had already set his camera up inside the car and started filming as the doors of the two unlabelled factory units slid open a couple of feet. With perfectly co-ordinated timing several dozen Chinese workers poured out of the vans and trailed inside the two units. As the last man entered, the factory doors slammed decisively shut behind him. They were to stay shut for the rest of the day.

Our plan was to visit all the other work-units in

the warehouse. Hopefully, one of them might offer the possibility of access or at least a good view into the ivory factories. Our first stop was at an oil-analyzing laboratory where we gave the manager the trade-film story and were welcomed in. Inside, while the others talked, I did a quick reconnaissance. I noticed that the concrete-block walls of the unit did not reach all the way up but stopped about eight feet short of the warehouse roof. That looked promising.

We visited a food-processing company on the other side of the warehouse and found it was constructed in the same way. Again the owner was happy to let us move freely around his unit. Explaining to him, quite truthfully, that I was checking out possible vantage-points for filming, I climbed on to a high platform next to a giant food-mixer and found that from it I could just see into both the ivory factories. In each unit Chinese workers were standing in front of what appeared to be band-saws all along one of the walls. But the view was too distant and restricted to be any good for filming.

We visited three other units close to the ivory factories without finding the ideal unobstructed filming viewpoint of either of the Poon operations. By the time we walked into the last possibility, a distribution warehouse for Black & Decker, we were tired, thirsty and despondent. It was nearly noon, and the temperature in the shade, if you could have found any, was well over a hundred degrees.

We must have looked in a sorry state, because one of the workers beckoned us into his office and offered us soft drinks. 'What about Ramadan?' I asked. He smiled conspiratorially. 'Just drink it out of sight!'

From the handbook we knew that the Black & Decker warehouse occupied three combined units directly adjacent to the ivory factory known as MK Jewellery. Its huge storage area was lined with several rows of high shelves each laden with boxes of the company's electrical appliances stacked on wooden pallets. We gave the manager one of the business cards I'd had printed as a precaution. It described us as being from Film London, a real company I'd set up when we were filming whaling off Norway. He happily agreed that we could film in his factory. 'I have to go out, but just ask Babu if you need anything.' He indicated our soft drink benefactor, who grinned and carried on moving pallets with his yellow forklift truck.

With the manager gone, only Babu and one other worker remained to witness our activities, and neither seemed in the least suspicious of us. From next door a shrill whining noise started up again, almost drowning out the harsh Chinese music which had been playing continually since we came in. While Clive moved around filming the stacks of Black & Decker drills, irons and mixing machines, I used his sound-recorder to tape the sounds coming from the other side of the wall.

It was immediately obvious that the best view into the ivory factory would be from the top row of shelves. The highest one, right at the back of the warehouse, was some twenty feet above the floor. I climbed to the shelf below it. From it I could clearly see Chinese workers sawing and drilling pieces of ivory. But I was conspicuous. If any of them glanced up I would be certain to be seen. There was no chance that we could stand on the top shelf with our cameras trained on them without being noticed. And in our jeans and T-shirts we certainly didn't look like Black & Decker workers.

'Could we borrow some of your overalls?' I asked Babu. 'It's a bit dusty on the shelves where we want to film.' Babu produced three khaki overalls displaying the Black & Decker logo. Now at least we might look as if we were on official business if we were spotted. But there was no disguising our cameras. What we needed was some sort of screen.

My eyes fell on a large empty cardboard packing-case lying against the wall. I pulled the box over to a pallet.

It fitted on top perfectly. I walked over to Babu. 'We've got a bit of a problem,' I said apologetically. 'I'd like to get some shots from the top shelf – artistic shots. But the film cameraman is afraid of heights.' I raised my eyebrows derisively. 'He doesn't want to climb up there. He says he'd feel happier working with something around him. I wondered if you'd mind lifting him up to the top shelf in that packing-case for five or ten minutes.'

Babu looked amused. 'No problem.'

'We might need some photographs. Why don't you go, too, Dave?' I called. The pair of them climbed in, grasping their cameras.

Babu pushed the forks of his truck under the pallet and disappeared down the back aisle with his human load. Within moments the box reappeared, rising into the air towards the topmost shelf of the back row. When it was safely in place Babu parked the forklift and went over to join his colleague, who was engaged in packing boxes. I followed him, pretending a great interest in this procedure, and questioned them in depth as they first stapled the boxes together, then filled them with appliances. When they finished their task, in desperation I interviewed them about their jobs and the company. Anything to keep their attention away from the activities of Clive and Dave.

DAVE

The box was barely large enough for the two of us with all our equipment; but somehow Clive and I squeezed ourselves in and sat down. From the sinking feeling in my stomach I guessed that the forklift was lifting us up. We exchanged apprehensive looks. We had worked together uncovering wildlife stories many times before, but this was certainly the strangest situation we had ever found ourselves in. And possibly the most crucial. 'Do you feel as bad as I do?' I asked Clive. He grimaced expressively. The pallet under the box suddenly stopped shuddering.

Looking up, I found we were just feet from the ceiling. Cautiously I peered over the top of the cardboard. I could clearly see carvers working all around the walls of the next unit. If they looked up, I would be visible to them, too.

I ducked back down and squatted next to Clive, who was preparing his film camera. 'There's no way we can just stand up and film. They'll spot us,' I said.

Clive looked around our container, searching for an idea.

'What if we cut a hole in the box?'

'With what?'

Smugly Clive produced a penknife out of his pocket. The box was made from heavy-duty reinforced cardboard and was not easy to cut, but after ten minutes' determined sawing we had a jagged flap about four inches across. Big enough to allow us to stick a lens through without, hopefully, giving much of a view into the inside of the box.

We were getting more cramped and stiff by the minute in the confined conditions, and the heat was becoming unbearable. Our once immaculate Black & Decker overalls were soaked with sweat. Clive put his eye up against the hole and squinted out. 'God, I can see them all down there working. There's a Portakabin in the middle and two big containers like the ones at the port.' He shifted his position slightly. 'There are lots of sacks, too, all piled in a heap on the floor. They're full of something. I don't know what. I can't make it out. Here, you take a look.'

Clive leaned to one side so that I could peer out of the hole. Now I could see where that sound that had reminded us of the dentist was coming from. Along the workbenches at the side of the unit were band-saws and drills at which men stood, working on pieces of creamy material. It had to be ivory. Some of the men were simply chopping large pieces into smaller pieces. Others seemed to be carving designs with drills, smoke rising steadily from the ivory as they worked.

I noted down the registration numbers on the containers, and my eyes moved to the bulging sacks on the floor beside them. From the top of one a long, curved, dirt-ingrained spike protruded. 'Those sacks,' I whispered hoarsely to Clive. 'They're *full* of tusks. There must be hundreds of sacks of ivory down there.' The volume was incredible. I calculated we must be looking at easily two thousand tusks in these sacks alone.

The Chinese music whined on, jarring with the noise of the carving, as Clive and I took turns to push our camera lenses through the flap in the box. Methodically we used both movie and still cameras to record the entire scene. No more than forty feet away from us, seated on circular metal stools on either side of a trestle table, two men were counting small cylinders of ivory and packing them by the hundred into polythene bags. From their size, about four inches long by half an inch across, I guessed these cylinders to be the signature-seals or *hanko* which were in such demand by the Japanese.

I took several pictures of them, and of the sacks of tusks. But the edges of the hole were restricting my view of the carvers. Some of them were directly below us, working on what looked like whole tusks, chopping them into rough segments with the band-saws. I desperately wanted a record of this and eventually decided to throw caution to the winds. 'I'm going to stand up now,' I warned Clive. 'If you see anyone looking, tell me.' We took it in turn to peer over the top of the box and complete our record of the factory's activities.

'I think I'll make this my final shot,' said Clive at last.

As he spoke I looked through the hole and spotted a carver on the other side of the factory staring intently at the box. A moment later he put down his work and stood up. 'Clive,' I warned. 'That guy over there. I think he's spotted us.'

Instantly, Clive dropped down beside me, and we

crouched peering through the hole. The carver was walking over to the Portakabin.

'What if he's telling Poon that someone's filming the inside of the factory?' Clive asked softly.

We waited tensely for the man to re-emerge but he didn't. The heat in the box was unbelievable. We were sweating so much the cardboard was becoming soggy underfoot. It was time to go.

ALLAN

It had been forty minutes rather than the 'five or ten' I had requested, and I had run out of stalling procedures. Babu had finally grown impatient with my increasingly inane questions and left the 'box' room to check on the film team. I followed him. Just as I entered the main warehouse the sliding door opened and sunlight flooded into the factory. Silhouetted in the doorway, with their faces thrown into dark relief, stood two Chinese men staring in at us. My pulse quickened. Babu hadn't seen them and had already disappeared behind the shelves heading for his forklift. Luckily, from where they were standing, the rows of shelving prevented the intruders having any view of the box. They made no move to come further in, and I decided the best policy was to ignore them. In what I hoped looked a calm manner I walked after Babu and watched as the box on its pallet was brought down on the forklift.

But my mind was buzzing. The men had to be from the ivory factories. What did their presence mean? Had they seen the other two filming? Or was this just a routine visit?

Clive and Dave clambered out of the box, their faces dripping. Their overalls seemed to have changed colour, and I realized that they were absolutely drenched in sweat. Together we walked back towards the entrance. The two Chinese men had gone.

While Dave and Clive were peeling off their overalls I slipped back into the manager's office. A sudden uneasy thought had struck me. The Film London card I had given him had my home address in London on it. To my relief it was still there on his desk. Quickly I picked it up and dropped it into my pocket.

After giving fulsome thanks to Babu and his colleague we loaded the film gear into the car. 'Let's get the hell out of here,' said Clive. Dave needed no urging. He flung the car into gear, and we drove towards the Free Zone exit as quickly as we dared. I watched the rear-view mirror anxiously, half expecting to see the two Chinese men emerge. Clive, too, was staring intently at the road behind us. But no-one appeared.

A few minutes later we were waved unhindered through the checkpoint, and gradually, as it became clear that we were not being followed, we relaxed.

'A clean getaway,' I said.

Dave was beaming with elation. 'We did it! We filmed Poon's secret ivory factories!'

We returned to London the following day. As a precaution, before leaving we photocopied all our documents: the notebook entries, the permits, the sketches of the layout of shed 65A at Jebel Ali, and the cards of the contacts we had made there. We sent copies to three separate addresses in Britain. Just in case.

Back in London, I felt a stronger sense of relief than I'd ever experienced before at the end of an investigation. It took us all a surprisingly long time to unwind. The aura that hung around the murky world of the ivory dealers had made a deep impression. I was uncomfortably aware that I had handed out the Film London card with my home address on it to several people around Dubai, and for several weeks I found myself checking for strange cars parked near my flat and taking a second look at Chinese faces passing me in the street. We might have penetrated the world of the ivory smugglers, but there was no escaping the unwelcome fact that they in return had invaded ours.

DAVE

Shortly after our return I met up with John Hanks, WWF International's Director of African Programmes. WWF's policy was still to support the continuation of ivory trading in the belief that eventually the CITES ivory controls would prove effective. After our discoveries in Dubai we now regarded this approach as dangerously naïve, to say the least.

On hearing that we'd been to Dubai, Hanks's interest was immediately aroused. 'What did you find out? Were you able to get an idea of how much ivory is going through the United Arab Emirates?'

I wasn't disposed to give him too many details. We wanted to complete our investigation before revealing to the world what we'd been doing. The more comprehensive and startling we could make our report when it came out, the more effective it would be. But it was doubly frustrating, knowing what we now knew, to listen to the continuing complacency of WWF over the fate of the elephants. I felt John Hanks should at least learn that there was a problem.

'We have discovered huge amounts of ivory coming out of Dubai,' I said carefully.

'Oh? Where is it going to?'

'To Hong Kong, Taiwan and Singapore mainly, but other countries as well.'

Hanks looked sceptical. 'I think you're wrong about Taiwan. Our information is from top contacts, and they assure us that all ivory imports into Taiwan stopped in mid-1987.'

My briefcase, containing copies of the Dubai printout and other documents, was beside me on the floor. I couldn't resist it. Silently I handed him two air-cargo manifests showing ivory exports to Taiwan. One manifest, for 1½ tonnes of ivory, was dated March 1988; the other, also for 1½ tonnes, was stamped April 1988. Hanks was clearly shaken. For me the episode underlined a crucial point – that WWF policy was often not based on fact. They were too willing to rely on governmental assurances without checking the validity of the statements they were given.

ALLAN

Fortunately we were not alone in wanting dramatic action on the elephant situation. A United States Congressman had proposed a law which would ban or restrict ivory imports into the United States. It would be quite a significant move. American imports accounted for over 25 per cent of the carved ivory leaving Hong Kong. Several American animal welfare groups, including Christine Stevens's group, supported him. In June I attended Congressional hearings in Washington, DC.

At the hearings, although most of the welfare groups claimed that a total ban on ivory coming into the United States would have a significant impact on the illegal ivory trade, Bill Reilly, president of WWF USA, disputed it. 'I feel it would be counter-productive,' he said. 'A unilateral ban by the US would undercut African conservation efforts.' There it was again, that blind dedication to the 'sustainable use of wildlife' theory: the old intransigent WWF argument that only by selling their ivory could African countries be persuaded to conserve their elephants as valuable assets. It was a theory which in most African countries was being completely disproved by the facts. What could we do to open WWF's eyes?

'The point is that Africans don't want a ban,' Reilly continued. 'They are the people closest to the problem, and we must respect their wishes.'

I had heard this argument before, too. When we got to

Africa I intended to find out just how much truth there was in this claim that 'Africans don't want a ban'.

After the Congressional hearings were completed I met Clarke Bavin, head of the United States Fish and Wildlife Enforcement Division, hoping that by briefing him on our discoveries from Dubai I could help move the United States closer to a ban. And not only the United States. American policy on threatened wildlife influenced countries all over the world. The European Community nations, in particular, often followed the American lead.

'In 1987 the following countries imported ivory from Dubai,' I recited. 'The People's Republic of China – two tonnes; Hong Kong – six tonnes; Singapore – thirty-five tonnes; Taiwan – eighty tonnes . . .' I paused before the next figure. 'USA – two tonnes.'

Bavin looked up from the file in which he was noting down my figures.

'Did I hear that correctly?'

'Yes, sir,' I confirmed. 'Two tonnes into the USA in 1987.'

Under American law, as we both knew, no ivory should have been imported from Dubai into the United States because the United Arab Emirates were not members of CITES. If even the super-vigilant United States Customs were not able to control illegal ivory shipments, what hope had the rest of the world?

Bavin put his notebook down and looked at me thoughtfully. 'That's very interesting. Unfortunately the figures for 1987 aren't going to be relevant when the new US restrictions come in this year. But after August, if any country is shown to be importing illegal ivory, they can be certified. Ivory from those countries wouldn't be allowed into the US. In addition any country that does trade with those nations would also find they were banned from exporting ivory to the States . . . Now, Mr Thornton,' Bavin smiled encouragingly, 'if you can come up with evidence that Singapore or Taiwan or other countries are

46

still importing poached ivory from Dubai after August we could bring action to suspend ivory imports from those countries.'

I nodded, trying not to worry about where the money for such an investigation might come from. 'I'm sure we can do that.' I spoke with more confidence than I felt. 'The ivory will still be going somewhere after August. I doubt very much that the Dubai factories are going to close down just because of a new US law.'

Smiling, Bavin stood up. 'This is the most detailed information we have ever received on the ivory trade in Dubai. It's superior to any of our other sources.' He shook my hand warmly. 'Nice work.'

As I packed my suitcase to return to London, Dave was about to land in Hong Kong to pursue the next stage of our investigation. I looked forward to seeing his face when I told him we would have to go back to Dubai . . .

5

JUNE 1988,
HONG KONG

DAVE

I arrived at Kai Tak airport on one of those hot humid days for which Hong Kong is famous. Only minutes after I'd stepped out of the air-conditioned terminal building my shirt was sticking unpleasantly to my back.

Hong Kong had seemed the obvious second stop in our investigation. Charmian Gooch's report had revealed that the British territory had long been at the heart of the world's ivory trade. For decades, factories here had been reducing the tusks of Africa's elephants to tourist souvenirs, so it was not surprising that most of the ivory air waybills we'd seen in Dubai had revealed consignees with Hong Kong addresses. We were certain, too, that the Poon empire, the name behind the Dubai factories, was based here. While in London we had done our homework and had discovered that the name Poon was associated with a Hong Kong shop and company called Tat Hing Ivory. I had no address as yet, but one of my priorities was to locate that shop.

The Hong Kong connection proved fortuitous for us. Because of the territory's British links, WWF UK had given EIA a grant to help uncover the true extent of Hong Kong's involvement in illegal trade. The money was sufficient for a two-week stay.

I flew to Hong Kong on a direct flight from Auckland where I'd been attending an International Whaling Commission meeting. The rest of the EIA team planned to join me the next day from London. Once again Clive was our film cameraman. Allan was attending the American Congressional hearings, and when he returned to England would be tied up with Greenpeace work, so in his place Charmian Gooch was to act as our sound-recordist and help with research. Since completing her report on ivory she'd become totally committed to the elephants' cause.

Hotel accommodation in Hong Kong is expensive, and I'd booked into the YMCA hotel in Kowloon, the sprawling mainland city opposite Hong Kong Island. I was exhausted from the flight, but it was impossible to sleep in the stifling heat, and at about 10 p.m. I decided to take a stroll outside.

Even at that hour the pavements were teeming with people. Away down the street neon lights flashed into the distance. The YMCA stands near the corner of Nathan Road, a mecca for tourists, and the shops that night were doing a roaring trade selling videos, cameras, stereos, jewellery and, as I soon discovered, ivory.

Only yards from the YMCA I halted in front of a shop window crammed full of ornate ivory carvings. There were bridges of elephants holding each other's tails, carved out of complete tusks; grotesque statuettes of fat men like sumo wrestlers; chess sets and mah-jong sets by the dozen. The prices were displayed in Hong Kong dollars and started at around $100 for a small ornament, rising to $10,000 for a particularly large 'whole tusk' carving, presumably worked by hand. Next to them were packed displays of cheaper ivory bangles and necklaces selling at prices between $10 and $200. I moved on. After a few paces I passed another ivory shop. Round the corner yet another.

I carried on walking, but I had company now. Something about my appearance must have shouted 'new arrival', and I found myself besieged by a pack of street-hawkers.

'Copy watch? Copy watch?' a voice shrieked in my ear,

and an arm braceleted with a dozen watches was thrust in front of my face.

'Where you from? America? Australia? England?' another voice demanded. At this last guess I nodded automatically and immediately cursed myself.

Encouraged, they pursued me. 'I like the English. I do you a special price.'

Shaking my head, I pushed my way through them until one by one they fell away.

A wave of tiredness swept over me. I'd been under unrelenting pressure since we returned from Dubai, struggling to keep EIA's other campaigns going. In the past three weeks, as well as petitioning WWF UK for the grant for our present trip, I'd paid a three-day visit to Pennsylvania where I'd testified to Congressmen at hearings on wild bird imports. Then, less than a week after returning from the United States, I'd flown the 12,000 miles to New Zealand to represent EIA at the International Whaling Commission meeting, where I'd spoken in support of the continuing fight to end the slaughter of whales and dolphins in the Faroes. Ten days after my arrival I'd flown directly to Hong Kong. It had been a heavy workload with a lot at stake, and now without warning my body was reacting to it. I felt disoriented and light-headed.

To escape the noise and bustle of the shopping area I turned right down a narrow side-street. Not wanting to lose my bearings, I noted the street-name: Cameron Road. It was darker and quieter here. These shops seemed to be closed, their windows guarded by heavy metal shutters. I paused, conscious that my pulse was racing and my body was shaking slightly. Typical jet-lag symptoms. I took deep breaths. Experience told me that a good night's sleep would probably lift me. It was stupid to keep walking. I turned around and started to head back for Nathan Road.

On either side of the street the illuminated signs of the shuttered shops flashed aggressively. As I passed in front of the entrance to an Underground station a small group of Chinese shoppers, turning in to catch their train home, bumped into me, and I spun around jumpily. Over the past few weeks, the thought had occasionally occurred to me, as it had to Allan, that the ivory traders might now be investigating *us*. Suddenly that uneasiness crept up again. I turned and scanned the shop behind me: it was closed and shuttered like all the rest. My eyes were drawn to the sign above the shutters, and as I read it I felt my spine tingle. Below the Chinese lettering, gold letters spelled out in English the words Tat Hing Ivory. It was the name we had been told in London to look out for. This was Poon's shop. The heart of all his operations. From behind these shutters the tusks from thousands of poached elephants had been sold and exported around the world.

My jet-lag was jolted away. Elated, I walked briskly back through the hawkers to my room at the YMCA. At least, I reflected, as my head hit the pillow, we had chosen a convenient base from which to start our investigation of the Poon empire!

Charmian and Clive arrived on a flight late the next morning. They were accompanied by 100 kilos of 16 mm film equipment; not a welcome burden in this heat, but essential. We were aiming now at a big public exposé of the poached ivory trade rather than an internal report for the environmental movement. The elephant issue was too big for that. A public exposé would involve the media; and to interest them, as we knew from our whale campaigns, what we needed was film – reels of it.

Our first three days in Hong Kong were taken up with company searches of ivory trading companies in the Hong Kong equivalent of Company House. The records were not computerized, so it meant ordering copies of company accounts and photographing the details. Our research in London had also identified several potentially useful contacts in Hong Kong, and I phoned round to make appointments with them.

I had been advised to get in touch with the Hong Kong Independent Commission against Corruption (ICAC), a body answerable only to the governor of Hong Kong. The Commission's task is to root out crooked dealings at all levels, and there are plenty of those in Hong Kong to keep them busy; they had recently been responsible for putting some top officials behind bars. Most of the staff have been seconded from Scotland Yard on two-year contracts and work from an unlikely base on the top floors of a multi-storey carpark.

It seemed probable that these men might have at least an inkling about the illegal ivory trade, and we were keen to talk to them. We found our entrée when Charmian learned that fifty-two tonnes of ivory, imported to Hong Kong from the Sudan in January and March, had no permits registered on the CITES computer in Cambridge. Ultimately it turned out that this ivory had been imported legally using 1987 permits, but in the course of investigating the shipment one of the officials admitted to feeling a lot of sympathy for our cause. 'Let me tell you, Dave,' he confided, 'whoever devised those CITES regulations knew nothing about trade. They're so full of loopholes that they're absolutely useless. If the future of elephants depends on them, then frankly they've had it!'

I was still digesting his statement when we visited the Agriculture and Fisheries Department. There, an official assured us confidently that they were doing everything they could to clamp down on illegal ivory imports. 'Each year our department makes several confiscations,' he said proudly. 'We have a room here full of wildlife products which people have tried to smuggle in.'

'Would it be possible for us to see them?' I asked.

'And perhaps film them?' put in Clive.

The official looked dubious, then relented. 'I don't see why not.'

He led us to a set of strongroom doors and unlocked the padlock. Inside was a small box-room. Along three of its sides were shelves stacked with booty: spotted cat skins, a tiger skin, a heap of twenty rhino horns, a holdall full of ivory seals and two boxes of semi-carved ivory. On the floor I noticed with some satisfaction a sack of tusks marked prominently 'Tat Hing Ivory'. It appeared Mr Poon did not get away with everything.

'How recently was this ivory confiscated? Was it all found this year?' I asked.

The official frowned. 'Oh, no. It came in over a long time – maybe last year, too.'

It seemed a very tiny haul considering the amount of ivory we knew to be flooding into Hong Kong.

The man described in detail to us the loophole in the CITES regulations which allowed carved and semi-carved ivory to pass through Customs without permits.

'Is much ivory coming in this way that you know of?' I asked.

'Oh, yes, I think so. There is no way to stop it.'

'Do you know which traders are bringing it in? Could you give us any names?'

He shook his head vigorously. 'No, I can't do that.'

'But it's not illegal. Why is there a problem?' Charmian persisted.

'I cannot tell you any names,' he repeated firmly. 'Anyway, after August 1988 it will all stop. The dealers will not be able to do this any more. We are closing the loophole. After this date they will need CITES certificates for all ivory being brought into Hong Kong whether it is carved or raw.'

We were already aware of this. We also knew that, with what seemed crass stupidity, the authorities had given the traders several months' notice of this tightening-up of regulations. 'Does your department know that at this moment the Dubai factories are flooding Hong Kong with semi-carved ivory to beat that deadline?' I asked.

'Yes, of course I know this is happening,' he said defensively, 'but we are not responsible for what Hong Kong traders do in Dubai. That is outside our control.'

'Well, perhaps you can tell us why it has taken two years to close this loophole if you're really so keen to stop illegal trading. Other countries haven't allowed semi-carved ivory in for a long time, especially from non-CITES countries.'

He smiled enigmatically. 'We are closing the loophole next August,' he repeated as he motioned us out of his strongroom.

We left his office with the impression that the Hong Kong government had very little genuine commitment to stopping poached ivory entering the territory.

A contact of ours in Hong Kong had given us the name of an ivory trader – trader X – who owed him a favour, and the following day we telephoned to introduce ourselves. We had not pressed our colleague for details of the favour, but it must have been substantial because in return for a promise of confidentiality trader X agreed to give us some inside information on poached ivory. Charmian and I visited him in his office, three floors up in an ageing tower block in the centre of Hong Kong city.

We sat in his office for twenty minutes while he held forth about how the trade had changed for the worse. How honest companies had gone out of business while a few traders had benefited by circumventing the CITES regulations. 'They buy people off. They have so much money they can corrupt anyone,' he asserted.

'Oh? Give us an example,' I encouraged.

He thought. 'The stockpiles. You know about the Burundi stockpile?'

'A little.' I knew that when the latest CITES regulations had come into force several stockpiles of confiscated poached ivory had been given an amnesty and legitimized. One of them had been in Burundi, a tiny East African country sandwiched between Zaïre and Tanzania. It had been a very odd decision and had caused quite a furore at the time, particularly since Burundi no longer had any elephants left. To allow a country with no elephants to continue to export ivory seemed to be actively encouraging smuggling from neighbouring countries.

'What do you know about Burundi?' I asked curiously.

Trader X smiled at my interest. 'In 1986, just before the new regulations, I had a visit from a very important man in the Hong Kong ivory business. He wanted me to pay him some money. He wanted all the traders to pay him some money. You know what for?' Not waiting for an answer, he said triumphantly: 'To help to get the Burundi ivory legalized.'

This put a shocking new slant on the ivory story. His claim sounded disturbingly credible. CITES had never come up with an adequate explanation for their action in legalizing that stockpile. Had the ivory traders really handed over money to someone? If so, to whom? CITES was the very body which was supposed to be protecting the elephants' future. What was going on here?

'Did that happen with any of the other stockpiles?' I asked.

He looked knowing. 'Everyone believes it happened in Singapore, too,' he said. 'CITES were advised against legalizing it by people in the legitimate trade. But they did it anyway.' He nodded. 'Three traders got very rich out of that deal. One of them is Mr Poon. I think your friend told me you are interested in this man?'

I had been wondering how to get the conversation around to the Poons. 'What can you tell us about the Poon family?' I asked.

Trader X replied carefully, measuring his words. 'The Poons have got really big in the last few years through this poaching business. I think maybe they are the biggest traders of all now in Hong Kong.'

'How have they been so successful?' Charmian asked.

He smiled. 'It's because they're clever. Too clever to

get caught. It used to be a small family firm. In those days it was run by the old father Poon, but now his sons have taken over. They're the ones who have taken advantage of the loopholes in our import system here. Very successfully. They're investing a lot of their profits in property now.'

According to trader X, the Poon brothers now divided the responsibilities for their ivory empire. One brother, Poon Tat Hong, was in charge of the Hong Kong side of the enterprise; while another, known as George Poon, was in charge of setting up companies abroad. It was George who ran the Dubai factories, though other members of the family were also said to be involved.

'Do you think Poon Tat Hong would talk to us?' queried Charmian.

'He might. He might invite you in.' Trader X smiled to himself. 'On the other hand, he might have you thrown out. It just depends what mood he's in. He sits in his shop in Cameron Road most days. You can't mistake him. He's a large man. Very large.' Thoughtfully he added: 'If I were you, I'd take the direct approach. Just go up to him and ask to talk to him. But be careful what you say. Remember what I told you. Poon is a clever businessman.'

He paused, seemingly pondering something. Then he leaned forward confidentially. 'I don't know if it is of any interest to you, but George has a shop and office in Paris. He and his wife live there now.'

It was of considerable interest to us: this sounded like quite a new branch of the ivory trail. The Paris link could well be worth following up. If we could show a direct European involvement, our campaign would have much more impact.

I was still mulling over his revelation when our 'mole' followed it up with another.

'One more thing,' he added. 'You seem very interested in what the Poons are doing in Dubai. I hope you don't think they are the only people there. There are five carving

56

factories in that area altogether. The Poons only own two of them.'

I stared at him. 'Do you know the names of the other companies?'

He looked evasive. Evidently he felt he had more than repaid his favour to our friend. 'I can't tell you any names.'

The news that there was still an entire network to be uncovered in Dubai was disturbing. Almost certainly it would mean another trip there.

Charmian and I discussed our discoveries with Clive that evening. Now that we knew the identity of the Hong Kong boss of Poon Enterprises we wanted to try to find a way of persuading him to face us on film. It seemed likely that this would be one of the riskiest parts of our investigation, so it might be wise to finish any other business first. We decided to try to get some good film inside an ivory shop and a Hong Kong carving factory before we confronted Poon Tat Hong.

The following day we had been granted permission to film inside Shing On Ivory, a large store in a Kowloon shopping-centre. It held a double interest for us as it was owned by Lee Chat, chairman of the Hong Kong and Kowloon Ivory Manufacturers' Association, whom we were anxious to meet. Today, as far as Lee Chat was concerned, we were an independent film company making a commercial film about Hong Kong trade. We even had a name for the film: *Trade Winds*.

As we'd done before the Dubai trip, we'd had some cards printed. This time the logo declared us to be 'Box Films', an in-joke which referred to our exploits in the Dubai factory. The card showed a convenient London forwarding postal address.

Anxious not to be found out, we played our roles convincingly, enthusing over each carving shown us. Meticulously we filmed and photographed every corner of the shop. Occasionally I put my camera down to hold the clapperboard and chalk up the shot-numbers for Clive.

Charmian strolled behind us, holding the long microphone like a pistol, the Nagra tape-recorder nonchalantly slung over her shoulder. No-one could have guessed that her previous recording experience consisted of two brief practice sessions in our hotel.

On the shop wall a notice proclaimed in English: 'Ivory purchased here may legally be taken into the United States.' We filmed that, too, hoping we might prick American consciences as well as European ones. American tourists bought a large proportion of Hong Kong's ivory as holiday souvenirs. Even more important, a third of Hong Kong's output was exported directly to the States, largely as jewellery, where it was sold openly in shops. If the United States could be persuaded to ban all ivory imports, it would severely undermine the Hong Kong industry.

Exactly on cue, two middle-aged American couples came into the shop. Clive's eyes met mine, and I nodded. We watched as they browsed around the shop exclaiming to each other in loud Midwestern accents. One of the men bought a pair of ivory ear-rings for his wife, and while the assistant was wrapping them Clive stepped forward. 'Excuse me, sir. We're just making a film about tourism and trade in Hong Kong. I wonder if you'd mind if we filmed you looking around the shop.'

Far from minding, they revelled in it. It was just the sort of 'different' holiday experience they were looking for. Clive filmed shots of an assistant showing them a carving of a complete tusk. By its size I guessed it had come from an elephant around twenty years old.

'Oh, it's beautiful. How much is it?' asked one of the women.

'Five hundred dollars,' the shop assistant responded.

'You know what? It's worth it,' she hammed.

'Who's this film being made for?' enquired her husband.

'British television and magazines,' I smiled. 'You never

58

know, you might end up on the cover of *Time*!' Though I suspected they wouldn't have been too pleased if they had.

We finished filming, thanked them all, and were moving away when one of the men pointed to the whole-tusk carving and demanded of his wife: 'Do you wannit?'

'But it's five hundred dollars,' she protested.

'I didn't say how much is it. I said do you wannit?' he swaggered.

Looking embarrassed, she chivvied him out of the shop after their friends. He was still loudly demanding 'Do you wannit?' as the door closed behind them.

Charmian passed Clive the headphones so he could check whether her amateur recordings had made the grade. His smile broadened as he listened.

'What a team,' he confirmed.

Our next stop was the Kowloon ivory factory which produced the carvings for the shop where we had just filmed. Our guide was to be Lee Chat himself. We now learned that, in addition to his other roles, he was a government adviser on the ivory industry.

Lee Chat shook hands formally with each of us. He was a short man, even by Chinese standards, and his manner was stiffly formal and correct. His expression, despite a fixed smile, was classically inscrutable; it was impossible to guess at what was going on in his mind as we told him about the film. I did, however, get a definite feeling that this was not a man I would want to cross.

Through an interpreter, we asked Lee Chat to describe what went on in his factory, and he led us round, gesturing theatrically towards the various machines and carvings with a long cigarette-holder through which he smoked continuously. He painted a very rosy picture of his business. We kept up our naïve act, hoping he would think we were just badly informed film-makers; it had proved a useful ploy in the past when we were doing undercover work. People tend to be careless about what they let you see if they think you won't understand its significance.

The factory was closing down for the day, and only a few workers remained. Their equipment was much the same as we had seen in Dubai: benches supporting band-saws and drills, and tables where the *hanko* seals were chopped out by the hundred. There was no sign of any of the hand-carving tools used by the sort of craftsmen who took a year to fashion a tusk into a work of art. This was a mass-production factory specializing in tacky souvenirs.

We paused in a corner of the factory beside one of the small religious shrines you often stumble across in incongruous places in Hong Kong. It was draped with dark red and gold material, and illuminated by a flickering sweet-smelling candle.

'How big is your business?' I asked Lee Chat through our interpreter.

He considered. 'Medium-sized. I only use about ten tonnes of ivory a year.'

Charmian on my far side hissed sardonically: 'Only a thousand elephants!'

Lee Chat waved his cigarette-holder towards the benches. 'But I don't have much in stock, as you can see.'

I ran my eyes over the raw tusks stacked on shelves around the factory. At a rough estimate there was a tonne of ivory here waiting to be carved. Many of the tusks were pathetically small.

'I'll just film this pile of tusks here,' Clive said suddenly, switching on his lights. I squinted down, trying to see what had caught his attention. The tusks he was focusing on were marked in indelible ink with a CITES code: BI 86. I knew from Charmian's report that BI was the code for Burundi, which had no elephants. These tusks had to be from the confiscated stockpile that was legitimized in 1986.

I looked sideways to see Lee Chat's reaction to our interest and met a bland smile as he carefully inserted another cigarette into his holder. I wished I could see into his mind. Did he think that it was just coincidence that we had chosen to film these particular tusks? Something about his expression reminded me of a picture I remembered from a childhood book, of a dragon defending its lair, surrounded by the remains of its victims.

Most of the air waybills we had uncovered in Dubai had been for consignments bound for two addresses, one in Kowloon and one in the New Territories, the mainland district of Hong Kong which borders on China. We decided to hire a car and go out there for a day to see if we could track down the person named on the bills: Mr Chan Pik Wah of 44 Hung Sek Road, Tai Pat Yuen, Yuen Long.

We drove out of Kowloon to Tsuen Wan City and up the winding road into the hills. At one point we stopped the car to look down on the city and harbour. It was a letdown: an environmental mess. Ugly blocks of high-rise flats spiked the plain below. Winding through them, stained by dye from Hong Kong's clothing factory workshops, was a river so unnaturally green it was almost fluorescent.

We reached our initial destination, the town of Yuen Long, without much difficulty, but locating the address on the air waybills presented problems. Outside the main city it's not easy to find anyone who speaks English, and we asked dozens of people for directions without success.

'This is getting silly,' said Charmian as we travelled up the same street for the third time. 'We're never going to find it at this rate. Why don't Clive and I hail a taxi and tell the driver to take us there? Then you can follow us in the car.'

Like most of Charmian's solutions it was simple but effective. Ten minutes later the taxi stopped and Charmian and Clive were directed down a narrow alleyway with market stalls on either side. Parking the hired car, I rejoined them and we wandered down between the stalls.

Small fires glowed beside many of them, and people were ceremonially throwing coloured paper into the flames in some mysterious rite. With the suddenness typical of the Far East, warm rain started to pour down in torrents, and we took shelter under the corrugated-iron roof of one of the stalls. A minute later, as though someone had switched off a tap, the rain stopped, and we continued on our way.

The address we were seeking was tucked away at the end of a labyrinth of footpaths with open drainage ditches on either side; we would never have found it unaided. To our surprise it was a private house. Ferocious-sounding dogs barked behind its flimsy boundary fence, and we mutually agreed that further investigation was unnecessary.

Back in Kowloon we located the second address. This time it was a shop which sold hydraulic equipment. We introduced ourselves to the proprietor, gave him our Box Films card and were given his card in return. His name was Chan Lim To – the name of the consignee on the air waybill. It was clear now how Poon and his colleagues got much of their ivory into the country from Dubai. These were obviously accommodation addresses; there were possibly many more. Shipments of semi-carved ivory would be delivered here to be picked up later and taken secretly to the Hong Kong factories. It seemed an unnecessarily devious ploy when semi-carved ivory could be brought into Hong Kong quite openly with no need for permits. Perhaps the Poons reasoned that this way no-one could be sure of the amount of laundered ivory they were importing. The scale of the problem could be hidden from people like us who might be interested in clamping down on it. But I had an uneasy feeling that there might be another reason for this subterfuge of which we were not yet aware.

The following day we did some filming in and around the airport, and with the co-operation of British Caledonian filmed their Dubai flight arriving – an air-steward contact in London had told us this particular flight was known among the crew as 'the ivory run'.

In the afternoon I had an appointment with a young woman journalist, Tsang Shuk Wa, from the news magazine *Asiaweek*. A colleague in London had fixed it for us; Shuk Wa was helping prepare a major feature on the ivory trade, and we had agreed that it would be sensible to pool our knowledge. I told her the real purpose of our visit on the strict understanding that she would not mention EIA in her article, and gave her copies of Charmian's research and a summary of our discoveries in Dubai. Shuk Wa was eager to use our photographs, too. They, after all, were the proof of our claims and would increase the impact of her article. Despite some misgivings, I decided to offer her our 'box' photos from the Dubai factory. It would rankle not taking a credit for photos which might help the cause of EIA, but if we blew our cover now we would sabotage any further investigations. And, hopefully, co-operating with *Asiaweek* would bring its own rewards. It did. One of those rewards came almost immediately.

'How would you like to meet a trader who used to be involved in Dubai?' asked Shuk Wa.

'Very much. But will he talk?'

Shuk Wa flashed me a scheming smile. 'I think I can persuade him to tell you about it.'

We met in a restaurant. Mr Hang (not his real name) was, I guessed, in his late twenties, rather nervous and obviously quite smitten by Shuk Wa's charm. She introduced me as a commercial film-maker, and in response to her coaxing he started to talk.

What he had to say was extremely interesting. Mr Hang claimed that for some time he had worked in Dubai with the Poons, and he and his partner had supplied the workforce and equipment for the factories in Jebel Ali. George Poon's part of the deal had been to rent the factory, negotiate with the Dubai authorities and supply the raw ivory. His claims fitted in exactly with what I already knew. He confirmed that there were four or five factories operating in Dubai including the two run by George Poon in Jebel Ali.

Hang's own involvement, he claimed, was on a smaller scale than the Poons'. Though he had no direct connection with poaching, his operations were of dubious legality. He described them euphemistically as 'business tricks'. One of his 'tricks' was to import ivory into Hong Kong under his own name rather than under that of his business. That way he avoided paying business tax. But recently he had come unstuck. One of his shipments had been confiscated by the Government.

'Was it illegal?' I asked.

'No,' he said indignantly. 'It is carved ivory imported from Singapore. They seem to be picking on me. I don't know why. Everyone does this business trick from Singapore.'

'Can you explain it for Mr Currey?' Shuk Wa persuaded. She was skilfully milking him for information. Without her feminine wiles he would never have told me all this.

From across the table he assessed me cautiously. 'The point is that there are huge stocks of poached ivory in Singapore,' he said. 'They were given CITES permits in the amnesty in 1986. I buy some of this stockpile, which comes complete with the legal paperwork. Then I have it carved in Singapore and send it to Hong Kong without using the documents, because for carved ivory they don't ask for them. This leaves me with Singapore permits but no ivory. So I then get hold of raw poached ivory, usually from Dubai, and import it using the spare permits.'

He spread his palms in appeal. 'What's wrong with that?' his gesture demanded. 'Clever business trick!' And indeed it was. It meant that those CITES amnesty permits could be used for laundering purposes – bringing poached ivory into Singapore .and from thence to Hong Kong. There had been 270 tonnes in that Singapore stockpile.

How many more tonnes had been brought in on the amnesty permits? Twice that amount? Ten times? No-one could know. The permits would only be produced when the tusks were intercepted. For smugglers they were insurance against detection. The Singapore amnesty had been like an open invitation for poached tusks to enter the Far East. Between that and the activities of the Dubai factories it was obvious to me now that these ivory traders were running rings around the CITES control system. The reason for the elephant holocaust was becoming depressingly clear.

'Would you repeat what you've just said on film?' I asked Hang.

He spoke rapidly to Shuk Wa in Cantonese. 'He says "No",' she translated. 'He dare not because he is still in court with the Government over his seized ivory.'

Damn, I thought. A film testimony by an admitted trader in poached ivory would have added a valuable weapon to our armoury.

I suddenly remembered the August deadline, when the Hong Kong government had promised to close the main loophole. After August, even semi-carved ivory coming into Hong Kong would require permits.

'What will you and your colleagues do after August?' I enquired. 'You won't be able to use that trick for much longer.'

Hang shrugged. 'We will probably try to get the raw tusks into Singapore via Malaysia.'

'Why Malaysia?'

'There is a causeway between Singapore and Malaysia, so it is easy to bring ivory in. That way there is very little chance of Customs officers finding it.'

'And what about semi-carved ivory? Will you smuggle that into Singapore, too, or do you think the Dubai factories might close down once the loophole closes?'

Hang looked unperturbed. 'Perhaps. But there are other carving factories – in Taiwan and South Korea. We do not depend on Dubai. And even if all those carving factories close we will find a way.' He smiled confidently.

The scale of this operation continued to stagger me. When we had started our investigation I had envisaged large numbers of small-time smugglers, not a professionally run international business network. How could CITES possibly have been unaware of its existence? It seemed incredible.

6

DAVE

It was time for us to meet 'Mr Big'. Poon Tat Hong. The dilemma was how to make our first approach. If he refused to talk, or threw us out, there would be little chance of trying again. What would be the best time of day to approach him? The best expression to wear? What should our first words be? The possibility that Poon might have got wind of our activities in Dubai concerned me. For all we knew, he was expecting us and had set a trap.

After an evening of debate we settled on our approach. I would go alone to the Tat Hing Ivory shop, walk in unannounced, and hope to catch Poon off his guard. Even if he refused to speak to me, that would leave Clive and Charmian with a second opportunity to approach him.

Cameron Road looked less threatening in daylight than it had on my first night in Kowloon. I'd chosen to make my visit at 11 a.m. on the premiss that the best time to catch someone in his office is just before lunch. Twice I strolled past the shop doorway, polishing my camera lens and psyching myself up. The interior of the shop was well lit, and through the glass door I could see an overweight Chinese man sitting behind a desk at the far end of the shop. I remembered trader X's smile when he described Poon as 'large'. This had to be him. Near the shop entrance a second man and a woman shop assistant hovered beside a display of carvings.

It was my third trip past the shop. Another would be asking for trouble. I paused, mentally assumed my role of innocent film-maker abroad, and pushed open the door.

Giving the woman assistant what I hoped was a confident smile, I walked decisively past her towards the fat man at his desk and held out my hand. 'Mr Poon?' The man looked up, obviously taken aback, and let me shake his hand. I had the advantage of surprise and pressed it home. 'So good to meet you,' I enthused. 'My name's Dave Currey from London. I'm a producer with Box Films, and we're making a film about trade in Hong Kong with special emphasis on the changes leading up to Chinese rule in 1997.' I paused for breath and passed him my Box Films business card. Without speaking he exchanged it for one of his own. I scanned it quickly, noting that it bore three addresses: the Hong Kong shop, the Hong Kong factory and Tat Hing Ivory, Paris. I tucked the card carefully into my shirt pocket.

Poon Tat Hong was looking slightly disconcerted. It can't have been every day that an ebullient Englishman accosted him on his own territory. He was indeed very plump compared with the average lean Hong Kong resident and slumped inelegantly in his chair. Hearing my name did not seem to have provoked any untoward reaction – unless he was acting as hard as I was.

I continued my monologue about the film we were supposed to be making. Even to me it sounded abysmally boring. 'The reason we thought we'd look at the ivory business is that it makes better film than just lots of shots of containers. More local colour,' I explained.

Poon looked noncommittal.

'I believe you're a major importer?'

Poon's eyes narrowed, making him look faintly pig-like. 'I don't import ivory. I just sell it. You want to talk to the big traders.' He shuffled the papers on his desk into neat and unreadable piles. 'Man Hing or Nathan Ivory. They import a lot. They have two thousand square feet of factory. Here . . .' He scribbled down two telephone numbers and pushed them over the desk to me. 'You go and see them.'

I risked pressing him a little further. 'Oh? I was told by a number of people that you are a big importer.'

He stared at me coldly. 'No. Only a little from Japan.'

A change of tack was clearly called for. I looked up at the shelf behind him. 'Those carvings really are extraordinary, especially those balls with all the other carved balls inside them. How on earth do they do that?' There was no response, but I breezed on regardless. 'What I'd love to do is to film some of them in the shop if you'd let me bring my film crew in here. And perhaps we could get some shots inside your factory as well?' I held my breath.

'I'll have to see,' Poon said.

He dialled a number on his phone and spoke to someone in quick-fire Cantonese. Discreetly, still keeping my eager smile, I looked around the shop. The woman assistant smiled solicitously back. Propped on a cabinet next to me I recognized the familiar lettering of an air waybill. I shifted my position so I wouldn't have to crane my neck too obviously. Whatever it accompanied had come from 57 Faber Crescent, Singapore, and was addressed to Chan Pik Wah, Yuen Long, Hong Kong. I recognized the second address. It was the private house, the accommodation address, that we had visited in the New Territories. So Poon, too, was involved in bringing in ivory via Singapore. Was he like Mr Hang using the 'business trick' of re-using permits? I memorized the Singapore address.

Poon put the phone down. My interest in his air waybill had not escaped his attention. Picking it up, he folded it neatly away.

'It is not possible to film in the shop, but you may film in my factory,' he said shortly. I was nearly caught unawares. I had been quite sure he would refuse to co-operate.

'That's wonderful,' I declared. 'I'll fetch my camera crew and we'll be straight back.'

Clive and Charmian were waiting in Nathan Road, just around the corner; but, to our frustration, when the three of us returned to the shop Poon Tat Hong had disappeared. Clearly he had no intention of being filmed. We were met instead by a male employee who ushered us quickly outside again. He led us a few doors down the street and up some rickety steps. As we followed him through a doorway we were greeted again by the cacophony of dentist's drills and Chinese music that had become so familiar in Dubai. I pulled Poon's business card out of my shirt pocket. This was not the address of the factory named on it. I wondered how many unofficial places like this one he operated.

The assistant led us around. The factory had two workrooms, in each of which carvers were busy at benches, carving out small ivory ornaments with electric drills. A third room I guessed to be an office. A Chinese woman constantly walked in and out of it, each time shutting the door firmly behind her.

Clive set up his camera and lights while the carvers looked on agog, welcoming our intrusion as a break from the monotony of their day. As usual the film camera had a magnetic effect, and everyone was eager to help and pose.

'Would you mind facing this way a little more?' directed Clive, enjoying himself. While he and Charmian filmed I wandered around, taking photos and trying to talk to the staff. A box of partly carved figurines on the floor in the larger workroom bore a British Airways sticker. I bent down to take a closer look. The box had come from Singapore – that country kept cropping up. We were obviously going to have to go there at some stage.

'Where does all this ivory come from?' I asked one of the carvers.

'Africa,' he replied with a helpful smile.

'Yes. But why does it come through Singapore?' I pointed to the British Airways label.

His face went blank, and he shrugged and mumbled:

'I just carve.' The workers had been well briefed by someone. All assumed vacant expressions the moment I asked 'Where from?'

I stooped to photograph the figurines in the box. As I straightened up again the woman appeared once more and headed towards the office. 'Excuse me. Would you mind if I took some photos of you at your desk?' I asked ingratiatingly. 'You know. To show the business side of the craft.'

She eyed me suspiciously. 'No! You can't,' she snapped. 'You are not allowed in the office.' She slammed the door behind her.

I started to photograph the workers as they drilled the fine detail on to the semi-carved figurines. To my eye they looked quite hideous. I couldn't imagine why anyone would want to have such things about the house. A pile of tusks was lying on the floor in the corner, and I walked over and photographed them. They were unmarked. That meant they were either very old stock, pre-1986, or they were poached. Behind them on the white-painted wall, messages and phone numbers were scrawled in English and Chinese in felt-tip pen. Furtively I copied the details in my notebook and took a couple of photos.

Clive and Charmian walked in from the smaller workroom and started filming the carvers near me. Clive beckoned me over on the pretext of getting me to look in his viewfinder.

'What do you think, Dave?'

'Great!' I approved, then lowered my voice. 'She won't let me into the office. Why don't you and Charmian just walk in innocently and see what's in there?'

'OK. Right.' Then loudly, for the benefit of the workforce, he added: 'Let's see if another angle would be better.'

Charmian edged over to Clive with the Nagra tape recorder, and out of the corner of my eye I watched them conspire. Gradually I managed to attract all the

71

carvers towards me with a few strategic flashes from my flash-gun. 'Act naturally, please,' I commanded – a sure way to stiffen them up! Behind them Clive and Charmian moved towards the office door.

'Just a few more shots,' I requested, not sure how many of the workers had a clue what I was saying. Clive had stepped inside the door now. Charmian followed.

'Great. Good. Wonderful. Only a few more—'

Suddenly there was an angry shout, and the next moment Clive and Charmian were pushed out of the office by the woman I had spoken to. She looked quite distraught at the intrusion and, taking a key out of her pocket, pointedly locked the door before stalking angrily out of the room. Clive and Charmian came over to me looking innocent and bewildered, as though they had blundered in there by mistake.

'She didn't seem too pleased.' There was a twinkle in Charmian's eye.

'But we were in there long enough to film,' Clive murmured. 'We saw six boxes, all addressed to that same house we visited in the New Territories.'

'What did they have in them?'

'Bangles and ivory seals mainly. They've got quite a turnover going through here.'

The following day I ventured once more down Cameron Road and went into Tat Hing Ivory, intending to thank Poon Tat Hong for his help. Until our cover was broken I thought no harm could come of maintaining friendly relations. Poon was out, but I startled a man unpacking boxes of semi-carved ivory: roughly hewn statuettes with the fine detail still to be completed. He looked up at me like a startled rabbit, guilt written over his face; a complete contrast to Poon Tat Hong's confident attitude the previous day. I took a good look at the boxes. Written on the side was the name Chan Lim To. That was the man who ran the hydraulics shop in Kowloon, at the second of the accommodation addresses; so this shipment, too, like the crates we had seen in the factory, had not come directly to Poon, but via an intermediary. But it was still legal to import semi-carved products into Hong Kong without permits. Why was Poon going to so much trouble to obscure his trail? The question had been niggling away at me ever since we'd visited the house in the New Territories.

By now the man was frantically packing the carvings back into the box in a futile effort to stop me seeing them. As I watched him, a possible explanation for the subterfuge occurred to me. What if the Poon brothers were establishing these new routes in anticipation of the loophole being closed in August? If the route through the New Territories was already running smoothly by that time, they could simply continue operations in the same old way and no-one would be any the wiser; whereas, if they had been openly bringing tonnes of semi-carved ivory into the country prior to August, they would be put on the spot when permits were required. If they suddenly started using accommodation addresses at that time, then it would mean the amount of ivory they officially imported would drop dramatically. Some enterprising official might well notice that the amount of ivory the Poons sold was unchanged and put two and two together.

As trader X had told us, the Poons were clever businessmen. If my theory was correct, it seemed highly unlikely that any new law would be allowed to hinder their ivory laundering operations.

Our venture had been far more successful than I had dared hope. The film material we had gathered tied in so neatly with the Dubai film and documents that the Poons' operation was now in the film-can. It was a pity that Poon Tat Hong had managed to evade our cameras, but our main objective had been achieved.

The following day Charmian and Clive loaded up their equipment and documents and caught a plane back to London. My flight was not due out until later in the day, and I was packing my things in the YMCA when the phone rang. It was Shuk Wa, the reporter from *Asiaweek*.

'I interviewed Poon today. God, he was difficult. How about lunch? I've something you might be interested in.'

Over lunch in a restaurant in Nathan Road, Shuk Wa told me that she and an *Asiaweek* photographer had walked into Tat Hing Ivory unannounced. She had explained who they were, but after a few minutes Poon realized that she was recording the conversation. 'He tried to call his lawyer!' she laughed. 'But I managed to calm him down. In the end he had quite a bit to say. I think he saw it as a way of getting at his competitors. He told tales about quite a few other traders who were smuggling poached ivory. I'll give you details. But the main reason I called you is that he said something very interesting about CITES.'

Shuk Wa saw she'd hooked my curiosity. 'He suggested that there might be serious irregularities within CITES.'

She gave me a copy of the transcript. When she had gone I read through it again. In the final paragraph Shuk Wa stated that as she had been about to leave Poon Tat Hong's shop her photographer had tried to take a photo of the proprietor, but Poon had refused, saying cryptically: 'Men don't like to be known. Just like pigs don't like to be fat!'

If EIA has its way, the whole world will see pictures of Poon Tat Hong, I thought with relish, as I picked up my bags for the flight home.

7

November 1988,
Kenya

Allan

The *Asiaweek* article on elephant poaching was published
in August 1988. Only a handful of people knew that we
were responsible for the uncredited photographs of the
Poons' ivory factories in Dubai, and there was considerable
and (to us) quite amusing speculation within the conservation movement as to who could have taken them.

Shortly afterwards I resigned from the executive direc-
torship of Greenpeace and returned to work full-time for
EIA. It meant we could now pull out all the stops on the
elephant campaign and start planning a trip to Africa. The
sheer size of the continent made it a daunting prospect. We
decided to concentrate on East Africa, which was the area
on which we had obtained most information. Since Dave's
return from Hong Kong news had reached us that the Poon
brothers had set up yet another ivory carving factory in
Kisingani, northern Zaïre. That was one possible port of
call. Another was Burundi, which, because it had still not
joined CITES, was able to act as a funnel for much of the
poached ivory destined for Dubai.

But our initial stop had to be in Kenya. Not only
was this a country being badly hit by ivory poachers, but
also many outspoken conservationists lived there. Meeting
them would give us a much clearer picture of what
was really going on. Coincidentally the CITES African
Elephant Working Group was meeting for the first time in
Nairobi at the same time as our visit. This group had been

formed in 1987 to look at the effects of the ivory trade and any problems associated with it. Very few conservationists had been invited to attend even as observers, but somehow I hoped to be able to wangle my way in.

Clive wasn't coming on this trip since it was our intention to pose as tourists rather than as a professional film crew. Because filming of wildlife was subject to strict controls in most African countries, we were taking only a Video 8 camera, loaned to us by ITN, which hopefully might pass as a home movie camera. We had persuaded Ros Reeve to spend her vacation helping us out. Ros, who held a doctorate in microbiology, was a good photographer and had helped EIA to photograph the Faroes whale killings in 1986. In addition she spoke fluent French, which would be useful in Burundi. Once again our unflagging supporter Christine Stevens passed the hat round various American groups to raise some money for us. It was at her instigation that we had started this project and she had no intention of allowing lack of funds to hamper it now.

Acting on an impulse, a few days before we were due to depart I drew up a will, assigning my meagre assets to a few friends. I also wrote a letter to my bank authorizing the transfer of funds to EIA in the event of 'an emergency'. I gave both documents to Jenny for safe-keeping. I did not discover until later that Dave, troubled by similar unspoken qualms, had drawn up his will, too, before we left.

DAVE

Nairobi seems to balance uneasily on the edge of two cultures, its African roots entwined with the European influence of colonial days. Nowhere is the contrast between the two civilizations more obvious than on the taxi drive out to Iain Douglas-Hamilton's home in the Langata district of Nairobi.

The road on the outskirts of Nairobi is jammed with small overcrowded buses belching dark exhaust fumes as they discharge their black passengers into ramshackle shanty-towns. But approaching Langata the vista changes and you pass large elegant houses, each with six or eight bedrooms, most of them patrolled by guards with dogs and surrounded by high security-fences. Many of the white Kenyans we were to meet in the coming weeks lived in this opulent part of the city.

As we ventured into Langata I noticed our driver looking around him curiously.

'It's a very smart area,' I commented.

'Oh, yes, sir,' he agreed, his head swivelling. 'I don't come out here too often.'

The house where Iain Douglas-Hamilton and his journalist wife Oria lived was less ostentatious than its neighbours, being built of wood rather than of brick or stone and with no perimeter fence. We received a very warm welcome, though it was the first time Allan and I had seen them since the Ottawa meeting sixteen months earlier.

Iain and Oria had devoted their lives to the study of the African elephant and had written many books and appeared in wildlife films over the last fifteen years. Recently they had publicly condemned the ivory trade for the elephant's decline, and as a result of taking this stance Iain had been ostracized by several other elephant experts who were more sympathetic to the traders. Over a cool drink we told the Douglas-Hamiltons of our discoveries in Dubai and Hong Kong. They listened with interest.

'So what are you doing in Kenya?' Iain asked when we had temporarily exhausted the subject of the Poons.

'We felt it was time to find out more about the ivory trade in Africa,' Allan replied. 'We wanted to follow up the leads we have here.'

'Film footage of live and dead elephants would be useful, too,' I put in. 'We're hoping to get enough film material for a documentary feature on ivory poaching.'

Iain looked dubious. 'You know that you won't be

77

allowed to film in the national parks here in Kenya? The Government's very sensitive about this right now. They don't allow film crews in.' He smiled ironically. 'After all, it might put the tourists off if they see what's happening. But in any case you wouldn't be allowed off the roads into the bush where most of the poaching happens.'

As a result of this information, we decided to build up our contacts in Nairobi. One man we spoke to was a tour operator whose living depended on his customers seeing wildlife and especially elephants.

'It's getting too close for comfort nowadays,' he complained. 'I was at a camp in a park two months ago and in the early afternoon we saw a herd of elephants from the camp. At six-thirty I heard about forty to fifty shots. As soon as it was light the next morning we went to look and we found four dead elephants lying in a row. Every one of them had had its tusks removed.'

'How often would you say something like that happens?' Ros asked.

'Often. You hear reports like that all the time. The poachers use automatic weapons now: AK47 rifles. That means they don't even bother to aim to kill. They just spray the elephants with automatic fire and wait for them to drop. They don't stand a chance.'

'What about the local people? Do they want to protect the elephants?'

'Oh, yes, some do. The wildlife is a part of their tradition. But the traditions are changing like the times. I met a seventeen-year-old Masai warrior the other day. We were sitting by my camp-fire at night and he was admiring my leather briefcase – it's got pictures of the big five game animals embossed on it. He told me the Masai names for the animals, one by one. But when he came to the rhino he didn't know what it was. My guess is it'll be like that for the elephants, too, before long.'

WWF's repeated claim that Africans didn't want an ivory ban was not standing up to close scrutiny. Here in

Kenya where people's livelihoods were being threatened by poaching we'd so far heard very few words in favour of ivory trading. Even the official viewpoint seemed to be in favour of a ban. Richard Leakey, the well-known anthropologist and chairman of the East African Wildlife Society (EAWS), had recently accused the Minister of Tourism and Wildlife of being dilatory in acting against ivory poachers. Nehemiah Arap Rotich, the director of EAWS, took the same position as his chairman. 'Personally I think there should be a worldwide ban on ivory trading for at least twenty years,' he told us when we met him privately.

Another group, the African NGO Environment Network, also supported this view. Simon Muchiro, its director, told us that their scientific committee, which represented thirty-seven countries, had proposed an international ban on the ivory trade 'until populations grew back'. Despite WWF's claims to the contrary, it seemed that a fair number of Africans did want a ban. It wasn't the first instance we had discovered where WWF's research had proved to be woefully inaccurate.

The crowd of Americans stood around awkwardly, weighed down by cameras and video equipment, city folk transplanted overnight to the African bush, trying vainly to harmonize with nature. Looking at them, we realized how incongruous we, too, must appear to the natives of Kenya. Twenty feet away from us two baby elephants and two baby black rhinos frolicked in the evening sun.

We were all guests at Daphne Sheldrick's famous elephant orphanage in the Nairobi national park. Here Daphne and her daughter Jill devoted themselves to rearing the baby elephants and rhinos which had been spared by the poachers' bullets because the youngsters had no tusks or horns. Though 'spared' was hardly an apt word as the woman guide was now explaining. 'In the wild a baby elephant can't survive for more than twenty-four hours without its mother,' she said. 'If the lions don't get it, it'll die of exposure.'

Daphne had a good propaganda programme operating. Once the tourists' hearts were captured by the young animals, the guide told them of the rapid decline in elephant numbers caused by the poachers and followed it up with a graphic account of the state of shock in which the orphan babies were often found, after witnessing the deaths of all their family around them. She described the close-knit elephant society where every weak member, whether very young or very old, is cared for and protected by the stronger members. Some of her listeners looked horrified by what they were hearing. Poaching seemed to be a completely new concept to them. If only we could provoke the same reaction on a worldwide scale, we'd have achieved our aim.

We had asked if we might meet Daphne privately, and were invited up to her house after the public tour was over. Smiling, she came out to meet us, a grey-haired matronly woman whose fondness for her charges was immediately apparent. A tiny elephant stood near her back door, playing with its keeper. 'This is Fiona,' Daphne introduced us proudly. 'She's only been with us a week. She's the youngest elephant that I've been able to save, because it's only recently that we've found a satisfactory formula to substitute for mother's milk.'

We told Daphne about the Environmental Investigation Agency and explained that we were interested in making a film about the ivory trade. 'We need to keep the purpose of our visit confidential, if you don't mind,' I requested.

'Good idea,' Daphne responded. 'I can tell you what's going on here in Kenya. Why don't you tell me what you know about the trade first?'

Daphne was used to dealing with the media. A long line of ill-informed film-makers had visited her orphanage for cute (and cheap) footage of baby elephants. She had no reason initially to think our motives were very different.

However, when she heard that we had actually visited Hong Kong and Dubai and were planning a major campaign to ban the international ivory trade her cool blue eyes grew instantly alert and I knew she had started to take us more seriously.

'Why don't you come through to the balcony and have a beer?' she offered. We followed her through the house to an open veranda which overlooked an artificial waterhole. A family of warthogs were making the most of the last of the evening sunshine, racing around with tails erect like flagpoles. Daphne brought in a tray of beers, and we were joined by her daughter Jill and Jill's boyfriend Jean François, known to everyone as JF.

'Now. You want to know what's happening in Kenya,' said Daphne. 'What I can tell you is that the situation is very serious. I've been keeping a record of every incident of poaching that's been reported in Tsavo national park. About a thousand elephants have been killed there so far this year. There are probably less than ten thousand elephants left in the park now. It's organized crime – there's no doubt about that.'

'Is it locals?' I asked.

Daphne shrugged. 'Sometimes it is. There's a strong suspicion that some game scouts are involved. But more often it's *shifta* or Somali bandits. They're well armed and they go around in gangs. We've no effective force to oppose them, you see. Unfortunately the Ministry of Tourism and Wildlife doesn't make enough money available to protect the wildlife here.'

'You mean nothing's being done to stop it?' asked Ros.

'Nothing at all,' JF confirmed. 'All that happens at the moment is that the authorities deny there's any poaching going on so the tourists won't be put off.' It was just what Iain Douglas-Hamilton had told us.

'Have you ever heard of the Poon family?' I enquired of Daphne.

'Oh, yes, I've heard of them,' she said instantly.

'Ivory traders, aren't they? That's the whole problem. The massive demand for ivory. There's only one way to stop profiteering crooks like the Poons causing our elephants to be killed, and that's to close the ivory market. Ban the sale of ivory worldwide, once and for all.'

I looked at Allan. The same thought had occurred to both of us. 'Would you say that in a filmed interview, Daphne?' asked Allan. 'Would it be safe for you to call for an ivory ban?'

Her face broke into a broad smile. 'It's the only answer. Of course I'll say it.'

We agreed to film her the following morning and were finalizing the arrangements when there was a crash in the kitchen behind us. Daphne jumped up. 'Excuse me one moment. I think Fiona wants to be fed.'

We followed her and discovered the baby elephant sniffing hungrily round Daphne's kitchen shelves. 'We have to bottle-feed her every four hours, and she knows when it's due,' Daphne explained, deftly mixing powder and water in a jug. 'One of the keepers sleeps with her in her stable at the moment. At this age she must never be left without company. In the wild she'd never be out of her mother's sight and the two of them would always be touching each other. Physical contact is terribly important for these babies. It seems to give them the will to live.' Somehow Daphne managed to make having a baby elephant rummaging around the kitchen seem the most natural thing in the world.

The next day we returned to film. We were convinced that an interview with Daphne, given against the emotive backdrop of these orphaned baby elephants, the tiny casualties of poaching, could prove the key to swaying public opinion. We had to get it right.

Fiona was very playful this morning. John, her keeper, dragged out an old tractor inner tube and an umbrella for her to play with, and she sat on the tyre and rolled the umbrella around with her trunk. While Allan operated the video-camera, Ros and I took still photographs. I noticed some raw patches on Fiona's back. 'She was badly sunburned when she came in here,' explained Daphne. 'Normally baby elephants stay underneath the shade of the mother, but after Fiona's mother was shot she was exposed to the sun. It's one of the things that kills them when they're orphaned, but I hope with Fiona we got there in time. The blisters are starting to heal now.'

Fiona was starting to get impatient, and John took her off to be fed. We followed and were surprised to see him walk over to a large sheet of heavy tarpaulin slung hammock-style between two trees. He held Fiona's bottle up beside the tarpaulin and the baby elephant instantly nuzzled up and seized the teat, guzzling contentedly with the tarpaulin resting on her back.

'The tarpaulin makes her feel secure,' John explained. 'For her it's like being under her mother's belly.'

We were completely captivated by the baby elephant and the trust she showed in her new 'mother'. If John walked away, Fiona would stop playing and immediately trot off behind him, nudging and shoving him boisterously.

'It's very difficult for the keepers,' Daphne said. 'I don't like them to get too attached to each other, because it's important that the orphans retain some independence so we can eventually return them to the wild. But it's hard not to fall in love with them, isn't it?'

When the babies were weaned and healthy, Daphne told us, she took them down to the Tsavo national park. There, a thirty-year-old elephant known as Eleanor took over the duties of foster-mother from the keepers. Although Eleanor had never produced young of her own, she had a well-developed maternal instinct and was an expert at teaching the orphans to forage and cope with life in the bush.

While Allan was setting up the camera to film the interview Fiona ambled over to join Daphne, and we decided to include her in the shot for as long as she chose to stay. Daphne was evidently used to talking on camera, and her sincerity and dedication to the elephant cause shone through as she spoke. She talked concisely and movingly about the orphans and the killings.

'Something must be done to stop the demand for ivory, to stop people in America, Britain and places like that buying the end result, carved ivory. After all, nobody needs ivory, and as long as there is a demand for ivory elephants are going to be killed in Africa.'

It was evening by the time we finished filming. Daphne was expecting guests and after a while she left us to welcome them. We stayed outside to watch Fiona and talk to John before going back into the house. We found the living room full of people, and it was obvious that a propaganda campaign was in progress. I slipped in at the back of the room next to JF.

A ruggedly good-looking man was speaking forcibly on the subject of the Kenyan army's General Service Unit, which had been entrusted with anti-poaching duties.

'You can't imagine how badly organized they are. They have no training at all to deal with poachers. In fact it's said that they run away if they come across any.' His remarks seemed to be chiefly addressed to a woman dressed in a smart safari-suit who was sitting opposite him.

'Who's the man speaking?' I asked JF quietly.

'That's Marcus Russell,' he whispered back. 'He's a safari tour operator. He's always having a go at the ivory trade. The woman he's lecturing is Janet Bohlen, the wife of Buff Bohlen, the vice-president of WWF US. Janet's a journalist and wants to write a story about elephants. I know Marcus wants WWF to change its policy. Maybe he thinks this is the way to influence it.' JF winked. 'Actually, if she could be persuaded to follow up this side of the business instead of just writing another story about baby elephants, it could help a lot.'

Daphne sat in the corner quietly listening to Marcus,

and displaying unashamed emotion at his descriptions of the massacres he had seen. Occasionally she put in a few confirming words of her own. 'Marcus says that there are only a fraction of the elephants there once were in Tsavo East,' she interrupted at one point. 'There were forty-five thousand in the park twenty years ago. The few that remain now are frightened. They huddle in a triangle between Aruba, Voi and the south-east boundary because they feel safer round the tourists. They're smart animals, you know.'

Janet Bohlen seemed sympathetic to what she was hearing and was taking copious notes.

Allan, Ros and I moved out on to the veranda, not wishing to be too conspicuous. Daphne joined us a little later and sat down next to Ros. 'If you want to film elephant carcasses, Jill and JF are going to Tsavo at the weekend,' she said quietly. 'They have permission to go off the tourist roads into the bush. Lissa Ruben, one of our helpers, saw two dead elephants there last week. She could show you where they are, if you'd like. But don't talk about it and, whatever you do, don't tell anyone that you intend to shoot any film.' With a smile of collusion she walked back into the living room to rejoin her guests.

We met Jill, JF and Lissa at a house inside the park gate at Voi which was owned by Simon Trevor, the film cameraman. Simon was perhaps best known for his film *Bloody Ivory*, produced in the mid-seventies, which had documented the start of the ivory poaching era. He and his assistant, Barbara, were currently working on a film for Anglia Television's 'Survival' series about the dung beetle – a creature for which Simon displayed an amazing enthusiasm. In our ignorance we hadn't realized how much the dung beetle depended on the elephant, but Simon soon put us right in forthright terms.

'Did you know that four times a day an adult elephant produces a heap of dung which weighs six kilograms? That dung is buried by forty thousand dung beetles feeding and breeding on it.'

Simon was a mine of information about elephant dung. 'It contains the seeds of the baobab and acacia trees. The seeds germinate by passing through the gut of an elephant. There's something in the elephant's digestive tract which produces a chemical change in the seed-coat. What that means is that if you have an Africa without elephants you'll also have an Africa without acacia and baobab trees. How many people realize that, do you think?'

That evening we listened fascinated as Simon expounded on the ecology of Africa and the elephant's contribution to the complex web of life found in the bush. Elephants, he told us, had evolved with the environment in which they live. They are what is known as a keystone species, which means that in addition to the dung beetle the well-being of many other species depends on them. Their impact on forest and savannah helps create a less hostile environment for other animals. During droughts they are able to sense water beneath the surface and dig new waterholes where other species drink. In 'impenetrable' bush they create pathways where other animals follow. The appearance of Africa would change if the elephant disappeared. The environment would degrade. The diversity of the vegetation would be lost. And as inevitably as night follows day other species would follow them into extinction.

It was by now obvious to us that the importance of the elephant went far deeper than the value of its tusks. The balance of nature in Africa had taken millions of years to evolve. It was rather presumptuous of human beings to think that they could upset that balance without paying any penalty. Previous interferences by man had caused famines, droughts, and desertification of parts of Africa. But we seemed to have learned nothing from past mistakes.

There was a distinctly spartan air about Simon Trevor's house. The floors were of bare concrete and his mod cons consisted of a fridge and a cold-water tap. But he made us very welcome. We were to spend the night sleeping on camp-beds under mosquito-nets and would make a very early start the next morning. We were firmly instructed on the rules of the house. 'Make sure you bring your washing in before dark,' Lissa advised. 'There are lions around.'

'And keep your eyes open when you're wandering around the house, too,' warned Barbara. 'I was attacked by a spitting cobra in the shower last week. It spat venom in my eyes.' She grinned. 'Luckily the shower was running, so the venom was diluted.'

'What if it hadn't been?'

'Oh, I'd have been blinded probably,' said Barbara matter-of-factly.

I decided to postpone my shower until daylight.

It was dusk when we returned from photographing the two elephant carcasses the following day. Our faces were ingrained with red dust, and we were tired and hungry, but we also felt a sense of accomplishment. Our cameras had recorded one more vital piece of evidence against the poachers. Our case for the abolition of the ivory trade was growing stronger daily.

8

ALLAN

I had managed to engineer a last-minute invitation from Perez Olindo, the acting chairman, to attend the meeting of the CITES African Elephant Working Group at the United Nations building in Nairobi.

The declared purpose of this working group was to find new ways of controlling the ivory trade. The meeting was made up largely of representatives of the main ivory exporting countries of Africa and of the main ivory importing countries: the United States, Hong Kong, Germany, China, Japan. The big ivory traders' associations were also present. Only a handful of carefully selected 'moderate' conservationists had been invited to attend. The WWF were represented, as were a few of their affiliated groups, but there was no spokesperson for any of the wildlife organizations which publicly supported an ivory ban. (I was there undercover, since Olindo had assumed I was representing Greenpeace and I had not bothered to correct him.)

As Jacques Berney, the deputy secretary-general of the CITES secretariat, looked over in my direction, I saw his mouth literally fall open. He obviously remembered me from a meeting a few weeks earlier when I had rather outspokenly represented the views of Greenpeace. Now in his eyes I was branded a troublemaker. Fortunately not everyone saw me in the same light. The one man I really wanted to talk to at this meeting came into the room soon after I sat down: Ian Parker, an expert on the international ivory trade, a leading opponent of an ivory ban and a man occasionally employed by CITES as an ivory consultant.

I was very anxious not to alienate Parker at this stage. Before I nailed my colours to the mast I wanted to tap him for all the information I could about illegal ivory. Earlier in the year I'd met him in London on Greenpeace business and had carefully prepared the ground for future meetings. I had spent a day being thoroughly obsequious, worming my way into his confidence. A slightly built man, he had an undeniable charm. 'I loathe conservationists,' he had declared gleefully at our first meeting. I'd played along with him. Every statement I made had been deliberately moderate and noncommittal, intended to lull him into believing that the radical image of Greenpeace was exaggerated.

I'd even nodded sympathetically when he maintained that the ivory trade was not responsible for the decline of Africa's elephants.

'The drop in numbers is simply due to increasing human populations and a lack of investment in national parks,' he'd asserted confidently.

'Really? I hadn't realized that,' I'd responded, wide-eyed. I'd praised his knowledge of the ivory trade, and played very dumb, pretending to know nothing whatsoever about the elephant issue. I had wanted him to think that I could be useful to him; that he could influence me to sway Greenpeace policy on elephants. Without quite spelling it out, I had also planted the idea in his mind that Greenpeace were looking for an elephant expert to act as their consultant. I'd suggested that since Greenpeace was now a very big and successful organization it would probably pay a substantial fee to the right person. Consultancies were one of Parker's chief sources of income, as I well knew.

It seemed the ploy had worked. As Ian Parker entered the Nairobi CITES meeting he looked around and made a beeline towards me, smiling affably. 'Hello, Allan. Do you mind if I sit next to you?'

He introduced me to the man near him: Rowan Martin, deputy director of research from the Zimbabwe Wildlife Department, and another supporter of the continuing ivory trade. 'Mr Thornton and his Greenpeace group have become successful moderates,' Parker announced patronizingly. I shook Martin's hand and assumed what I imagined to be a moderate expression.

The meeting was called to order. One of the first speakers was the American delegate, Ron Lambertson. 'This is the most important CITES meeting since Ottawa in 1987,' he declared. 'The adequacy of CITES ivory controls to ensure elephant protection is coming under increasing scrutiny. If there is not substantial progress in improving ivory controls, the US may have to support the end of the ivory trade.'

So the writing was on the wall. How would CITES respond to the challenge?

The answer was disappointing, if predictable. Very soon the meeting became bogged down in a side issue, the legalization of Burundi ivory. The Burundi story was a complex one, confused further by Burundi's rapidly changing governments. Part of it we knew well already from Dave's Hong Kong investigation. In 1986 the Burundi government had said they would join CITES and respect the ivory controls. In return the CITES secretariat was persuaded to legalize eighty-nine tonnes of their illegal ivory.

The amnesty was great for Burundi. Their ivory was now worth more than twice its previous value. They sold it, did not join CITES, and carried on importing poached ivory from the rest of Africa as before. Not surprisingly, they now had another stockpile without permits; ninety tonnes this time, potentially worth $20 million on the legitimate market, though much less if it could only be sold without CITES permits. The Burundi government – a new one by now – wanted CITES to legalize this stockpile, too. But they assured the meeting they had now stopped ivory imports, and of course if their request was granted they promised this time they really would join CITES . . .

Jacques Berney spoke strongly in favour of granting the Burundi request. The Burundi delegate spoke strongly in favour of it. Furious though I was, I had to bite my tongue. I hadn't got what I wanted from Parker yet. In the end the meeting compromised, recommending that a third of the Burundi ivory, the fraction that had been confiscated by the Government after they had banned imports, be legalized straight away. The proceeds were to be used to benefit conservation in Burundi. A decision on the remaining two-thirds was deferred until the main meeting of CITES in October 1989. Parker seemed to know a great deal about this ivory. He leaned over to me and said quietly: 'That other two-thirds is still owned by independent traders, and there's no way the money from that ivory is going to be used for conservation.'

Next the illegal ivory trade in the United Arab Emirates was discussed. 'We do not know what is going on,' Berney admitted. 'We are still working to try to send a delegation to UAE. We know it is being used as an entrepôt, but we don't know what is happening there.'

It exemplified what was wrong with CITES. Crucial decisions appeared to be taken despite a lack of information. Rumour and hearsay about the ivory trade were recycled so often that they eventually became accepted as fact. It seemed to me that CITES members either had extremely poor judgement or were being manipulated. Perhaps both.

The meeting was only scheduled to last three days, and already the first day was over with nothing concrete being suggested in the way of new controls. The second day was as bad: it was devoted entirely to discussing a proposed study of the ivory trade which the 1987 CITES meeting had mandated this group to produce. Both Parker and

Rowan Martin spoke against conducting any inquiry outside the boundaries of Africa. 'There is too much of a myth about the ivory trade affecting elephant conservation,' claimed Rowan Martin. Jacques Berney then announced that the CITES secretariat had already employed Parker ('because he is the best connoisseur of the ivory trade') as a consultant to complete a report on the ivory market within Africa. That, he implied, should be sufficient. By the time they did get around to doing this study there'd be no elephants left to worry about anyway, I reflected.

By the third day of the meeting I had given up hope of these people achieving anything that would benefit elephants. Across the conference room I spotted Jorgen Thomsen who was head of Traffic US, the WWF-affiliated body which looked at wildlife trade controls, and only last year he had defended the CITES ivory controls to me, claiming they would work if given time. Now he was looking deeply depressed. I guessed that his long-standing loyalty to the quota system was being severely tested. An Australian scientist had just predicted that elephants would be extinct in East Africa within the next six years. In Africa as a whole he gave them twenty-five years. Other experts had given them as little as ten years. Despite those dire prophecies, this extraordinary meeting had taken decisions that not only favoured continued ivory trading, but could actually encourage it to escalate.

'How about going for a drink tonight?' I asked Jorgen during a coffee break.

He laughed morosely. 'Make it two drinks and you've got a deal.'

I was still hoping to get useful information out of Parker, but time was running out. We had continued to sit side by side during the conference, and our chumminess had caused raised eyebrows around the meeting room. But, although he had dropped several little snippets of information my way during the previous two days, I wanted something more specific.

'You should write a book about the ivory trade,' I flattered him now. 'You know more about it than anyone else in the world.'

He smiled wryly. 'I'd get bumped off by the ivory traders if I did that.' He looked at his watch. 'It's nearly time for us to finish for the morning. Would you like to join us for lunch?'

We ate with Rowan Martin and George Panghetti of the Zimbabwe Wildlife Department. I had a sudden inkling of how Daniel must have felt. All three of these 'lions' were powerful advocates of continued ivory trading. As I pretended to concentrate on my meal I listened avidly to their conversation.

'I've got to find the Burundi delegation,' Parker announced. 'They want to have dinner with me tonight. They've asked me to go out and register that ivory they've got, the way I did in 1986.' He chuckled. 'The trouble is they still owe me the fee for that job. They say it was incurred by the last government; and tough luck, they're not going to pay it. Still, I suppose it's not so bad. I was paid by the trader who owned the ivory and I got another fee from the CITES secretariat as a consultant. I was collecting three separate fees for doing the same job!'

Disguising my shock at this dramatic revelation, I said admiringly: 'How ever did you manage to do that?'

Parker rose to the bait. 'Well, in 1986 a Burundi ivory trader contacted the CITES secretariat and said he wanted to legalize his ivory. He wanted to get out of the illegal trade and go legal. The CITES secretariat arranged to meet with the trader, and when they did he offered them fifty thousand dollars. But the secretariat told this trader: "There's a consultant in Nairobi you can contact." Meaning me.'

'So what happened?'

'A few days later I got a phone call from this trader asking me to lunch. I went along, and the guy wanted to know how to legalize his sixty tonnes of ivory. I said I

93

would tell him how he could do it, but my fee for doing that would be three per cent of the value of the ivory.'

'And he accepted that?' I asked, my mind doing rapid mental arithmetic.

'Oh, yes.'

'So what did you tell him?' What sort of advice was worth hundreds of thousands of dollars, I wondered.

Parker grinned. 'It was quite simple. I told him that to get his ivory registered he would have to get the Burundi government to join CITES. He said that was no problem and that he just had to bribe the right people. And, sure enough, the guy got the Burundi government as far as stamping the CITES application papers.'

Nice work, I thought. But Parker hadn't finished yet.

'Then the CITES secretariat hired me as a consultant to go to Burundi to register the total ivory stocks there. I registered the whole eighty-nine tonnes in nine days and marked them all myself with CITES numbers.'

'How did you go about organizing it?'

'I told the traders they had until the twenty-fifth of September to get their ivory there and that I wouldn't accept any more after that. The traders even offered me $750,000 to delay the deadline for registering the ivory. They said they had more ivory coming in from Tanzania and Zaïre, but it wouldn't be there in time.'

I could hardly believe what I was hearing. The CITES amnesty had been for the existing ivory stocks in Burundi. But the Burundi traders had gone so far as to ask Parker to use it to launder any additional poached ivory they could get their hands on.

'Were you able to do that?' I asked.

Parker shook his head ruefully. 'In any case I didn't trust those guys to pay the money into my account and I didn't think I was going to be able to carry three-quarters of a million dollars in cash out through the airport, so I backed out. When I refused to extend the deadline, a group of traders took me into a room and one of them pulled a knife on me. They knew my home address and threatened my wife too. But, anyway,' he concluded, 'the whole situation would have unwound. CITES was already getting criticized for registering these ivory stocks, and the CITES secretariat were starting to panic when I told them the traders wanted to extend the deadline.'

I was overcome by an almost physical sense of outrage. Parker's revelations were just incredible. Employed as a CITES consultant, he had nevertheless just admitted that he was prepared to accept payment from illegal ivory traders. And this was the man who the secretariat had just recommended should take charge of their official trade study! Would the WWF still have confidence in the CITES regulations if they could hear this?

After leaving the restaurant to return to the meeting I excused myself and went to the men's washroom where I wrote Parker's story down verbatim. I was determined that other people should hear about this and be awakened to the implications. If what Parker said was true, then it threw a very different light on this week's heated discussions about the new Burundi stockpile. What deals might be going on there behind the scenes?

The meeting was about to end. The Hong Kong delegate had put a question to the United States and the European Community representatives. Would they allow ivory imports if the CITES certificate did not give a country of origin? It was obvious why they wanted to know. Certificates which did not name the source were usually only given for poached ivory which had been given an amnesty. Hong Kong was clearly interested in buying the ivory stockpile in Burundi, but first they wanted a guarantee that they could sell it through the United States and Europe.

So far I had not addressed the meeting at all. But now that I had got the information out of Parker there was no reason for me to keep silent any longer. Hong Kong's attempt to undermine the stand which the United States was making against poaching was just too blatant to allow it to pass. The time had come to show my true colours. I put my hand up.

Perez Olindo in the chair spotted it. 'Yes, Mr Thornton?'

I stood up.

'Mr Chairman, I have listened to the request that the Hong Kong delegate has just made. The whole world should be outraged at the despicable behaviour of Hong Kong's ivory traders and we should denounce their reprehensible role in wiping out Africa's elephants. Their request for other countries to accept such ivory is an appeal to support poaching, bribery and corruption, and should be completely rejected.'

I paused, wanting my next words to have maximum impact.

'My organization is a newcomer to the elephant debate, but I pledge our commitment to save the elephant. That means we have to stop the ivory trade and we will work with anyone else who is dedïcated to that aim.' I sat down.

Dozens of startled faces stared in my direction. From the seat on my left Parker glared at me, thunderstruck. 'Traitor!' his eyes declared. The cosy sense of *bonhomie* which had pervaded the meeting up to now had evaporated. No-one had ever denounced the Hong Kong ivory barons in a CITES meeting before.

From his seat at the other side of the room Jorgen gave me a thumbs-up signal.

'You should have seen Berney's face.' Jorgen took a gulp of the cold beer I'd promised him and smiled grimly at the recollection. 'And when he saw me encouraging you – well, if looks could kill!' He clapped me on the back. 'Anyway, it was a great speech. Everyone was talking about it afterwards.'

'It was a terrible meeting, though, Jorgen. You can't

still believe that the ivory trade can be controlled after that, can you?'

'It was very depressing,' Jorgen admitted gloomily. 'I thought we would make a lot of progress in three days, but we made none.'

'The only way we're going to stop poaching is by a total ban,' I said. 'I'm more convinced of that than I've ever been.'

The heat of the Kenyan evening had given us both a thirst. Jorgen drained his glass before giving me a reluctant smile.

'Yeah, you're right,' he conceded. 'We just have to destroy the trade.'

It must have been a difficult thing for Jorgen to acknowledge after all the hard work he had put into trying to make the control system work, and I respected him for it. But if Jorgen was now on the same side of the fence as EIA I wanted to capitalize on it before he had second thoughts.

'Jorgen, if you really think we need a ban, why don't you write an Appendix One proposal for the African elephant to be presented to CITES?' I suggested.

In order to consider upgrading a species to the Appendix One list, which would mean a ban on trading, CITES required a country to present a detailed scientific and technical proposal setting out the arguments for the suggested change in status. Because of his position within WWF, Jorgen would have access to the most up-to-date scientific information available, which would greatly strengthen the impact of the proposal. Even more important, in writing the proposal he would be declaring his personal commitment to achieving a ban. Such a commitment from one of their chief representatives could in turn trigger a fundamental change in WWF's policy.

To my relief Jorgen didn't hesitate. 'OK, I'll do it. I can take a month off from work to write it. I'll come back here to get hold of the data. The only thing is . . .' he hesitated, embarrassed. 'I obviously can't do it as WWF business. Could EIA help me out with air fares?'

I gave a hollow laugh. 'We're broke as usual, but don't worry. I'll find the money somewhere. Now, we've got eleven months until the next CITES meeting and all proposals have to be submitted five months before the meeting. That means it's got to be with CITES by May. And before that we have to get a country to agree to put it forward, so we need all the time we can get. Can you have the Appendix One proposal done by March?'

'I'll get it to you before the end of March,' Jorgen promised.

For the first time that week I felt optimistic.

9

November 1988,
Tanzania

Allan

'I've been thinking about Burundi and Zaïre,' I said. 'I'm not so sure now that it's the most productive use of our time to go there.'

Ros, who was busy copying the jottings from her notebook, looked up in surprise. 'Where else do you think we ought to go?'

'Well, we've received lots of information relating to Tanzania. First, there was that ship, *Fadhil Allah*, picking up ivory off the coast; then, when we were in Dubai, we found records of imports from Tanzania; and now, on this trip as well, Tanzania's name keeps cropping up. It sounds to me as though it could be a major centre for ivory smuggling.' I reached into my bag and pulled out a loose-leaf file. 'Iain Douglas-Hamilton has lent me a report on the poaching around the Selous game reserve and we've been given the names of several contacts. We'd have specific leads to follow up if we went to Tanzania.'

Dave frowned as he flicked through the file. 'Yes, but the trouble is that if we do that, we won't get to Burundi on this trip and we know there are ninety tonnes of ivory there right now.'

'Frankly, after what I heard at the CITES meeting I think our chances of finding out anything new about the Burundi ivory are pretty slim,' I said. 'They've already had a lot of people digging about trying to find out what's going on there. Their defences will be up. If we feel it's necessary, we can always go there some other time. But right now I definitely think it would be more productive to fly to Dar es Salaam for ten days.'

'I think you've got a point,' Ros agreed.

Dave hesitated. 'Come on,' I said. 'You're outnumbered. Don't forget Serengeti's in Tanzania, Dave.'

He laughed. 'Pull the other one. You can't kid me there'll be time for that!'

Tanzania had fascinated me for some time. I'd discussed its ivory problems with Chris Huxley, a former member of the CITES secretariat, when I met him in England earlier in the year. 'You won't get any co-operation from the Wildlife Department in Tanzania,' Huxley had predicted. 'Fred Lwezuela, the Director of Wildlife, is not all that keen on conservationists.'

I made a mental note to look more closely at Tanzania some day. Huxley must have read my mind. 'By the way,' he said, 'I think you ought to know that the last guy that was investigating the ivory trade in Dar es Salaam and got too close to the ivory dealers had his head chopped off. They stuck his head on the front of a Land Rover and drove around town for a day to warn off other people.'

'Who told you that?' I demanded sceptically.

Huxley looked mysterious. 'I can't tell you. I'm just advising you. That's all.'

It was Huxley who had first introduced me to Ian Parker, and Parker had confirmed the story. 'Yeah, the guy had his head chopped off and put on a Land Rover,' he said. I didn't believe them. The tale was too far-fetched to take seriously. But why had they both repeated it to me? To warn me off going to Tanzania? What did they think I might uncover there?

Our arrival in Dar es Salaam was enlivened for Ros and Dave, if not for me, by the loss of my vaccination certificate. For over two hours I argued with an airport 'doctor' who, wielding a filthy-looking syringe, threatened me with an instant injection. My only alternative, he explained with a sinister smile, was to make him 'a little gift'. Fortunately I managed to avoid both options by pointing to my Canadian passport. 'Canada and Tanzania are very good friends. Canada gives many gifts to Tanzania,' I repeated over and over again until finally he waved me through, his patience exhausted.

Dar es Salaam (literally Haven of Peace) came as a shock after Nairobi, which, for Africa, is a relatively affluent city. Here in contrast the streets were dusty and pot-holed, the buildings decrepit, and there was no street lighting. We spent our first night swatting mosquitoes in a seedy waterfront hotel which had neither air-conditioning nor working telephones. The next morning by mutual consent we moved to the Kunduchi Beach Hotel fifteen miles outside the capital, which was one of the few places that had rooms available.

It was an improvement, though only a slight one. The Kunduchi Beach had seen better days, and its once smart sixties décor was badly faded. The doors to our rooms appeared to have been kicked in on more than one occasion, while the walls were ingrained with ancient grime. It was even hotter in Tanzania than it had been in Kenya, but this hotel did at least have a few struggling fans to keep the air circulating, and, more important, it had telephones. Our rooms also had an unexpected bonus: magnificent views over an idyllic tropical beach.

Whilst in Kenya we had been advised to contact someone called Neil Baker on our arrival. An engineer and ornithologist, Neil was heavily involved in wildlife conservation. We left a message at his house asking him to contact us, and while we were waiting for a response we drove back into the city. We had hired a red VW Beetle which came complete with driver for a very reasonable charge. We felt it was a wise precaution in view of the primitive state of the roads, which in places looked as though they had been carpet-bombed. John, the driver, wove the Beetle expertly around the craters; even so, it took us three-quarters of an hour to traverse the fifteen miles into town.

We were looking for someone else who had been recommended to us: a sport hunter called Jason who took clients – usually rich Americans – into the bush to shoot elephants by permit. Despite our disapproval of any form of elephant killing, we recognized that sport hunters could have information that might be useful to us. WWF argued that sport hunting was a good example of their 'sustainable use of wildlife' policy in action. Americans and Europeans who were obsessed with the idea of big game hunting would pay huge amounts of money for a permit to shoot just one elephant.

As a sport hunter, Jason's livelihood was just as much threatened by elephant poaching as that of the tour operators, so we were keen to hear what he had to say on the subject. Jason turned out to be a swarthy man of indeterminate Mediterranean origin. 'President Mwinyi banned ivory trading inside Tanzania at the end of 1986,' he informed us. 'He's very keen on conservation. In fact he's the president of the Wildlife Conservation Society of Tanzania. But it was never going to be easy for him. There was a lot of opposition to the ban from people within the Government.' Jason looked knowing. 'It's understandable. Some of them are involved in the ivory business. But the Customs department have been quite determined about enforcing the ban here, and there've been a lot of seizures of ivory since 1986. It would be interesting for you to have a look inside the ivory room. That's what they call the warehouse where they hold the impounded ivory. Mind you, it's not as secure as it ought to be.'

'What do you mean?' I enquired.

He smiled knowingly. 'Oh, ivory disappears from it from time to time.'

'Can you suggest anyone it would be useful for us to talk to about poaching?' Dave asked.

Jason considered. 'Costa Mlay is a good person. He works in the Wildlife Department. You should see him.'

'Really? We've heard some bad things about the Wildlife Department here,' I said doubtfully.

Jason chuckled. 'And I'm sure a lot of them are true. But Costa is a clean guy. Very honest. Very dedicated towards wildlife protection. He was put into the Department two years ago to keep an eye on Fred Lwezuela. Have you heard of him?'

I nodded. Lwezuela was the Director of Wildlife whom both Huxley and Parker had mentioned. I had seen him at the Nairobi meeting.

'There are rumours that Fred knows something about the ivory that keeps disappearing from the Customs shed,' Jason continued. 'He's certainly a very influential guy. I think President Mwinyi wants to see Costa replace Fred as Director, but Fred has some very powerful supporters in the Government who don't want to see him go. So all Costa can do for the moment is watch what he gets up to. You'll like Costa. He's a man of integrity. That's quite rare in this business,' he admitted.

'Fine. We'll speak to him. Do you know anyone else who might help us?' asked Ros.

'Well,' Jason considered, 'there is someone who'd talk to you. But he's not so reliable. A guy called Rex. He takes hunters out, too. He can tell you a lot about ivory, but don't tell him too much about yourselves. He probably shoots elephants himself when he gets the chance.' Jason wrote a phone number and address on a piece of paper. He pushed it over to us. 'Be careful.'

Breakfast at the Kunduchi Beach Hotel the following morning was a memorable experience, not so much because of the quality of the food – toast with canned butter and tar-like jam – but because of the frenetic character of the service. There were very few guests at the hotel, and the waiters descended on us in a swarm. No less than four separate waiters asked us for our order. Unfortunately they were obviously out of practice at communicating with the kitchen, and twenty minutes later we were still waiting for our coffee.

There was a message for us that Neil Baker would call at the hotel at six o'clock that evening. Since it was Sunday we decided to award ourselves a day off, and after breakfast we retired to the beach to soak up the sun. The deserted white sands were straight out of a hedonist's dream, shaded by palm trees and cooled by the gentle breeze which blew in from the Indian Ocean.

'I wonder if it's snowing in England,' Ros mused contentedly.

Late in the afternoon, relaxed and slightly sunburned, we retired to the hotel bar to sample a killer-strength local brew called Safari Lager.

'Are you Allan Thornton?'

I swivelled around on my bar stool and found myself facing a thin man in shorts accompanied by a smiling, vivacious-looking woman and a young girl of about eight.

'Neil Baker?' I guessed.

'That's right.' Neil shook my hand. 'And this is Liz Boswell. She's honorary secretary of the Wildlife Conservation Society of Tanzania. And this is her daughter Katie.'

Introductions over, we settled at the bar to talk.

With Liz and Neil we made no pretence of being a film team. Their credentials as conservationists were too well established. Even the teddy bear Katie carried with her went by the name of Rainbow Warrior!

We had seen a copy of *Miombo*, the magazine of the Wildlife Conservation Society of Tanzania, and had read several authoritative articles by Liz. When we explained that we were researching the ivory trade, Neil invited us over to their home in Dar es Salaam where we could talk in more privacy.

Two hours later, after some difficulty in finding our way out of the hotel owing to a total blackout of all the lights

– a regular occurrence, according to John, our driver – we found ourselves confronting half a dozen baying guard dogs at the front of Neil and Liz's house. Fortunately Liz had assured us before she left the hotel that they were 'all noise', and by the time the front door opened the dogs had lost interest in us.

'Come in,' Liz smiled, and we filed into a large entrance hall lined with shelves containing an impressive library of books and wildlife magazines. Liz led us into the dining room, which was furnished with yet more bookshelves, and we seated ourselves around the big dining table.

'I hope you're going to make more use of what we tell you about ivory than the last person did,' Neil began.

'Who was that?' Dave asked.

'Buff Bohlen from WWF USA. He came through here last April on his way to a meeting in Lusaka.'

Liz looked scornful. 'We tried to give him and his colleagues all our information on the ivory trade, but they didn't seem interested. They said: "We've got it all under control." They think they're the experts.' She laughed derisively. 'They really believe they're in command of the situation.'

So we weren't the only ones with reservations about WWF.

'Well, we *know* it's not under control,' I said. 'We're under no illusions about that after what we've seen in Dubai and Hong Kong. What we're trying to do is to get the material together for a campaign against the ivory trade. We want to prove that poaching is destroying Africa's elephants. And what we need is contacts – people who can tell us the inside story.'

Neil was enthusiastic. 'I think that should be possible,' he said. 'Hang on a minute. I'm just going to make a phone call.'

Twenty minutes later he returned bearing Tusker beers and two big bags full of cooked chicken and French fries. It had been nearly twelve hours since our unappetizing breakfast, and we ate with gusto. We had almost finished when the guard dogs let out a warning howl and Neil disappeared outside. Shortly afterwards he returned accompanied by a smartly dressed black man. 'I'd like to introduce you to Costa Mlay,' he said.

Liz, Costa and Neil went through the elaborate ritual of polite greetings which we were to discover were part of social etiquette in Tanzanian society. It made our Londoners' tendency to dive straight into discussions without preliminaries seem terribly crass.

Costa pulled a chair up to the table. 'Now,' he said when everyone was settled, 'Neil told me you are investigating the ivory trade. I would be most interested to hear what you found out in Kenya.' I summarized the information we had gathered there and gave him a résumé of the fruitless CITES meeting I had attended in Nairobi before I broached the subject of Tanzanian ivory.

'How does the ivory trade work here?' I asked. 'From what we've heard it's very complicated.'

'It *is* complicated,' Costa agreed. 'There are many different routes that the ivory can take. But one thing's for sure. It's a very big trade.'

'Is Burundi involved?' asked Ros.

'Burundi has a lot to do with it. It's the cause of a lot of our problems. Without Burundi the poachers would find it much harder to get the ivory out of Africa. There are at least two ways that Burundi is involved. One established link concerns ivory that has been poached in the Selous game reserve. It's taken into Burundi by Somali truckers. They have a favourite route: Dodoma, Singida and finally Kigoma in the north. It ends up at Bujumbura in Burundi. There is no problem getting it through Customs, because Burundi allows anything of value to be imported tax free even if it's illicit. They only tax the ivory when they export it.'

'And you said there was another way Burundi is involved?'

'Ah, this is quite different. What happens here is that someone will send a container full of second-hand clothes, or something else like that, from Dubai to Burundi via Tanzania. But the container never gets to Burundi because halfway across Tanzania it stops. It's unloaded; the clothes are taken out and poached ivory is put into the container instead. Now, next comes the cunning bit. The poachers have a collaborator who works for the Customs department of Burundi. When the poachers contact him to say the shipment is ready he flies into Tanzania, meets the lorry, now loaded with ivory, attaches a Burundi Customs seal to the container and issues false papers complete with official stamps which describe it as something else! Sealed transit cargo cannot be opened of course. But the container vehicle never goes to Burundi. Now it simply turns around and heads back for Dar es Salaam; then it's loaded on to a ship and goes back to Dubai. No problem.'

'How did you find out about this?' Dave asked.

Costa smiled and helped himself to a piece of chicken. 'Because,' he said, 'we've intercepted one of these shipments of ivory near Dodoma when the lorry had an accident. The driver was killed, and the container was damaged so badly that its load was revealed. We found three hundred and eighty-three tusks. Then we found a secret compartment that had ninety-two more tusks hidden in it. All of the false Burundi papers and seals were in the truck.'

He beamed as he regarded our stunned expressions. 'You come to my office tomorrow and I will give you more details.'

We did not go immediately to Costa's office on Monday as we had a prior appointment to view the Government's ivory room, home of the ivory confiscated by Customs officers since Tanzania's recent trading ban. We had declared ourselves to be 'tourists'. The security was rather tighter than it had been for the ivory room in Hong Kong.

The man at the gate gave us a pass, and we then had to wait in a small office for the man with the key to the ivory room. On the desk lay a visitors' book. Idly I opened it and flipped through the pages. Suddenly I froze as my eyes alighted on a familiar name. George Poon.

'Dave, can you get a picture of this?' I indicated the signature.

With a soundless whistle Dave raised his camera. But he was thwarted by the sudden appearance of the warehouse guard. He shrugged frustratedly at me as the guard beckoned us to follow him.

'Never mind. Later,' I said.

The guard led us through two huge doors into a dark tomb-like area. The air inside was still and very hot. At first, after the blinding sunlight outside, we could see nothing, but gradually our eyes adjusted and we gaped as we discerned the shapes of thousands upon thousands of tusks laid out in neat rows, all stacked in piles according to size and weight.

'How many are there?' gasped Ros.

'About six thousand tusks. Weighing twenty tonnes.' From the way the guard reeled off the figures, I guessed visits from 'tourists' were a fairly regular occurrence. Had George Poon, too, declared himself to be a tourist as he assessed the confiscated stock? What had he been doing here? Buying ivory?

We walked up and down the rows. There were dozens of piles. Most of the tusks were small, around five kilos in weight. In one corner there was a small pile of really tiny tusks, ranging from five to sixteen inches in length.

'Those are just babies,' Ros exclaimed.

'Yes.' The guard nodded sympathetically. 'Just babies.'

The sheer volume of the confiscations was daunting. Most people accept that with ivory, as with drugs, what is confiscated represents only a small percentage of the amount that gets through. It was horrifying, therefore, to see the size of this cache. If they had impounded the tusks of three thousand elephants, how many had actually been killed by the poachers in recent years?

'May we take pictures?' Dave enquired.

'Yes, yes. Please,' invited the guard. Dave and Ros spent forty-five minutes snapping away, while I took out the Video 8 camera which had been loaned to us by ITN to record this African trip. At the hotel that morning I had taken it out of its too professional-looking metal case and slipped it into a small canvas knapsack thinking it might more easily pass as a standard home video-camera. The ploy worked. The guard watched indulgently as Dave, Ros and I filmed each other wandering through the rows of tusks. We even got the guard to join in, holding up various tusks and estimating the age of elephant they had come from.

'This one maybe one year,' he said, indicating the five-inch tusk.

'And those?' asked Dave, pointing to half a dozen huge tusks propped against metal supports.

'Oh, those are old.' The guide shook his head. 'They weigh fifty to sixty kilos. They come from very old bull elephants. But we don't find those any more. There are none left. Those tusks were confiscated twenty years ago.'

After an hour in this stifling tomb we were drenched in sweat. Satisfied with our filming session, we returned to the guard's office. He seemed completely unsuspicious of our activities so far, and I decided to risk a final request.

'May we take some photos of the visitors' book? Just out of interest?'

He made no objection, and Dave snapped shots of several pages including the one with George Poon's signature. What would the guard say, I wondered, if he knew that the hand that had written this name had most probably also signed the death warrant for many of the elephants at whose tusks we had just looked?

We had intended to try to see Fred Lwezuela while we were visiting Costa, but were told he was out of town that day. Costa's office was on the ninth floor of the Ministry of Lands, Tourism and Natural Resources, with a magnificent view over the harbour. He greeted us warmly and, opening a locked filing cabinet, took out a thick binder bursting with documents.

'These are the details of the shipment involved in the road accident that we discussed last night.' Costa put them down on the table in front of us. 'I also have details here of another ivory shipment seized in Belgium which I thought might interest you. It was discovered because Belgian Customs officials became suspicious of some containers on a ship from Tanzania. They were addressed to Dubai via Antwerp, and their documentation said they contained beeswax. But the Belgians thought it might be drugs and opened them. Altogether they found nineteen hundred tusks.'

'How had they got out of Tanzania?' I asked. 'Which route? The same as the accident shipment?'

'No. These containers had been sent via West Africa, so that's another route we now know the poachers are using. There was a big dispute over that shipment. It was all addressed to a firm in Dubai. They demanded that it be sent on, but the Belgians held it. They did tell us about it, but they wouldn't hand it back to us, either. In the end they sold it for $750,000 to ivory merchants and kept the money for themselves.' Costa shrugged philosophically. 'It is not the first time Belgium has got involved in poached ivory. It's a disgrace, but there is very little we can do about it. Now, perhaps we can help each other. Is there anything else you can tell me that you have found out about Tanzanian ivory?'

'We do know that a great deal of it was turning up in

the UAE all last year,' said Dave. 'At least eighty tonnes into Dubai alone.'

Costa was instantly alert. 'Do you have any proof of that?'

'Yes, we have documents from the statistics department in Dubai. We'll let you have copies.'

'That will be very useful. We have never had proof of the amount of ivory received in Dubai.'

Again Ros brought up the subject of Burundi. 'What do you think will happen there, now they say they've banned the ivory trade? Surely the poachers won't be able to use it to export their ivory any more.'

Costa shook his head. 'The indications we have are that Burundi will continue to receive ivory for the next few years. The market is prepared to receive ivory and to organize the shipments. The traders seem to be confident they can bribe or outwit the officials there. If the Burundi government gets very tough, I think the traders might go to a very lawless country like eastern Zaïre or else go through Uganda and Rwanda to Mombasa. There will always be ways as long as the traders are rich enough to buy people off.'

And as long as people can be bought off Burundi's Customs officers are going to continue to allow the ivory in, I reflected. So it wouldn't be stopped at the border.

'What about patrolling the roads in Tanzania? Couldn't you stop these containers getting out if you had regular road-checks?' Dave asked.

Costa stood up and walked to the map displayed on the wall. 'If we threw all our resources into patrolling this stretch of road leading to Kigoma, then, yes, I think we could stop the illegal trade here almost overnight. This is where most of the illegal ivory moves. It was planned to do this, but the plan had to be suspended. It would cost too much. The Tanzanian government doesn't have the money to spare for something like that. We are not a rich country.'

In the short time since we'd met him Costa had given us important insights into the ivory trade. So far, apart from a brief résumé of our Dubai and Hong Kong discoveries, I felt we had given him very little in return.

'What can we do to help *you*, Costa?' I asked.

He considered. 'Two things. Find out more about the men involved at the final end of the ivory trade. And, most important, find out who their agents in Africa are. If we could identify them, it might give us a chance of controlling the situation.'

We had an appointment to meet the sport hunter called Rex, described by his colleague Jason as being 'not so reliable'. Rex was a larger-than-life Hemingway sort of character. Although he had glanced casually at our Film London card, he seemed totally unconcerned about incriminating himself. Obviously he did not consider that three small-time film-makers presented any threat to him.

'Do I know anyone killing elephants illegally?' he repeated incredulously. 'You'll have to arrest half the foreign diplomats in this country if you want to stop that. They're all doing it, and sending it home in their luggage because they've got diplomatic immunity.' His manner suggested he found this quite amusing. 'I've taken guys from embassies out myself to shoot elephants,' he admitted. 'It costs them ten or twenty bucks to get the ranger to look the other way. But that sort aren't the worst.'

'Oh? Who are the worst?' prompted Ros.

'Well, some of these embassy guys are into this racket in a big way. Not just shooting a couple of elephants for themselves. They've got whole gangs out shooting for them. They're moving a lot of ivory out in diplomatic baggage. To nail them the police have to catch them red-handed with the ivory. But if it's in an embassy car there's nothing the police can do, because the car has diplomatic immunity too.'

'Which embassies are involved?' I asked.

'Oh, it's no secret. You can read about them in the papers here. At least,' he grinned, 'you read about the ones that do get caught. The Iranians, the Pakistanis, the Chinese. They're all doing it. Why not? It's risk-free.'

'And what about safari hunting?' I asked. 'Does everyone keep to the rules with that?'

'Don't make me laugh,' said Rex. 'I'll tell you what happens. You get a permit which allows you to shoot an elephant, a leopard, whatever you like. So you shoot the elephant. But it's not a very big one. Your client is a fat old American who has just spent twenty-five thousand dollars on this safari, and he's not happy. He grumbles that the tusks aren't big enough. So what do you do? Another elephant comes along with bigger tusks. There's a ranger with you who's supposed to make sure you keep to the rules, so you give him ten or twenty dollars to look the other way and then you shoot the bigger animal as well. He goes off with the big tusks and you're left with a spare set of tusks to sell. Who's going to find out? Most of the hunting outfits do it. If they don't, they're gonna be out of business. None of their clients will come back again. Sure it's hard on the elephants but . . .' He shrugged. 'You have to make a living.'

'Karibu.' Liz smiled as we walked into the office of Tanzania's Wildlife Conservation Society. Both she and Neil always met their visitors with this greeting – the Swahili word for 'welcome'.

'Hey, guys, come on in.' Neil beckoned us into his inner sanctum – a small room from which he ran his engineering business as well as his conservation work. 'There's someone here I want you to meet.' A man stood up as we entered. 'Sidney, meet Ros, Dave and Allan. This is Sidney Mabawiki. He's a Tanzanian journalist. And he's been investigating the same problem as you. Take a look at this. You might find something of interest. It's all Sidney's work.'

Neil handed me a thick orange file. I riffled through the pages with growing interest. It was full of accounts of incidents concerning the illegal ivory trade. All were described in the most comprehensive detail. Dates, places, names, amounts. Sidney's notes rivalled any police file ever compiled. I passed a handful of the loose-leaf pages to Dave and Ros to study.

'This is very impressive. How long have you been putting this together, Sidney?' I asked at last.

'Oh, I started about three years before I met Mr Baker. He has helped me to do more,' Sidney said diffidently. 'I have always been very concerned about ivory poaching. I wanted to make a record of what is going on in Tanzania.'

'Have you published any of it?'

Sidney shook his head. 'If there is a prosecution, then I report on it for my paper of course; but, the way things are now in Tanzania, it would be unwise for me to draw attention to what I am doing. I think a lot of people would want to stop me investigating, you know.'

'And have you discovered any sort of organization behind the poaching?'

Sidney nodded. 'What we know is this. The primary collection point for ivory is Ifakara. From there it is taken by small vehicles to secret depots in Dar es Salaam. Different routes are used to move ivory from national parks or reserves. Most of it comes from the Selous game reserve. In the Dar es Salaam depots it is loaded into trucks, and different routes are used to take it into Burundi.'

'And how do the smugglers avoid the ivory being discovered? What happens if the police stop them before they get to Burundi?' Dave asked.

'Ah,' Sidney smiled. 'They have three ways of dealing with that. The first is to have a secret chamber in the truck. It is sealed off from the main compartment, and it can only be loaded or unloaded from the top. Outside the length of the truck is ten metres, but the chamber inside is only eight metres long.'

I nodded. That must have been the type of truck involved in the crash Costa had told us about.

Sidney took a scrap of paper from Neil's desk and drew a rough diagram of a truck. 'The second way is to build large petrol-tanks holding six hundred litres, one tank on each side of the truck, like this.' He sketched two torpedo-shaped objects down the side of the truck. 'The drivers say they are to hold the extra petrol they will need to get to Burundi. One of them is really for that purpose.' He gave a dry chuckle. 'But the other one is filled with ivory. And they have a back-up in case they are discovered. A car accompanies the truck carrying a lot of cash. If officials stop a truck, they are offered bribes to allow it to continue.'

'And the third way?' Ros enquired.

'The third way is to use sealed containers. An arrangement is made with crooked Customs officers from Burundi to rendezvous secretly with the containers, seal them and issue papers saying "transit cargo to Burundi". Then, even if they are stopped before they get to Burundi, they cannot be opened.'

'That's similar to the method that Costa told us about with a different twist,' I said. I described the operation Costa had outlined where the trucks supposedly *en route* for Burundi did an about-turn after being sealed and documented out in the bush. Sidney listened intently. I realized that his unassuming manner concealed an immense knowledge of the complex workings of the ivory trade.

'Yes. That sounds quite possible. They probably do the same as the containers which actually are going to Burundi and change their licence plates between each town to make it more difficult to keep track of their movements.'

I listened to his revelations with growing excitement. This was all immensely important information. It was like stumbling on a gold-mine in the middle of a desert. It would have taken us years to uncover all this information by ourselves. I asked Sidney if his knowledge extended into the way the poachers worked.

'Oh, yes,' he said matter-of-factly. 'When they have killed the elephants they hack out the tusks with machetes. They move them some distance away and then usually they bury them in the bush. They are left there for some time. I have spoken to collectors whose job it is to retrieve this ivory from the bush. They hide it in sacks of food on farms. They are just couriers really; they are paid only a few thousand shillings, but that is not bad money for them. The average monthly wage here is fifteen hundred shillings or ten US dollars, so you can see why there is no problem finding people to do this work. Also, they are usually supplied with a vehicle: a pick-up truck. These collectors are the men who pay the poachers. The leader of the poaching gang gets about one thousand shillings for each kilo, and he divides that between his gang. On average it takes about two months after an elephant is killed for its tusks to reach Dar es Salaam.'

I was curious to know how much money the dealers could expect to make out of a truckload of poached ivory. After all, it was only worth half what legal ivory would fetch.

Sidney did not have to consult his notes. 'The average shipment is a hundred tusks at five kilos. That will bring seventy-five thousand US dollars. What the dealer does is to use the money in Dubai to purchase about twenty pick-up trucks, which are greatly in demand here. He ships them back to Tanzania and sells them at an enormous profit – it nearly doubles the money he got for the ivory. Then he spends that money again to buy more ivory from the poachers.'

'How on earth did you find out so much information?' Dave was visibly as impressed as I was.

Sidney said modestly: 'Oh, I've been a journalist for a long time – seventeen years. And I've worked all over Tanzania. I know police and Customs men in each district, and over the years you find out the ones you can trust. Some of them let me see the police files on the traders. I record it all. That's the important thing. To record it.'

'It's remarkable work,' I said sincerely.

'Thank you. If you like, I can also give you the names of the big dealers. Why don't you borrow the file tonight? Read it. Then let's meet again tomorrow.' Sidney smiled. 'I want to help you. There is no point in having all this information unless someone uses it.'

'Aren't you putting yourself in danger with this work?' I asked.

Sidney shrugged philosophically. 'Well, I was once threatened by a Somali poacher who was checking up on me. But he got killed in a road accident near Dodoma. Maybe I'm just lucky!'

In our hotel that evening we pored over Sidney's file and by the following day had prepared a long list of questions to ask him. We wanted to know the biggest dealers; where they traded ivory; how they organized it.

We met as arranged at the Oyster Bay Hotel, outside Dar es Salaam's city centre. 'Hello, my friends.' Beaming, Sidney shook us each by the hand. We ordered sodas and settled down for a long session.

'A man called Zaidi Barakah is the main collector from Ifakara,' Sidney revealed. 'He is of Asian origin. He lives in Burundi but he has a lot of relatives in Dar es Salaam. There was a case recently where one of Barakah's drivers was arrested who admitted to making twenty-three ivory smuggling trips in less than three years. But there has been very little progress in investigating Barakah, I'm afraid. Whenever the Security Office and officers from the Criminal Investigation Bureau start to look at how he gets his ivory out of Dar es Salaam, they tell me their initiatives get blocked by a senior police officer. They also say that this police officer is often a guest at Zaidi Barakah's house. What can they do?'

Sidney continued with more revelations of corruption, of major ivory deals, the traders involved, their political allies, and the bribes they paid.

'Did you know that one of Tanzania's MPs has just been sentenced to prison for selling ivory?' he said suddenly.

I sat up. 'No. Tell us more.'

'It's a very complicated story, but I will tell you the part that I think will be of most interest to you. It concerns deals with Europe. You see, this MP was selling ivory in the southern region of Tanzania through a middleman. And among his customers were some missionaries who exported the ivory to Germany.'

'You're kidding!' Ros exclaimed.

'No. It's true.'

'Do you know details?'

'Not too many. The MP wouldn't talk about who else was involved. He said he wanted to live to be an old man. But I do have an article about the case.' Sidney delved into his folder and produced a much-folded newspaper cutting. It was a page from a 1987 copy of the *Tanzanian Daily News*. I scanned the article quickly. It concerned a priest from a church in Mtwara who had been charged with having possession of 224 ivory tusks and subsequently sentenced to a gaol-term.

'This priest was working for another "father" who controls the illegal ivory trade in various missions,' said Sidney. 'The boss priest is known locally as "the king". He is very powerful and has much influence over all the local government officials and police there. He collects the poached ivory from all around the southern region of Tanzania and sends it out to Germany on container ships.'

'And has it stopped now?' Dave asked.

'Oh, no,' Sidney said. 'Even though the first priest who was charged was sent to prison, they have continued to collect ivory.'

'How do you know this?'

'I have been to the area,' said Sidney simply. 'I have talked to people in the villages near the mission, and they all know. Some work in the mission, and they told me how this MP comes there after midnight to deliver sacks. And when they have enough ivory they send it to Hamburg.'

'How often do the containers go out?'

'About every three or four months.'

I was poised on the edge of my chair. I thought of Peter Pueschel, my friend in the Greenpeace office in Hamburg, and how he would react to this story. Surely this meant that now Greenpeace Germany would be interested to help save the elephants.

'Could you find out when there will be another shipment?' I asked.

'I could,' said Sidney doubtfully, 'but it would mean going down to that part of the country. And I have taken all my paid leave.'

'We'll provide funds for research,' I said quickly. We couldn't let this story drop now. Priests smuggling tusks – what next? The deeper we dug, the more incredible this ivory trail became.

It was time to return to England. Liz and Neil drove us out to the airport. We had been in East Africa for a month and in that time had amassed more information than we had ever expected. Uncovering the Tanzanian connection was a huge breakthrough. It meant that we now had details of the whole illegal ivory trail from start to finish. It marked the end of the passive part of our work. From now on we would start to take charge of events. Now that we had allies in Africa the prospect of an Appendix One proposal for the African elephant no longer seemed an unrealistic dream, but a real possibility.

We were under no illusion that it would be easy. Too many influential people in Africa had vested interests in preserving poaching. Unanswered questions thrown up by our discoveries plagued us. Why hadn't the scandals regarding embassy staff been more widely publicized? Why had none of the 'experts' at CITES mentioned the corruption and bribery surrounding the ivory trade in African countries? Did they think it was irrelevant? To us it seemed now to be one of the key factors in the whole sordid business.

We sat back in our airline seats and started to work out a plan of action for when we were back in England. On one point we were already agreed. Before long these scandals would be spread across the front page of newspapers around the world as well as the *Tanzanian Daily News*.

10

December 1988–January 1989, London and Dubai

Dave

'Conservationists are warning that the African elephant will be extinct within ten years unless the world acts to curb the demand for ivory.' Newscaster Julia Somerville's announcement during the ITN news bulletin of 5 December 1988 marked the end of EIA's low public profile on the elephant issue. From now on we would be openly demanding a ban on ivory trading.

Making the decision to go public had not been easy. Usually we like to complete all our research before we launch a campaign, since undercover work is obviously more difficult if you've publicized your allegiance to a cause. But after our last trip we felt we had little option. Time was running out for the African elephant. Everything we'd heard or seen in Africa confirmed that the ivory trade was completely out of control. Somebody had to bring the issue out into the open. And, since no other organization seemed interested in doing it, that 'somebody' would have to be EIA.

We had all been conscious of a sense of urgency when we arrived back in London. There was a lot to achieve before the next CITES meeting in ten months' time: we had to influence WWF to change its position; before May we had to find a country to propose an ivory ban; and, most important of all, we had to stir up public opinion and create a climate where buying ivory was no longer socially acceptable. It was a tall order, and the sooner we got started the better.

A few days after our return from Dar es Salaam I'd telephoned Maggie Eales, ITN's senior foreign editor, and suggested she have a look at our film of Kenya and Tanzania. Maggie had been interested in our story since our first visit to the United Arab Emirates eight months earlier, and ITN had already given us a lot of support, lending us the Video 8 camera which we had used in Africa and also processing our film for us. When I outlined the content of the film Maggie was immediately interested. 'Can you come in tomorrow morning?' she asked.

At the studios Maggie introduced me to Paul Davies, the reporter whose job it would be to put together a news report from our material. We viewed the films together, and both of them seemed pleased.

'It's a good story, Dave,' said Maggie quietly.

The item went out the next day on all three of ITN's main news bulletins. It opened with shots of the second herd of wild elephant we had filmed in Tsavo, and moved on to the two poached carcasses we had found on that same trip. Then the scene changed to Daphne Sheldrick's orphanage where it showed Dika, a young elephant 'still in a state of shock after seeing his mother and the rest of the herd slaughtered'.

Daphne came on the screen and made her impassioned plea to the people of 'America, Britain and places like that' to stop buying the end results of the poaching – the carved ivory. 'After all, nobody needs ivory,' she pointed out, 'and as long as there is a demand for ivory, elephants are going to be killed in Africa.'

The next sequence was of the ivory room in Dar es Salaam accompanied by Paul Davies's commentary. 'Three thousand elephants died in agony to produce the tusks in this one room alone. Some had been just a few months old.'

Finally there was a shot of Eleanor, the elephant foster-mother, walking away from the camera into the fading evening light, eloquently symbolizing the end of the species. It made powerful television.

I had recorded a follow-up interview with Julia Somerville which was broadcast straight after the news item. During it I repeated Daphne's plea to the British public to stop buying ivory. We sat back and waited for reaction.

It was not slow in coming. The following morning found me in the BBC studios being interviewed on the 'Breakfast Time' programme. The interviewer expressed surprise that none of the big wildlife organizations was organizing a campaign against ivory poaching, when our film had demonstrated the case against the poachers so forcibly. I told her that I shared that surprise.

Soon after the ITN news feature was broadcast we sold our film to CBS News for showing in the United States. It brought in some much-needed funds which would help finance our next trip. We were now faced with a dilemma: whether to negotiate, perhaps lengthily, to sell the film to other television stations around the world, or to offer it to World Wide TV News, an international television news agency which satellites news programmes all over the world but which pays no fee to contributors. The latter option meant our film would be guaranteed immediate and extensive worldwide showing, and that consideration decided us. It meant forgoing desperately needed income for EIA, but it would strengthen the impact of the campaign and raise public awareness of the ivory trade, and that had to be our first priority. The decision paid off. Our revelations got newspaper coverage for days, and magazine articles on our work appeared for months afterwards.

We saw the CBS News version of our film, which was even more emotive than ITN's. It showed little Fiona playing at Daphne's orphanage while the voice-over commented poignantly: 'All that remains of her family can be found in a store near you.' CBS had also included archive film showing a whole herd of elephants being shot one after the other. It made traumatic viewing, the great animals seeming to leap in shock at the impact of the bullets before crumpling to the ground. Christine Stevens reported that the item had generated a tremor of revulsion against the ivory trade in America.

There was no doubt about it. The ivory ban 'ball' was now rolling. Early in the New Year, Allan came bounding into the office. 'Greenpeace Germany are going to support us for six months!' he announced exultantly. Greenpeace Germany had always had an active interest in endangered species, and Allan had undertaken investigations with them in the past. We'd informed them of the ivory smuggling missionaries as soon as we arrived back in London; and that, combined with their decision to help save the elephants, had persuaded the group to give us a grant of $50,000 to be spent on further investigations into ivory smuggling.

Around this time, too, we were approached by no fewer than four television companies, each planning a film on the ivory trade. We had lengthy discussions with Roger Cook and the team who produce the investigative programme 'The Cook Report' for Central Television. The company wanted one of us to go with them for a month to Africa to act as adviser on location; but we declined their offer. 'The Cook Report' was only likely to repeat our material and our investigations might have been hampered by our association with them.

My first responsibility was to return to Dubai. Clarke Bavin from the United States Fish and Wildlife Department had told us that, if we could obtain documents to show that Dubai had continued to export ivory to Taiwan, Singapore or Hong Kong after August 1988, the United States would be bound to blacklist imports from those countries. We were hearing rumours from the WWF that the Jebel Ali factories had shut down when the Hong Kong loophole had been closed, but we were unconvinced. Dubai was far from being our favourite place in the world, but at least one of us had to go back and see for himself if the factories were still there.

For obvious reasons we tried always to avoid doing sensitive or undercover investigations unaccompanied. But there had been dramatic developments in Tanzania, and Allan had to return there immediately. We had several volunteer workers in the EIA office, and I asked one of them, Susie Watts, to come to Dubai in place of Allan. She seemed eminently suitable. Born of English and Japanese parents, Susie had lived as a child in Tanzania and had fond memories of elephants from that time. She was also a lot prettier than Allan. 'Just smile at the Arab men, and I think they'll confess everything!' I teased.

A week later Susie and I parked our car in the Jebel Ali Free Zone and strolled towards shed 65A, enjoying the feeling of hot Middle East sun on our backs – a welcome change from London's chill January. Now that I knew the ropes, gaining entry to Jebel Ali had not proved too difficult, and we had been given permission to drive around the Free Zone for a few hours.

The doors to both the jewellery factories were bolted shut. I put my ear to the door of MK Jewellery. Silence: no ivory drills, no Chinese music, nothing. We visited a couple of adjoining units and asked what had happened to the ivory factories. 'They moved out last September. The Ruler of Dubai gave orders they had to go,' one of the unit managers told us.

'Did they go back to Hong Kong?'

He shook his head. 'I don't think so. I heard they moved up to Ajman.'

So much for WWF's complacency! Ajman was a neighbouring emirate, just an hour's drive north of Jebel Ali. Susie and I considered driving there that day, but decided against it. It would be better to do some homework first and see if we could get an idea of the factories' location and whether they were still working.

'I have this picture for you.'

The airport cargo manager took the photograph from me

warily, then smiled as he recognized himself. In anticipation of this visit I had brought a folder of the photos we had taken in Dubai on the previous trip.

'Do you remember me? We're finishing off that story we were doing last year on trade.'

'Oh, yes, I remember.' He smiled.

'You let me see the air waybills last time,' I continued. 'It was very useful for our film. We need some current contacts now – companies who have exported in the last year – just to bring our story up to date. Would it be possible to look through a few recent air waybills?'

The manager raised no objection and once more left us alone with the air waybill files.

Now that I knew which airlines to check it was not long before we turned up the vital evidence. 'Look at this,' I whispered to Susie and held up a sheaf of air waybills for carved ivory shipments to Taiwan. They were dated right up until the present month. This was exactly what we needed to clinch it for an American ban on ivory imports from Taiwan. If only we could find similar proof against Singapore and Hong Kong. These continuing exports almost certainly meant that factories were still operating somewhere in the United Arab Emirates. I photographed several incriminating air waybills before Susie slipped them into her bag. It was an insurance policy; double records meant two chances of getting our evidence out of the country. The air waybills were unlikely to be missed since the cargo had already been sent.

An office worker volunteered to show us the import records and help us with our research. We checked through the African airlines but, perhaps not surprisingly, found no shipments declared as ivory. Then the office worker held a document aloft. 'Look at this one,' he said with a smile. 'Hippo teeth from Tanzania.'

'How very interesting.' Susie frowned. Hippo teeth like elephant 'teeth' were a recognized form of ivory.

'Who were they sent to?' I asked.

He read the address aloud. 'Al Redha General Trading in Dubai.' The same company that the Scottish sailor had told us owned the ivory smuggling ship *Fadhil Allah*.

Pretending to have lost interest, I walked over to the other side of the room and asked the man to help me find the file for Uganda Airlines. Looking over his shoulder, I could see Susie's bag consuming the hippo teeth air waybill.

Back in my room we emptied Susie's handbag on to the bed and examined our booty. The details on the air waybills were interesting. The 'hippo teeth' waybill gave the name of a Tanzanian exporter: Al Waffa. Allan could look him up – he would be in Tanzania this week. Costa would be interested in this, too.

The other air waybills showed that the Poons' MK Jewellery factory was still the main exporter of ivory, sending shipments every two weeks to Taiwan, though they were now using a different shipping company. But there was another company exporting ivory, too, one we had not come across before, called Dubai Trade and Trust. Instead of an address, it gave a Dubai post office box number. I telephoned a journalist contact I'd met on our first trip to Dubai. 'Have you ever heard of the company called Dubai Trade and Trust?' I asked.

'Oh, yes,' he replied. 'Funnily enough, I was doing a story on his visit to Dubai only today. It was quite a state occasion. All the royal limousines and security were put at his disposal.'

'Whose visit? Whose disposal?' I had no idea who he was talking about.

'I'm sorry. I assumed you would know. Mohammed Fayed. Dubai Trade and Trust is owned by the Fayed brothers. You know them? They bought that famous department store in London – Harrods.'

We had to follow this up. Further enquiries revealed that the headquarters of Dubai Trade and Trust was in the Dubai International Trade Centre, a landmark skyscraper on the Abu Dhabi road. The following day I put ITN's video-camera in my holdall and set off with Susie to chase up the Harrods connection.

The Dubai Trade and Trust office was on the nineteenth floor of the Trade Centre. As we came out of the lift we found ourselves in a plushly carpeted foyer. A receptionist sat at a desk; behind her was a list of all the allied companies of Dubai Trade and Trust. At the bottom of the list was the one-word title 'Harrods'.

'I've got to get some video of that board,' I whispered to Susie. 'Good morning,' I greeted the receptionist cheerily. 'We would like to ship some of our belongings from Tanzania to Dubai. We've been advised to come to you.'

'Yes, sir. I'll call someone to attend to it for you.' She picked up the telephone, and a young man appeared and led us into his office. After ten minutes we returned to reception having promised the young man to contact him 'when we've worked out the dates'.

'Would you mind if we took a seat for a moment?' I asked the receptionist.

She smiled. 'Please. Help yourself.'

Susie sat down beside me. I unzipped the holdall and pulled out the video-camera. The board I wanted to video was behind us. It would look extremely suspicious if I stood up and filmed it openly. I fiddled with the camera for a few seconds then turned towards Susie. 'Oh, no! I thought I told you to be careful with the camera,' I bawled at her.

Susie looked bewildered.

'It's broken,' I exclaimed. 'There's no picture showing in the screen.'

'But I was careful with it,' she protested. 'It's not really broken, is it?'

I stood up and walked a few paces staring into the screen then turned back to face Susie. 'It's not working at all,' I said angrily. I pointed the camera at the board. 'No! Nothing! This will cost a fortune to have fixed.' As I'd hoped, the receptionist, embarrassed by this unpleasant marital scene, wasn't even looking at us now.

'Honestly, I really was careful,' Susie said. 'I can't think how it happened.' She looked close to tears. I hadn't realized she was such a good actress.

'We'll just have to see if we can find a camera shop,' I said coldly. 'Let's go. Come on.'

As soon as the lift doors closed behind us Susie started to remonstrate with me. 'Even if it had been working, I don't think we could have filmed that board without causing suspicion.' She looked desperately worried. 'Will it really cost a lot to repair?'

Guilt swept over me. 'I'm sorry, Susie. Didn't you realize what I was doing? I thought you were acting.' I grinned. 'The camera's fine. We've got all the video of the board we want.'

Susie stared at me perplexed for a moment, then slowly started to laugh.

We had agreed that on this trip we would visit Al Redha General Trading, the company which owned *Fadhil Allah*. We had found the address on one of the air waybills. Al Redha turned out to be a small clothes shop in the old part of Dubai. We parked the car in the carpark of the Commercial Bank, and Susie tested the microphone she'd hidden behind the brooch on her blouse and adjusted the small tape-recorder strapped inside the waistband of her jeans. For the first time on any of our investigations she looked nervous.

'We'll just make out we're tourists and we'll see what happens,' I reassured her. 'We won't ask for trouble, so there shouldn't be any. I tell you what – we'll pretend to be newlyweds, OK?'

Susie grinned uncertainly at me and we strolled hand in hand towards the shop entrance.

The shop was tiny, with a small office at the back. An Arab and two Indians looked on silently as Susie and I rummaged through a rack of tightly packed shirts and jeans. 'What do you think of these, darling?' I asked, holding out a pair of blue denims.

Susie gave me a mischievous look. 'I prefer you in black, I think. Why don't you try some on?'

I selected a pair of black jeans, and the Arab ushered me through the office to a small changing area at the bottom of a flight of stairs. I could see that at the top of the stairs there was a bigger office; that seemed likely to be the centre of Al Redha's operation. Putting the jeans on, I went back into the shop where Susie was chatting animatedly to the three men, showing no trace of her earlier nerves.

'They're too small. I'll try another pair,' I muttered, not wanting to interrupt their conversation.

Susie looked over to me. 'He's put on so much weight since we were married three months ago!' she exclaimed. 'We'll probably be here all day waiting for him to find a thirty-two-inch waist that will fit him!'

I pulled a wry face at her. The men guffawed at my expense. Picking up another three pairs of jeans, I disappeared out the back a second time. The sound of laughter continued in the shop. Furtively I climbed the stairs.

The room at the top was much larger than the office downstairs. Inside it was equipped with telephones and a telex machine, but there was none of the usual office clutter of paperwork – no incriminating documents. Whoever was in charge of this office was either very tidy or very circumspect.

Downstairs once more I put on another pair of jeans and rejoined Susie. She and the men had moved to the far corner of the shop now and were inspecting a glass display table. I looked over Susie's shoulder. Under the glass a whole range of African currency was set out in neat rows.

'What lovely notes,' Susie exclaimed. 'You must visit Africa a lot. I didn't know jeans came from Africa.'

Elephant carcasses found by following the smell of decay in Tsavo National Park, Kenya

Dave took this picture of Clive while perched inside the cardboard box overlooking Poon's ivory factory in Dubai

The view from the box

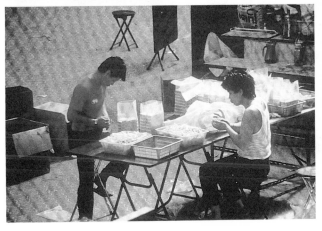

Stockpile of raw ivory in Lee Chat's factory, Hong Kong

American tourists shopping for ivory in Hong Kong

Carved tusks and ivory seals (hanko) for sale in Hong Kong

Fiona, John, Daphne Sheldrick, Allan and Dave at the elephant orphanage in Nairobi National Park (Ros Reeve/EIA)

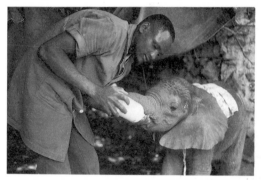

Fiona, one month old

Encounter with a solitary bull elephant in Tsavo National Park

Eleanor, foster mother to Daphne's orphans

The Ivory Room in Dar es Salaam

Anti-poaching unit in
Selous Game Reserve,
Tanzania

Indonesian ambassador's
cache of ivory confiscated
by the Tanzanian
authorities

Costa Mlay, Tanzania's
Director of Wildlife

Clandestine shot of George Poon in Ajman moments before he jumped on Des and Dave's moving car

ITN's Desmond Hamill talking to Simon Li in Belhon Trading, Dubai

Eugene Lapointe (Tom Stoddart/*Sunday Telegraph Magazine*)

Ian Parker

Rowan Martin

A reprieve for the wild elephants of Africa

'Oh, no,' answered the Arab man, 'I don't go for jeans. I smuggle ivory!'

'Really? How exciting! Where do you go to?' said Susie innocently.

'Oh, Tanzania, Burundi, Zambia, Rwanda, Kenya – all over the place,' he bragged.

I feigned a lack of interest and, exchanging the jeans I was holding for another couple of pairs, left Susie to carry on with her interrogation for five more minutes. When I returned, having finally decided on the jeans I wanted, I joined in the conversation.

'I suppose you send the ivory on to other countries. It's not needed here, is it?' I casually asked as I handed the jeans over to be wrapped.

'Some we send on, but there are factories here that carve it,' he replied.

'In Dubai?' I said, rather too sharply.

Fortunately he didn't pick my tone up. Susie had got under his guard completely.

'Yes, and in Ajman, too, near the Municipality Building. We smuggle ivory from Tanzania to a small port called Hamriya in Dubai. Here the business is open. No problem,' he said complacently, handing me my change.

'It would be wonderful to visit these factories,' Susie sighed. 'Do you know who owns them?'

'Chinese,' the man answered dismissively. He thought for a moment. He was obviously eager to please Susie. 'It's their New Year and the bosses are all in Hong Kong now, but the factories may be open. The Dubai factory is near the Defence Roundabout.'

Susie looked around for a chair to sit down on and opened her handbag. 'Do you mind me smoking?' The three men didn't. Nor did they mind when she pulled her camera out of her bag and took their photo 'just to remind me of you all when I get home'. They obviously felt it was perfectly understandable that she should wish to remember them and posed and preened enthusiastically.

'What's your name?' she asked the self-confessed smuggler as we got up to go.

'Abdullah Yamvi,' he replied. His voice took on a respectful tone. 'And my boss is Sheikh Abdullah Ali Bamakramah.'

The Defence Roundabout stands at the edge of Dubai on the Jebel Ali road. We parked the car nearby and wandered around, uncertain quite what we were looking for until Susie spotted a wooden packing-case lying outside the 'Sheikh Rashid' building. There was lettering on the side: 'Made in Burundi, Kee Lung, Taiwan.' This had to be the place! Another box lay beside it labelled in Chinese and English, its contents described as dentist's drilling tools. Nearby was a small metal trunk with an Air Zimbabwe sticker on its side.

People were walking past us, and we asked one or two passers-by if they knew anything about this unit. We were told it was owned by a local company called Belhon Trading, but as Susie's friend Abdullah Yamvi had predicted it was closed on account of the Chinese New Year. It didn't matter. The fact that the factory existed was enough to shatter the myth that the Dubai ivory carvers had all been forced out of business.

I paid a visit to the Statistics Department to obtain the most recent import–export figures. Our main interest was in trading since August 1988, but to my frustration those records were not yet available. However, I did discover that over sixteen tonnes of ivory had been imported from Tanzania in the first nine months of 1988. Costa would be interested in that, too. I made a note of it. Dubai had also imported ivory from Burundi, Kenya, Zimbabwe, Cameroon, Greece and Britain. Hong Kong and Taiwan were the principal destinations. There was no mention of Singapore.

Following our usual policy, we had left what we expected to be the most risky part of our investigation – searching for the Ajman factories – till last. We decided to get some official cover before starting the hunt, and Susie called the offices of the Government of Ajman and arranged an appointment with an adviser in the Economics Department.

Ajman is very different from Dubai and the other Emirates. It is poorer and smaller than its neighbours, and the backstreets are deserted and unpaved. The officials, anxious to help us with our 'trade film', had laid on a guided tour of the Ajman Free Zone area for us. It was a ramshackle area in the port, quite unlike Dubai's modern development. We were shunted from one business to another, none of which had the remotest connection with the ivory trade. I tried several times to draw our guide on the subject of ivory, but all my talk of Chinese businesses, crafts and jewellery provoked only a blank look. We feigned interest in the other businesses, but for us the whole day was proving rather a waste of time until, as we wandered around the port area with our guide, we found ourselves walking towards a small coastal vessel. Something about her appearance intrigued me. She was obviously quite an old ship, but had been recently repainted in a rather vivid colour scheme; her hull was bright blue. I looked towards the bow to see her name and stopped in my tracks. She was *Fadhil Allah*, the ship whose smuggling activities had started us on this whole campaign.

Susie had registered the name at the same time as I did and, thinking quickly, stepped over to talk to the crew who were hanging about on the quayside. I had been right about Susie's effect on Arab men. Within minutes we found ourselves invited on board to meet the captain. Unfortunately what he revealed was disappointing.

'My company has only just bought the ship,' he said. 'We have just sailed to Bombay and back.'

So she did not belong to Sheikh Abdullah Ali Bamakramah any more.

Susie persevered. 'I've always been fascinated by ships' voyages. What's the history of this one?'

Smiling indulgently, the captain leaned over to unlock a cupboard. 'These are the ship's logs for the last few years,' he said, passing a tattered log-book over to Susie. 'Take a look if you like.'

Listed inside the book were the voyages, dates, crew names and ports of call for a couple of years earlier.

'Could I photograph some of these pages? Just to remind us of your ship when we get home?' I requested.

'Of course.'

Inside the front cover I had noticed the name of the Mombasa agent that the Scottish sailor had first given us two years earlier, Said Faraj. I focused my camera on it. As I turned the pages, the ports of call jumped out at me. Mogadishu, Lamu, Mombasa, Tanga, Dar es Salaam; all the big East African ivory smuggling ports. There could no longer be any doubt as to the accuracy of the information that had set us off on this campaign.

We had been quite unable to extract a single hint as to the whereabouts of the ivory factories from the Ajman officials. Our only information was from Susie's conquest, Abdullah Yamvi at Al Redha General Trading. Accordingly, after bidding farewell to our guides, we drove to the place he had named, the Ajman Municipality Building. It was dusty and very hot. Some new shop units had been built on one side of the building, and we strolled in that direction. As we approached the nearest unit I heard the unmistakable sound of ivory drills.

'We've found them,' I whispered. Susie's hidden tape-recorder was running, and the video-camera, though currently pointing at the ground, was switched on, too.

The glass door of the factory was covered with newspapers, effectively preventing anyone looking in, and the outer metal security shutter was pulled a third of the way down.

'Smile,' I instructed Susie. She grimaced back at me. Pushing open the door, we walked in.

Dozens of curious faces turned to look at us. Most of the workforce seemed to be Indian or Pakistani.

'Hello. We're from Film London,' I announced to the factory at large. 'We're filming industry in Ajman. This is fascinating. What are you doing here?'

'Nobody here,' one of the Indians responded. 'In one week Mr Poon come.'

I saw a Chinese man dressed in pyjama-like clothes rush out of the factory door. At his departure the other men stopped working and clustered around us, eager to find out what was going on. This factory was smaller than the ones in Jebel Ali had been. It consisted of two rooms, each with drilling machines ranged along the walls. On the floor a sack had fallen over, spilling tusks in an untidy heap. I could see no sign of seals or of large carvings; instead, all the men seemed to be making beads. Plastic bags full of beads were stacked against one of the walls.

I raised my camera, and instantly the mood of curiosity changed. 'You can't take pictures,' the man I had spoken to shouted. As the workers jostled around me Susie took advantage of their diversion and slipped into the other room with the video-camera.

'The Government of Ajman sent us,' I lied. 'They said we could film in here.'

That calmed them down a bit, though they still looked dubious. I carried on snapping urgently.

Suddenly the door swung open, and the Chinese man returned and started shouting at us in Cantonese.

'He's from Hong Kong. He's upset,' said the Indian rather unnecessarily.

I carried on photographing. The Chinese guy was quite irate by now. Pulling a piece of paper from his pocket, he started to dial a telephone number. From the number of digits I knew it had to be an international number. I walked over and looked at the paper; there were two numbers on it. Ignoring his glares, I jotted them both down in my notebook. Susie came back into the room, her smile beginning to look strained. 'Dave, I think we ought to get out of here,' she said out of the corner of her mouth. 'I'm not happy about the film I've shot. I've taken it all from waist level so they didn't see what I was up to. I don't think it'll be usable.'

'OK, give me the camera,' I said. 'I'll shoot some more now before we go.' I felt there was little point in trying to be discreet about what we were doing at this stage; since it looked as though our cover was about to be blown we had better make the most of this opportunity. It would probably be the only one we'd get.

Flashing the watching workers a confident smile, I focused the video on the bags packed with beads. As I did so I noticed the words 'Fung Fcty' written on the side. It was the name of Poon's Singapore factory, which had been sending semi-carved ivory into Hong Kong. Yet this year Singapore had not been recorded in the official statistics as one of the destinations for Dubai's ivory exports. If it had been, then the United States could have blacklisted Singapore. What circuitous route did it take to get there? Or was it declared on Customs forms as something else?

Susie interrupted my musings. 'Oh God, Dave,' she begged. 'Let's go.'

The only Chinese man left in Ajman during Chinese New Year was still dialling frantically when we left. Back at the hotel I searched through my files for the visiting card Poon Tat Hong had given me when we visited him in Hong Kong. I compared it with the two numbers the manager had been trying so desperately to contact. As I had suspected, one of them was the Poons' factory in Hong Kong. The other was the Tat Hing Ivory shop in Kowloon. It would only be a matter of hours before the Poons knew that their Ajman factories had been discovered.

I turned to Susie. 'Get your bag packed,' I said. 'I think it's time we were going home.'

II

JANUARY–FEBRUARY 1989, LONDON AND TANZANIA

ALLAN

> Attn: Allan and Dave. Urgent message. Indonesian ambassador caught with container of poached ivory as he tried to smuggle it out of country. Police seized from container: 184 raw ivory tusks, 24 partly worked tusks, 82 carved figurines, ivory necklaces, ivory walking-sticks. Please get this into the British press!
>
> *Liz and Neil*

I rang John Merritt of the *Observer*. 'I've just received a telex from Tanzania with some news that might make a good story for you,' I said. As the story developed I spoke to Liz and Neil by telephone. A few days later they told me the Indonesian ambassador had attempted to fly from Tanzania to Singapore with his wife but had been prevented from leaving when Customs officers found dozens of ivory carvings in his luggage. He had tried to claim diplomatic immunity, but this had apparently cut little ice with the Tanzanian Customs and Excise department.

On Sunday 22 January 1989 the *Observer* broke the story on its foreign page under the headline 'Diplomat Snared in Illegal Ivory Run'. John Merritt's article strongly condemned ivory poaching and the Hong Kong connection, and concluded: 'Britain should bear some special responsibility for controlling [the ivory's] seemingly unrestricted entry into the territory.' The British press, at least, were now firmly on the side of the elephant.

This latest development meant I would have to go back to Tanzania to follow up the story. The scandal of diplomatic involvement would make good campaign material. Now that Greenpeace Germany had come up with their grant I was committed to following up the missionary story there anyway. This would simply mean bringing my trip forward.

Just before my departure Jorgen flew in from Washington. With the money from our film sales I had been able to pay his air fare and expenses to do the research for the Appendix One proposal for CITES. He had taken a month's unpaid leave and was now *en route* to Nairobi where he would have access to new elephant population estimates produced by Iain Douglas-Hamilton as well as other vital data.

'But you will get it done by the end of March, won't you?' I pressed him. Time was short. Even if Jorgen met his deadline we would have only two months to find a country willing to propose the ban.

'I'll have it done,' Jorgen assured me. 'I'll keep you informed on how it's going.'

'Karibu.' Liz smiled her by now familiar welcome. 'Nice to see you again.' During the drive from the airport to Dar es Salaam she updated me on the case of the Indonesian ambassador. 'He's gone home now, but they say he's been retired from the Foreign Ministry in Indonesia without his pension. He had to leave all his ivory behind here, and it's still under seizure. It was all very embarrassing for the Indonesian government. There was a lot of international publicity – you had something to do with that, I think,' Liz smiled. 'At the time it happened the Indonesian Foreign Minister was in Peking, and it seems the Chinese press were critical about the incident.'

'That's rich!' I said. 'Rex told me the Chinese embassy staff had been caught doing the same thing!'

We went first to Neil's office. He was out on business but arrived back as Liz was showing me the copy she was preparing for the next issue of *Miombo*, the magazine of the Wildlife Conservation Society of Tanzania she edited. 'We're pulling no punches this time,' she said.

'Buying Ivory Kills Elephants,' the first-page headline blared. It introduced a major article by the chairman of the WCST, Ned Kitomari, calling for an international ivory ban.

As I read it an idea was germinating in my mind. 'If you've got any suggestions or changes . . . ?' said Liz.

'Yes. There is just one thing,' I said slowly. 'You ask CITES to ban the international trade in ivory. That's great. But what if you also called on Tanzania to propose the ban? We need a country to put forward the proposal for the Appendix One listing. CITES won't put it on the agenda otherwise. Tanzania seems the ideal country. Look how many elephants you've lost because of poaching.'

'A hundred thousand in the last ten years,' Neil reflected. 'Exactly.'

'All right, we'll have to OK it with the chairman, but that shouldn't be a problem. But how we'll convince the Wildlife Department to support it . . .' Liz's voice trailed off hopelessly.

'I don't think you should worry too much about that,' Neil intervened. 'I think there are going to be some big changes there soon. I just stopped by to see Mr Lumbanga at the Ministry of Lands and Tourism. He's very committed to conservation and he has just heard he is going to be made the new permanent secretary at the Ministry. Which is great, but what is even better is that I'm told there will soon be a new Director of Wildlife as well.' Neil winked at me mysteriously.

On this trip I was staying as Liz and Neil's guest at a large house cum hotel they were minding not far from the Kunduchi Beach Hotel where I had stayed last time. 'We rise at six,' Liz warned me as I retired for the night. 'That's if we sleep in!' added Neil. Sure enough, we left for the office the next morning at six-thirty. Since my last visit the pot-holed road had been repaired by aid workers, and we sped smoothly past the cool blue Indian Ocean, with its fringe of palm trees, towards the city. The view easily compensated for the early start.

I was sitting in his office when Neil strode in carrying a copy of the *Tanzanian Daily News*. 'What did I tell you?' he exulted.

A front-page article announced that Constantius Mlay had been made the new Director of Wildlife.

'Oh boy,' Neil spoke with relish. 'Are there going to be some changes in the Wildlife Department now!'

'And the Appendix One proposal?' I asked.

'We can start lobbying now,' Neil grinned.

Fred Lwezuela was out on his ear. He had been Director of Wildlife for the past nine years, during which time Tanzania's elephant population had been devastated. With him out of the way and Costa in his chair, who knew what might be possible? A few days ago it had just seemed an idle daydream that Tanzania might propose the ban on ivory trading to CITES. All at once it seemed a real possibility.

Costa had promised to come over on Sunday morning. We waited for him on the veranda of Liz and Neil's borrowed house which overlooked a slight slope down to the ocean. High above us a huge spider was busily weaving a web the size of a small hammock, while on the wooden floor lizards and the occasional frog moved about erratically. Neil and Liz's dogs lay watching them, ears pricked.

In Tanzania the skies, too, are always filled with wildlife. At night it was bats, skimming over the derelict swimming pool in search of mosquitoes. This morning the air was alive with brilliantly coloured butterflies, beetles and birds. Neil sat, binoculars at the ready, occasionally leaping up at the sight of some black dot a hundred metres up to shout excitedly: 'Oh, wow, Liz. There's a . . . !'

The sound of a car door slamming sent the dogs charging off the veranda, and moments later Costa appeared in the doorway.

'Congratulations.' I shook his hand.

Smiling diffidently, he sat down next to me. 'Now, what shall we talk about? Can I guess?' he asked.

I had just spoken on the telephone to Dave in Dubai and received the information about Al-Waffa, the Tanzanian ivory agent, and I handed the details over to Costa.

He looked at them with interest. 'Thank you, Allan. We will investigate this and see what we can find out.' He folded the piece of paper carefully and tucked it in his pocket.

'Costa, tell Allan about the Indonesian ambassador,' prompted Neil. 'Costa was there when they discovered the ivory,' he explained.

Costa smiled. 'The ambassador and his wife tried to bluff it out to the bitter end. The police asked the ambassador if he had any ivory in the container, and he said: "I think my wife might have a few pieces in her personal belongings." So we asked her separately: "Do you have any ivory in the container?" *Her* reply was: "Oh, I think my husband may have a few pieces in his personal belongings." A few pieces!' Costa threw his head back and laughed. 'We were unpacking it all night! Crate after crate of it.'

'I think the Indonesian ambassador may actually have done the elephants a lot of good,' Liz said reflectively. I could see her point. The scandal generated was out of all proportion to the amount of ivory involved: 184 tusks represented just a small drop in the ocean of poached ivory, but public outrage at the incident had greatly fuelled the support for a ban.

'I have some documents for you, Costa. I'll fetch them from my room,' I said. Before I left London I'd compiled a brief report from the Customs statistics of Taiwan,

Singapore and Dubai. It showed the ivory declared as being of Tanzanian origin that these countries had imported in recent years. I had also included an estimated figure for illegal exports via Burundi, aware now that a high percentage of their exported ivory was Tanzanian. Taken together, my figures indicated that at least 173 tonnes of ivory a year was leaving Tanzania.

'Of course, what the Customs figures don't tell us is how much of this is legal ivory,' I admitted, handing the file to Costa.

'I can tell you that,' he responded. 'Almost none of it. Do you know how much ivory Tanzania has legally exported in the past two and a half years? Less than twenty tonnes.' Costa contemplated my report and the copies of Customs statistics I had attached to it. 'Allan, I think you should come and show this to Mr Lumbanga, the new permanent secretary at the Ministry,' he said at last. 'This is very powerful proof of what is going on.'

'So do you think Tanzania will agree to propose the Appendix One listing?'

'It's possible.' Costa was cautious. 'It's something we can work towards.'

'How do you suggest we do that?'

'Well, maybe first we should call a meeting of the Wildlife Conservation Society's steering committee to endorse the policy. I believe the chairman has agreed to you suggesting it in the *Miombo* editorial, Liz?'

Liz nodded. 'I spoke to Mr Kitomari. It's fine by him, but I think we should also brief President Mwinyi of our intentions. After all, he's the Patron of the Society.'

'And how about writing to all the wildlife groups in Europe and America, the whole world in fact?' I suggested. 'Your group, WCST, could ask them all to write to your government to support them in calling on CITES to ban the ivory trade. I think it might have tremendous impact. We're always being told by "experts" in Europe and America that Africans don't want a ban. If an African wildlife group sends out a letter calling for one, it will send a lot of shockwaves through the conservation movement. People will be forced to think again.'

'I think that's a good idea,' Liz nodded pensively. 'It could drum up a lot of support. Why don't you write the letters and I'll ask Mr Kitomari to sign them, as chairman of the Society.'

'Hello, Allan!' Sidney shook my hand warmly. 'I have some very interesting information for you about the missionaries.' He had been down to southern Tanzania for a week-long visit. The result of his enquiries was an eight-page document. His report included transcribed interviews with both past and present staff from the mission. I read them avidly. One of the staff had confessed he was paid an extra 1,500 shillings (£5) a week to keep the key to the room where the ivory was kept, but he had begged Sidney not to use the information as he would be in 'big trouble'. It appeared that, to preserve the secrecy of the mission's extracurricular activities, the servants who worked there were never allowed to have family or friends for visits. 'If anyone does call like you have done, the Father asks everyone to watch them and listen to see if they ask questions about him,' this servant had told Sidney.

Another man had revealed: 'The Father has seven or eight carvers, and they are all locked in a room all day long. They carve ivory pieces and they send them to the mission in Germany.' None of the workers Sidney had questioned believed the work they were doing was illegal. 'The Father is a very important man here. He has many important visitors. He has permission to do this, we are sure,' one had said.

'This is excellent information,' I said to Sidney, shutting the folder.

Sidney smiled. 'But there is more, Allan. A shipment of ivory is to be sent out from the mission some time in April. I am trying to get the name of the ship that will carry it.'

'Do you know which port it will be shipped to?'

He nodded. 'To Hamburg.'

'Sidney, thank you. I'm sure my friends in Greenpeace Germany will be very interested in this.'

I wanted to obtain copies of the press photographs relating to the Tanzanian MP who had been gaoled for ivory smuggling. A staff writer at the *Tanzanian Daily News* was very helpful and produced dozens of photographs relating to both that case and others. There were pictures of the MP's vehicle stuffed with ivory, and of other seizures: from homes, from trains, and from trucks with secret compartments. He allowed me to take them away to be copied at the government information office down the street.

Returning later to pick up the copies, I was checking through them when a voice spoke over my shoulder: 'It's bad, isn't it?'

I looked up to see a young man studying the photographs. 'Very bad,' he repeated. 'The ivory trade is destroying all of Tanzania's elephants.'

His name was Raymond. He told me he was a teacher who'd been educated in England. 'Are you interested in ivory poaching?' he asked. I could hardly deny it.

'I'm conducting a research project at the moment,' Raymond informed me. 'My office is in the building behind this one. I know a few interesting stories about ivory. There is a lot of corruption. Do you want to come and talk some more?'

I followed him back to his office, which was plain and drab, like most government offices in Tanzania, with a simple wooden desk and an ancient manual typewriter.

Raymond seated himself opposite me. 'I've a friend who's a journalist in the south of Tanzania,' he said. 'He told me that one day last year three men were arrested for having ivory – over two hundred tusks. Two of these men were influential businessmen. After two days the three men were released from gaol. As for the ivory . . .' He shrugged.

'It just disappeared from the police station. My friend wrote about the arrests and posted it to his office in Dar es Salaam, but the story was never published. When he called to find out about it his boss said: "Just forget the story and don't send me any more information about it." '

'This sounds more like Sicily than Africa,' I said.

Raymond smiled. 'Listen. I have a very good friend in the police force. He told me that in early 1988 about three hundred tusks were seized by the police. They belonged to a local businessman and they were bound for Yemen. The ivory was taken to the police station, and certain senior officials were called in. After two weeks the tusks disappeared.'

'Maybe they went to the ivory room in Dar es Salaam,' I suggested.

Raymond shook his head. 'No. He checked that.'

'How do you know he is telling the truth?'

'He is my friend. We are the same tribe and grew up together since we were small boys. He told me all about the cases from the beginning because it made him angry. "There should be elephants when my children grow up." That's what he said to me.'

Those had been Jenny's words, too, I remembered.

'He knows people in Customs also,' Raymond said suddenly.

'At Dar es Salaam port?'

'Yes, and other places. In Customs, he says, everyone knows what is going on. The senior people get paid not to look in certain containers, not just for ivory, but for anything valuable. But many junior people don't get paid off, and they are often willing to talk.'

This sounded interesting. 'Can you find out about ivory going out through the port? I want to find out about specific shipments – who was sending them out, which dates, to whom and where.'

'Yes, I can ask my friend.' Raymond lowered his voice. 'I know that the ambassador from —— is sending ivory back home. My friend in the police can tell you the details. Do you want to meet him?'

'Sure. I'd like that,' I said.

Twenty minutes and a taxi ride later I was sitting at a restaurant table opposite a tall uniformed policeman. When we were introduced he was reserved and suspicious but gradually with Raymond's encouragement he relaxed. He confirmed Raymond's story about the ambassador from ——. 'He was posted here in January 1988 and he has sent at least three shipments of ivory since then. He arranges for the elephants to be killed in the Selous game reserve and has the ivory sent to him at the embassy.'

The quantities in the shipments were not large by Poon's standards. Twenty tusks here, fifty tusks there, but again the scandal element of a second ambassador being involved could bring valuable publicity if we released this story. I scribbled the details in my notebook.

'Thank you for this,' I said. 'I have a feeling I'll meet you both again.'

Back at Neil's office I got to work on the word processor, preparing a detailed briefing on the international ivory trade for Mr Lumbanga, the new permanent secretary to the Ministry of Lands and Tourism. Hopefully it would help persuade him to support an ivory ban.

Next I drafted the letters for the Wildlife Conservation Society of Tanzania to send to groups around the world. There had to be several different letters, their wording dependent on the current position of the group involved: one for groups which opposed the ban, one for those that supported it, others for those that were not yet involved in the issue or were undecided.

Over the next few days I printed out dozens of copies of each letter. To each one I attached a copy of the newly printed *Miombo* magazine with its cover illustration of an elephant and its eye-catching headline 'Buying Ivory Kills Elephants'. After addressing them to the relevant wildlife organizations Liz and I took the letters to be signed by Mr Kitomari, the Society chairman.

Mr Kitomari was also deputy governor of the Bank of Tanzania and it was obvious from his remarks during our meeting that the financial implications of the illegal ivory trade were not lost on him. Other countries were making fortunes out of destroying one of Tanzania's most important tourist resources while Tanzania itself was struggling to avoid devaluing its currency.

To my surprise Mr Kitomari seemed largely unaware of Burundi's role in the poached ivory trade. When I informed him that Burundi currently held a lot of poached Tanzanian ivory which they were trying to get legalized so they could sell it on to the international market he reacted angrily.

'I will call our embassy in Burundi. And the Society must send a telex to the CITES secretariat to protest at their efforts to sell this ivory. If it has been stolen from us, they do not have any right to sell it.'

'How important to Tanzania is the income from legal ivory sales?' I asked. Although Costa had assured me only 22½ tonnes had been exported legally in recent years, I wanted to clarify Tanzania's attitude to ivory dealing. 'Would the loss of money, if there was a ban, be a big problem for the Treasury?'

Kitomari was philosophic. 'We always need foreign exchange,' he said. 'That is a *very* endangered species in Tanzania! But we need our elephants more. And we have a duty to protect them.'

'Would you be able to talk to the Finance Minister to see that he will not oppose an ivory ban?' It was a crucial question.

Mr Kitomari smiled. 'Yes, I will do that,' he promised. 'He is a good friend of mine. It will be no problem.'

It was a good note on which to return to London.

12

MARCH 1989,
DUBAI AND SINGAPORE

DAVE

Early in 1989, EIA had moved into a new three-roomed office in Islington. The volume of work building up on the elephant issue meant that the old single-room office had become completely inadequate. Much of this work involved press releases and interviews; both necessary to spread the word. But our dealings with the press did not always go to plan.

In February one of the Sunday colour supplements published a long article on the elephant poaching in Kenya. My photograph of the two carcasses in Tsavo national park was spread across two pages, and other EIA photos were also used to illustrate the piece. It was good publicity. We had been aware that the article was being prepared, and Ros had even accompanied the author around Tsavo during our visit in December. Ruefully, we noted the absence of any mention of EIA in the article apart from one tiny photocredit. To our dismay the magazine had instead published the name and address of WWF and suggested that donations to help the elephant's cause be sent to them. Even though WWF were still fighting the very idea of a ban on the ivory trade!

To add insult to injury, I was interviewed on BBC Radio Four's natural history programme and found myself defending EIA's position against the arguments of WWF's international treaties expert, Simon Lyster. Despite the fact that people had been encouraged to send WWF money in the expectation that they were going to stop elephants being killed, Simon argued once more in favour of the sustainable use of wildlife. I suggested that his reasoning was seriously flawed, and appeared to be based on inadequate knowledge of the facts – criticisms which were not terribly well received.

In view of the widening gulf between us, I was surprised to get a telephone call from Simon a few days later. And even more surprised to hear him request a favour. Prince Charles was going to Dubai to play polo, and WWF wanted to brief him on the ivory situation there. Not surprisingly, since WWF knew nothing whatsoever about the ivory situation in Dubai, this was proving difficult. 'I wonder if you'd put together a report for us to give to Prince Charles,' Simon suggested affably.

Until the WWF were on our side of the fence I had not the slightest intention of playing ball with them.

'No, Simon, we won't. But we will tell Prince Charles the situation if someone from his office would like to contact us,' I offered, equally affably.

EIA never did hear from Prince Charles's office.

For the next few months Allan and I were to spend very little time in England. Allan was due to return for a third time to Tanzania, hopeful of making some progress in persuading the government there to propose the Appendix One listing at the CITES convention. While he was there, I would be in Singapore, once again accompanied by Susie. Her newly discovered acting talents promised to be an invaluable asset.

We broke our journey in the United Arab Emirates and spent a few days picking up more statistics. To my frustration, the figures for trading after August 1988 were still 'not available'. I couldn't help wondering if this meant the authorities now knew what we were up to and were deliberately dragging their feet.

The Chinese workforce were back from their holidays at the Ajman factories, and we did a little spying there. While parked outside we spotted the swish Mercedes and BMW cars owned, according to an informant, by the brothers George and Sam Poon.

Since we were in Dubai we decided to have a look at the most recent documentation in the air cargo office. Having removed the air waybills on our last visit, we entered the building with some trepidation. But once again everyone was very obliging and pulled out the folders of bills for us to examine. We asked if they had a small room we could take the documents to ('We don't want to disturb you!'), and we were shown into the kitchen or messroom. As we looked through the bills we discovered ivory had been regularly exported by 'MK Jewellery factory' but using a new Ajman address. The shipping agent was Al-Rais. The same agent had also shipped cargo described as 'fashion or imitation jewellery' to Germany and Belgium. Curiously enough, we discovered that these boxes were the same size and weight as the ivory shipments!

We photographed all the relevant waybills, depositing them in our bags as before. But it was far more difficult this time. The office workers seemed reluctant to leave us on our own; it was almost as though they had been delegated to keep an eye on us. I turned to the wall and surreptitiously extracted the waybills from the folders whenever I thought no-one was looking. I was taking a photograph of a waybill when a man walking past outside glanced through the glass door. After cautiously waiting a couple of seconds I pulled the waybill out of the folder and looked up to see the same man pass by in the other direction. There was no doubt that he'd seen me. I froze. If we were caught stealing documents, we were likely to be gaoled for a few days, at least, until the embassy was informed; maybe for much longer.

I turned to Susie. 'I think we should go,' I said urgently. As I spoke, the door opened. It was the supervisor. 'How are you doing? Are you finished?' he asked. His voice, though still polite, had lost its earlier friendliness.

'I think so. We were just going,' I replied with a smile.

'All this research is still for your film?'

I nodded. 'Yes. That's right.'

'I would like you to meet my director.' It was a statement rather than a request.

We picked up our bags, uncomfortably aware of their incriminating contents. Hastily I pushed a protruding piece of paper back into Susie's bag. The supervisor led the way into an immaculate office with a smoked glass table and travel brochures arranged in a neat display on a mahogany desk.

'So. You're from Film London, are you?' a voice asked. I turned around. It was the man who had seen me rip the waybill out of its folder. He was scrutinizing my fake business card. 'You're making a film on trade, I believe. You were here before?' It was obviously a rhetorical question.

I held my hand out. 'Pleased to meet you. I must say that your staff have been very helpful,' I said warmly.

He looked faintly amused. 'Yes, I'm sure they have. You should have come straight to see me, you know. I need to know what is going on around here.'

Just then the supervisor came back into the room with one of his clerks. Lighting a cigarette, the director drew deeply on it.

'Did you take any documents relating to some hippo teeth the last time you were here? This man remembers you paying particular attention to them.' He gave me a disquieting smile. 'And then they disappeared.'

'Do you remember that one, Dave? I don't,' said Susie innocently.

'I think I do,' I said slowly. 'Didn't we laugh at it, wondering what anyone would want with hippo teeth?' The clerk nodded confirmation. 'No, we certainly didn't take it. Maybe it got mixed up in some of the other papers we were looking through. I'm sorry. Perhaps we filed it somewhere else.'

'Perhaps.' The director looked unconvinced.

'Anyway, we've taken up enough of your time,' I said decisively. 'It was a pleasure meeting you all, and we can't thank you enough.' Susie and I stood up, shook hands all round and made our way towards the door.

'Just a minute,' the director called after us.

I turned.

He gave me a penetrating look. 'Are you sure that you've got all your bags?'

His meaning was unmistakable. I nodded. 'Yes, thanks.'

'Goodbye, then. Did you say you were leaving tonight?'

Something in his tone told me it was an instruction.

'Yes, in a couple of hours.'

He nodded. 'So we won't be seeing you again.'

'Not on your life,' said Susie under her breath as the door closed behind us.

We continued our journey to Singapore that evening and the next day. Because we always booked the cheapest seats to save money, our routing was seldom direct. On this occasion we landed at Bangkok and then Kuala Lumpur before finally touching down in Singapore.

By now we were pretty exhausted but we found ourselves unable to relax in Singapore. It is a city of contrasts; a strange mixture of permissiveness and repressive laws. We were staying at the Grand Central, a tourist hotel off one of the main shopping-streets. It has a seedy shopping precinct attached and a 'fitness centre' where 'massages' are on offer. The girls hang around openly near the doorway waiting for their names to be called and watching the American and Japanese clients pay by credit card. Yet out on the streets you can be fined for jaywalking or for stubbing a cigarette out on the pavement.

Singapore thrives on trade. Its port is massive, and there is free passage into some of the less well advertised free zones. A lot of Hong Kong businessmen started operating out of Singapore in the early part of the eighties. They included many illegal ivory traders who felt restricted by the mild CITES controls starting to be imposed in Hong Kong. We knew now that some of the first carving factories to exploit the Hong Kong loophole had been set up here. Singapore had not joined CITES until 1986 when its notorious stockpile of 270 tonnes of poached raw ivory had been given an amnesty. This had not been confiscated ivory. It was all owned by dealers, and its value when it was legalized had doubled overnight, making the Poons, the Lai family, K. T. Wang and others like them millions of pounds, and consolidating their domination of the ivory trade. By withholding the stockpile from the market-place they were able to manipulate ivory prices upwards, and many legal traders were driven out of business.

The enforcement of CITES restrictions in Singapore was obviously slack. We knew that in 1987 at least thirty-nine tonnes of poached ivory had arrived here from Dubai. We also knew that Fung Ivory still received ivory from the Ajman factory. The evidence we had collected in Hong Kong made us certain that Singapore was still being used as a stepping stone into the territory. What we were hoping to do in the short time we were here was to unravel that involvement.

During our first two days in Singapore we developed a routine. We would walk into an ivory shop and pretend to be interested in buying ivory seals or *hanko*.

'What do you do with these?' Susie would ask innocently.

'You have the tips carved with your signature,' the reply would come. 'You use them to sign documents.'

'What do you think, darling?' I'd respond. 'Shall we get a dozen made up as gifts for friends? I'll do the designs and then we can get them carved.'

Susie would flutter her eyelashes at me. 'What a great idea. I wonder if these people know where we could get them carved. Do you have a factory by any chance?' In this way we slowly gathered information on the companies operating factories in Singapore.

Next we went to Colombo Court, a government office

complex not far from the famous Raffles Hotel. In an office on the sixteenth floor there was another 'Company House' where anyone interested could get access to company files by computer. The information we found there described a web of Hong Kong involvement in the Singapore ivory business, with the name Poon and Tat Hing cropping up again and again.

We compiled a list of the names and addresses of Singapore shareholders in ivory companies and sifted through them to try to put the names in some order of importance based on the number of shares they held and the size of the company. We ended up with a list of two dozen addresses. When we checked them out, to our surprise most of them turned out to be small unimpressive tower block apartments in modest parts of town. But when we drove to the Singapore residences of the Hong Kong directors we found a quite different picture: villas and large expensive apartments in the best residential areas. Most of them had security checkpoints outside. It was obvious where the control of these companies lay.

Susie telephoned the government department responsible for implementing CITES regulations and asked for an interview. They were uncooperative and demanded to see a copy of our questions first, so we rearranged our itinerary and drove instead to the Sun Cheong ivory factory. It was owned by the Lai family of Hong Kong and had been set up in 1984. Michael Lai, we knew, had been one of the chief beneficiaries, along with the Poon brothers, of the 1986 amnesty.

The factory was situated on the third floor of a large building which had been divided into small business units. We walked up the stairs and found ourselves standing on an uncovered balcony with the sun beating down on our heads. Three large packing-cases were stacked at the top of the stairs, and I took down the shipment details written on the side. Somewhere close by we could hear the sound of drilling. I stepped through an open door leading off the balcony, and Susie followed. A young Chinese man approached us. Smiling confidently, I handed him a Box Films card. 'Hello. We wondered if we could have a talk with you. We're researching a film on the ivory trade.' I had decided in advance to use the open approach. This, after all, was not Poon's factory.

It paid off. The man revealed himself to be Lai Yu Key, a member of the Lai family syndicate. He seemed happy to show us round and led us into an area where men were marking out circular areas on tusks, preparatory to drilling out seals. The machine with which they did this was pumping water continuously as it drilled. Each seal took about five seconds to extract – it was a bit like coring an apple. Yu Key told us that even the fine fragments of tusk that remained were not wasted, but were used to make beads.

After drilling, the seals were packed into boxes, which when full contained a thousand seals and weighed twenty kilograms. 'We only produce one box a day now,' said Yu Key apologetically. 'I only have ten employees, but we used to be much bigger. When we first came to Singapore to avoid the CITES controls we had fifty workers.' With seals retailing at about twenty pounds each, his turnover was still not exactly small, I reflected.

'So coming here was a way of exploiting a loophole in the CITES system?' I probed. 'Was that because you could take carved ivory into Hong Kong?'

Yu Key nodded. 'That's right.'

'Are there any other loopholes in the system? Perhaps there are some that other people use?'

He smiled knowingly. 'There is one simple loophole that applies to jewellery companies making beads. They import fragments of ivory from Hong Kong – with legal permits. They must use these same permits when they export the beads. But with fragments the wastage is often 20 per cent. So for every hundred kilograms of fragments they only export eighty kilograms of beads. They are left with unused permits for twenty kilograms of ivory.'

'And how do they use them?' asked Susie.

'Well, you can still import finished products into Singapore without permits; you always could do that, but it's become a much more important route now that the Hong Kong loophole is closed. So they bring in finished products made from poached ivory – maybe carved in Dubai or Taiwan. Then they export them to Hong Kong and Japan using the spare permits.'

So that was how it was done. Now we knew another reason why Singapore was being used as a stepping stone from the Dubai factories. Singapore's role had increased in importance since August, when Hong Kong tightened up its regulations. Not only did they have this fragment permit scam going; they also had lots of amnesty permits still in hand which they could produce if any ivory was discovered while it was being smuggled into Hong Kong.

'Fascinating, but too complicated for our film, don't you think, Susie?' I said.

She adjusted the brooch concealing her microphone. 'I don't think I fully understood it anyway,' she lied. 'But it's been very interesting. Thank you for your time, Mr Lai.'

Driving back to the hotel, we discussed Lai's revelation.

'So we're looking for bead factories. Lots of them,' said Susie.

'The point about this fragment loophole,' I said, still excited by our discovery, 'is that it's really a way of buying permits. It's the paper that's valuable; it's used to legitimize poached ivory which then doubles in value. Ivory fragments are only worth twenty US dollars a kilo, while even raw ivory with permits is about two hundred US dollars now.'

'So they don't even have to make beads,' Susie reasoned. 'If they threw the fragments away and used all the fragment permits to export raw or carved ivory, they'd still be making huge profits!'

* * *

We walked into the hotel still pondering our discovery. There was a message on the notice board for someone called Naomi Watts. Naomi was Susie's first name. But she never used it. As far as I was aware, I was the only person in Singapore that knew she was called Naomi.

Susie waited until we were safely in her room before opening the envelope. Her hands shook as she read the message. 'It's on Singapore government paper,' she said unsteadily. 'It's to say we can meet tomorrow for an informal conversation.' Her face had turned white. 'If they know I'm called Naomi, it must mean they've been doing some checking up on us.'

Picking up a pencil, she scribbled something on her notepad and pushed it over to me.

'Let's not talk about ivory in our rooms from now on. I'm scared. Luv, Susie.'

The two government representatives were polite but cautious. One of them did most of the talking.

'You understand this is not an interview? We will just give you some information on how we enforce CITES regulations in Singapore. The Singapore government's attitude is very similar to that of Mrs Thatcher, your Prime Minister: we want as little interference with trade as possible.'

It was obvious he did not want us to interrupt his prepared speech. 'Singapore is the first country in this region to specifically bring in CITES legislation,' he boasted.

'Very impressive,' smiled Susie in an effort to relax the atmosphere.

'But when you joined CITES a lot of ivory was found in Singapore,' I intervened.

He clammed up immediately. He did not want to talk about the stockpile. Nor did he wish to discuss who owned it.

I tried another tack. 'Did you know that dealers have been using permits from ivory fragments to launder poached ivory coming into Singapore?'

He was on the defensive now. 'These are minor details.' His voice rose. 'We should concentrate on the elephants that are still alive! With our import regulations we are concerned with the big issues, like rabies in dogs and cats, not with details like these.'

His colleague couldn't resist a follow-up stab at us. 'The trouble with investigative journalists like you is that you divert the limited manpower of developing countries away from the major issues.'

I persevered. 'Is it true that thirty-nine tonnes of ivory came here from Dubai in 1987?'

'This is not an interview,' the first man protested angrily.

'But it is rather an important question, isn't it?'

'How do you know about this?'

'From Dubai statistics,' Susie answered him quietly.

'Their statistics are probably wrong,' he retorted. 'Off-hand I think it is very unlikely that the ivory came here.' He shrugged dismissively. 'Anyway, whatever happened, it will have complied with CITES regulations.'

His colleague adopted a more conciliatory tone. 'You see, ivory is a cultural issue in Singapore and all around this region. It's equivalent to Beethoven, Bach or the Great Masters in Europe. Its meaning is difficult to express to Westerners.'

I bit my tongue. I wanted to point out the absurdity of his comparisons. The ivory trade was supplying Europe, the United States and Japan with trinkets. What men like Poon were doing had nothing whatsoever to do with fine art. But it would have been a waste of energy. We were never going to alter their indoctrinated 'official viewpoint'. This meeting was leading us nowhere. Susie and I took our leave.

Encouraged by our friendly reception at the Sun Cheong ivory factory we decided to tackle Fung Ivory. Maybe it was pushing our luck to continue pursuing the Poons, but I felt it was important to try to form a complete picture of their activities. I was, I admit, also curious.

'Don't forget, Susie. No heroics,' I joked as I pulled the car up opposite the factory.

'Not much chance of that,' she said quietly. I was suddenly aware that all this tension was beginning to get to Susie. She knew as well as I did that I had been in Hong Kong, Dubai and Ajman already, investigating the Poon empire. Surely the Poon family would be on the lookout for me by now.

'If one of the Poons is in there, what will you do?' she demanded.

'I'll ask him if he's well and babble on as usual,' I replied.

Susie gave me a scathing look, then plugged the tiny microphone into the recorder strapped to her waist. 'Come on, then,' she said resignedly.

Carrying the camera, I walked by her side. The ivory factory was on the sixth floor, approached by a long corridor. The buzz of drills led us to it. Sitting at benches along the wall, a dozen workers bent in concentration over their tasks. A man approached us and started to speak in Cantonese, then seeing our blank expressions gave up and walked into another room. He reappeared with a woman who spoke to us in broken English.

'We have come to visit from a film company,' I explained.

'Film? Don't know,' she responded warily. She and the man exchanged a few words in Cantonese. She turned back to us. 'Yes. OK,' she agreed.

We didn't wait for her to have second thoughts. Taking out the video-camera, I focused it on the men at the side benches. It was only then that I realized what was going on here. All around us the men were working on fragments of tusk perforated with deep holes. On the floor were large plastic bowls full of beads and necklaces.

'This is it,' whispered Susie excitedly. 'It's one of the bead factories we're looking for. This is what Lai Yu Key was talking about.'

It was all beginning to tie in. Fung Ivory in Singapore had been the destination of many of the Poons' recent shipments from Dubai. Now it was obvious why. The carved pieces would probably not even be unpacked here but would be forwarded to Hong Kong using surplus ivory fragment permits. As far as Poon was concerned, it seemed that where one loophole closed another opened. Between smuggling, amnesty permits and fragment permits, the passage of ivory into Hong Kong was still running on well–oiled tracks.

The woman approached us again. 'Mrs Wong, she come tomorrow. She boss.'

'Oh?' I queried. 'I thought Poon Tat Hong was the boss.'

'Yes, he own factory, but he never here. You know Mr Poon?'

'Yes, I met him. We'll come and see Mrs Wong tomorrow. Will you tell her?'

Her voice was suddenly respectful. She was obviously impressed by our connections. 'Oh, yes. I tell her you come.'

But when Susie rang the factory in the morning the response was short and sharp. 'Mrs Wong not here. Called away. Family emergency.' The phone went dead.

In the circumstances it seemed foolhardy to try do any further prying. Our trip had achieved its aim. We had the names of dozens of people involved in illegal trading and had confirmed the laundering role of Singapore. I was due to fly to Kenya the next day before joining Allan who had returned for a third visit to Tanzania. That night, adopting our usual precautions, we photocopied all our documents and posted them back to Britain.

'Thanks, Susie,' I said. 'See you soon in London.'

13

MARCH 1989,
TANZANIA AND DUBAI

ALLAN

For a third time I had arrived back in Dar es Salaam, armed with a shipment of manuals, books, computer ribbons and other materials requested by Neil and Liz. There had been a massive response to the letters I'd drafted to the world's wildlife societies. Liz and Neil showed me the replies on my first day back in Dar es Salaam. Thirty-nine American groups had jointly pledged their support for an Appendix One listing and were appealing to Tanzania to propose it to CITES. There were also letters of support from various Greenpeace groups and from other concerned societies throughout Europe and the United States. The strength of the reaction was overwhelming. Even Prince Sadruddin Aga Khan, the vice-president of WWF International, had written personally in support of a ban, declaring: 'All else has failed, and we must move on to the next step.'

Virtually the only dissenting voices came from WWF. Buff Bohlen, Jorgen's boss, had written a wait-and-see letter to Mr Kitomari. But, although he did not support the ban, I thought I detected a slight shift in his attitude. I passed the letter over for Liz to reread it. 'What do you think, Liz? It sounds to me like Jorgen's been working on Buff.'

'H'm. It's interesting you should say that. He faxed a personal letter to Costa, care of our office, which seems to bear that out. Here, take a look. It's supposed to be confidential, but since he faxed it he can't be terribly concerned who reads it.'

I read Buff's letter with growing disbelief.

'Privately WWF USA supports an Appendix One listing as the only option to save the elephants. But for strategic and other reasons we do not wish to make this position public at the present time.'

'Who is it they don't want to offend, do you think, Liz?' I asked thoughtfully.

'I'm not sure. South Africa? Zimbabwe? Maybe the rest of WWF? Who knows?'

As I read the next paragraph I sensed Liz watching me to see my reaction.

'If Tanzania is willing to propose an Appendix One listing to CITES, we can provide you on an exclusive basis a fully documented proposal . . .'

My jaw dropped. We knew very well that WWF had not been working on a proposal. Jorgen would have told us if they had been. There was only one explanation for this generous offer. Somehow WWF had commandeered the proposal that we at EIA had funded Jorgen to write.

I was simultaneously shocked and delighted. I was furious that WWF were taking over our proposal but also knew that this was a crucial step forward in trying to stop the ivory trade. We *had* to get WWF to support the ban, and Jorgen had clearly used our proposal to enlist Buff's help to swing WWF behind a ban.

Neil came in and summed up the situation as he saw me holding Buff Bohlen's letter.

'Interesting letter, that,' he grinned. 'It's a good thing EIA is so generous – funding a little struggling group like WWF!'

Although a new WWF USA policy on ivory was starting to crystalize, internationally the WWF position was still very confused and it was clear a lot of people were still opposed to a ban. Liz and Neil told me that John Hanks from WWF International had recently flown in for two days on a whistle-stop visit and had a very stormy meeting with the steering committee of the Wildlife Conservation Society of Tanzania. 'He was arguing strongly against the Appendix One listing and trying to dissuade Tanzania from proposing it,' said Liz. 'He claimed that a ban on the ivory trade wouldn't do any good at all because according to him the Japanese import 75 per cent of all ivory and their traditional demand would not disappear just because of new CITES regulations. He said a ban would be counter-productive because the illegal trade would just escalate out of control.'

Hanks's attitude had irritated the local wildlife fraternity.

'This guy thought he could fly in and tell Tanzania what to do,' said Neil. 'But he actually didn't have the most basic information. He kept going on about how Japan consumed three-quarters of the world's ivory as though it was undisputed fact. But we outwitted him there. Do you remember I faxed you in London to ask for your figures on Japan?'

I did remember. I had replied that our information, based on the most recent statistics available, was that Japan did not import more than 40 per cent of the world's ivory.

'I presented him with your tables and then asked Hanks what his figures were based on. He didn't answer.'

Sidney, who had just arrived at the office, interrupted. 'Hanks kept saying that elephants must be used commercially to provide income for African countries. I asked him: "What about the ecological role of elephants? Isn't that important in African countries?" He had no answer to that, either.'

'This "commercial use" idea is very much Zimbabwe's policy,' said Neil. 'He should start listening to the rest of Africa instead.'

*

I had come to Tanzania hoping to tidy up several loose ends. Before leaving London I had spoken to Sidney over the phone. The news of his research on the missionary story had been encouraging. His contacts had told him that a shipment might be sent out from Mtwara over the Easter weekend. If everything went according to plan, I hoped to film its seizure by the Tanzanian authorities. Ivory smuggling priests would create even more of an international press uproar than poaching ambassadors!

But it was not to be. Sidney had been given the name of the ship which was expected to pick up the ivory, but when I checked with Lloyd's Shipping Registry it was not registered. This in itself didn't cause me undue concern. Many ships operating on the African coast were not Lloyd's-registered. But Sidney now revealed that no boat was reported due in Mtwara at Easter weekend. Either the priests' plans had changed or he had been led astray. It was disappointing. Greenpeace Germany had been hoping to catch these priests red-handed. But hopefully there would be another opportunity.

Dave flew from Singapore to Kenya to catch up on developments there before joining me in Dar es Salaam. Together we paid a visit to Costa in his new director's office to update him on our latest information relating to the Tanzania–Dubai connection. EIA's standing and credibility were increasing steadily in Tanzania. Since Costa's appointment as Director of Wildlife the authorities in Tanzania had been clamping down hard on ivory poachers (possibly explained why the priests had changed their plans). Following Dave's tip-off they had looked into the activities of Al-Waffa, and Costa told us that a massive haul of illegal ivory consigned by Al-Waffa had recently been located on board a dhow sailing for the United Arab Emirates. The police had been tipped off and had watched it loading up the coast from Dar es Salaam. But it had got away. However, Interpol had been contacted, and UAE had been asked to seize the boat, known as *Khairat Oman*, when it arrived in port.

'We're sending our team off to Dubai next week to try to get our ivory back,' said Costa. 'Interpol told us they have intercepted it and taken it to Abu Dhabi.'

I turned to Dave. 'Is there a chance that you could go back to Dubai to help their men there, Dave? You know your way around so well now.'

Dave gave a stoical grin. 'If they'll still let me into the country, I'll go.'

Costa smiled. 'Well, if you just happened to be in Dubai at the same time as our delegation, I'm sure that might be very useful.'

'And how about the Appendix One proposal? Is there anything to report?' I was anxious to get around to our main concern.

Costa nodded. 'Mr Lumbanga has let the Ministry know about all these letters from the different societies, and the Ministry is very encouraged by that support. I've written a paper for the Cabinet to discuss. It's looking hopeful. I feel confident that we'll move on the proposal.'

'How will it be approved? Can it go straight to the President?'

'The proposal can come from the whole Cabinet or from an Inner Cabinet meeting, or the President could make the proposal himself – in effect it would then be a decree. That would obviously be the best way. But don't worry. We'll get the support, whatever happens.'

Before we left we filmed an interview with Costa which we planned to submit with our next batch of film to ITN. Normally Costa avoided interviews, preferring to keep a low profile about his work, but he rose to the occasion. His final emotive words echoed Daphne Sheldrick's statement months earlier: 'People in the UK, Germany, France, the US and Japan must realize that buying ivory means killing elephants.'

*

At the weekend we took a break and drove with Neil and Liz to Mikumi Park; a four-hour journey west of Dares Salaam. It was nearly dark when suddenly huge ethereal shapes appeared beside the road and white tusks flashed out of the gloom. After all the depressing statistics it was wonderful to see live elephants again. We stayed with friends of Neil and Liz, an Irish couple who took us out the next day to film. A mile into the park we sighted a herd of thirty-five elephants. Our host turned off his Land Rover engine, and I used ITN's Video 8 while Dave snapped away. It was our first film of a herd of live elephants in the wild at close quarters.

The herd was composed mainly of females, all very young, probably less than twenty years of age. At the CITES meeting in Nairobi I had met a biologist called Joyce Poole, who was writing a paper on the collapsed age structure of Mikumi's elephants. She had found that poachers had wiped out most of the males and there were few of breeding age left. (Unlike the females, who may breed in their teens, the males do not breed until they are twenty-five to thirty years old.) This had caused a serious reduction in the frequency of births within the herds.

The elephants slowly surrounded us. Dave and I focused our cameras on a tiny newborn elephant as it ran clumsily between its mother and its aunts, half tripping over its trunk in its hurry, its little ears flapping madly.

The herd moved closer, some of them settling into a waterhole barely ten feet from us where they splashed water and showered themselves, rolling around in the mud, completely ignoring us. Our hosts told us that poaching had recently declined dramatically in Mikumi because of an intensive anti-poaching regime, and as a result the elephants were getting their confidence back. We left Mikumi revitalized. It had been just the boost we needed – a reminder of the real purpose behind all this hard work.

*

The night before Dave was due to leave for Dubai we ate what seemed at the time a delightful meal of fresh prawns. I woke up the next day with a violent case of food poisoning. Poor Dave didn't look too well, either, but was committed to catch his flight that day.

I struggled to keep an appointment with Mr Kitomari during which we discussed his attempts to recover the Burundi ivory and to arrange a meeting for the Wildlife Conservation Society of Tanzania and myself with the President. On both counts he reported no progress whatsoever. However, it was some compensation when Mr Kitomari offered me access to the Bank of Tanzania export files. There, despite my complaining stomach, I was able to check on the activities of Al-Waffa, the agent named on Dave's 'hippo teeth' air waybill, and confirm that they had dealt several times with Al Redha in Dubai. By chance I also found four documents that had been filed by the German missionaries. They related to containers of what they described as 'makonde wooden carvings' which had been addressed to a monastery in Germany. After copying them I left to meet Raymond, my schoolteacher contact from the last trip. He had still more paperwork for me: documents of recent suspect shipments obtained from his policeman friend, and allegations about politicians suspected of involvement. It was all necessary as proof of our allegations, but I was pleased it was Charmian back in London and not me who would have to collate all this accumulating paperwork into some sort of order.

Raymond and I were sitting in a café looking at the documents when two tall well-dressed men walked in. They were wearing sunglasses and looked rather sinister. After scanning the bar they walked straight over to us and stared impassively at me before shaking Raymond's hand and speaking to him in Kiswahili. Raymond looked deeply nervous. I saw them glancing at the papers on the table and covered them up as unobtrusively as I could.

When they'd finished talking, the men walked back to

the bar from where they continued to watch us openly. Raymond leaned towards me. 'They are from the secret police,' he whispered. 'They asked me who my friend is. They want to know all about you. I think there is another one of them over there.' The man he indicated was writing something in a notebook at a table just across the room from us. He met my gaze and scowled. Raymond lit a cigarette. His hand was shaking badly. 'I told them you were an old friend from England,' he said.

'Do you think they saw any names in these documents?' I asked.

Raymond shrugged uneasily. 'They didn't say anything about them, but you wouldn't know. I hope not. I really hope not.'

What could the secret police want with us? The likelihood was that they were concerned about my ivory enquiries. Raymond was implicating top people in his statements to me. If they had found out about that, it did not bode well for either of us. But there were other possibilities. Perhaps they had followed me from the bank. If they had seen me copying all those trading documents, maybe they thought I was a bank investigator looking for incriminating documents or even something more sinister. None of the possibilities was reassuring. The effect on my already disturbed stomach was extremely unpleasant. I stood up. 'Why don't we go somewhere else, Raymond?'

We walked out of the café and around the corner, resisting the temptation to turn around and check if we were being followed. As we turned a second corner, Raymond suddenly said, 'In here,' and dived through an open doorway. We went into a building, up two flights of stairs and exited through the back. A few yards further on we walked into another building and came out in the street behind it. There was no sign of the men. 'There's another café up here.' Raymond pointed. 'More private.'

We ordered drinks and resumed our conversation. Neither of us mentioned the incident again, but I noticed that Raymond's cigarette lighting was still shaky when we parted.

Later in the day Dave called Neil's office.

'How was your flight?' I asked him.

'Miserable.'

'It was the prawns,' I commiserated. 'How's Dubai?'

'I think they're giving the Tanzanians the run around. The ivory has gone, and it looks like the boat has gone, too. But I'm going to meet some more people this afternoon who might be able to tell me more.'

I packaged up our documents and videotape and took them to the offices of Swissair to be sent on ahead of me. While I was out Jorgen Thomsen called Liz. To my immense relief she said he had assured her the Appendix One proposal would arrive in Dar es Salaam in a day or so. We had arranged to supply the proposal directly to the Wildlife Conservation Society of Tanzania. They would work on it to make it acceptable from a Tanzanian point of view, and it was then going to be up to the Society to persuade the Government.

Before I left for London once more I had a small mountain of paperwork to attend to, which effectively kept my mind off the secret police and their interest in me. I drafted responses to the letters received from all the wildlife groups; then, since it seemed unlikely now that I would see him in person, I wrote a briefing on the Appendix One initiative for President Mwinyi. Finally I drafted a letter for Mr Kitomari to sign in his role as chairman of WCST, formally requesting the Ministry to ensure that the Tanzanian government propose the Appendix One listing to CITES.

For the last week Sidney had been up in Tanga on the coast of northern Tanzania. It was close to where *Fadhil Allah* used to load her ivory. We suspected that the ships currently owned by Al Redha still loaded tusks there before sailing for Dubai. Although he was a day late, Sidney was wreathed in smiles as he walked back into

Neil's office. On a farm outside Tanga he had discovered a cache of 800 tusks and 200 rhino horns awaiting shipment from the port.

'The man who owns the farm is very rich. His house is very big, and on its roof there is a large radio antenna. I think he uses this radio to talk to the ships which load the ivory to take to Dubai,' he said. I nodded. It would make sense.

Sidney produced details of four ships which were due to pick the ivory up. He also had information on dates of shipments and the names of local officials who had been bought off by the ivory traders. In addition there were transcripts of a dozen interviews, confirming the identity of the major illegal ivory traders in the region. Sidney had good cause to look pleased with himself.

DAVE

My unplanned trip to Dubai was not a resounding success. I had nursed a hope that the Interpol intervention and subsequent seizure of the poached ivory from Tanzania might make a big media story, keeping up the public interest without necessitating the premature publication of our own investigations. But it was not to be. The problems started when the Tanzanian delegation had their passports confiscated at the airport and continued when the first contacts I spoke to denied all knowledge of the dhow called *Khairat Oman* which Interpol was supposed to have intercepted. Blank faces met every enquiry I made.

We had decided that it would not be circumspect for me to stay at the same Dubai hotel as the Tanzanian delegation. My brief was to help them find their way around and assist in any way I could in locating the stolen ivory shipment. But the authorities were obviously already hostile to the Tanzanians, so it would not do the Africans' cause any good at all to be linked to me and my associations with stolen air waybills and bogus film companies.

Accordingly I booked into the Palm Beach Hotel where I had stayed on the last trip, very conscious that this time I was on my own – a situation we had vowed never to let happen when we were investigating.

I contacted Paul Sarakikya, one of the delegation, who was an official with the Tanzanian anti-poaching unit. Costa had introduced me to him the previous week. We joined up in secret, and I drove him around the area. After touring Hamriya Port in a fruitless search for *Khairat Oman*, we went for a drink at the Hyatt Regency Hotel bar. As we walked through the shopping and cinema complex we were suddenly faced by the Hyatt ice-rink, an extravagant creation which is kept frozen all year despite the ninety-degree heat outside. Adjacent to it were expensive jewellery and clothing shops. I became aware that Paul had fallen behind me and was staring at this flagrant display of wealth in amazement. Dar es Salaam has nothing which remotely compares with such opulence. Nor is it ever likely to have.

'Petrodollars?' he asked me ironically. 'Or ivory dollars?'

Paul became a good friend in the two weeks we were there. But it was soon plain that reclaiming the ivory was a lost cause. Working largely alone, I visited virtually every port in the area, including Port Zayed in Abu Dhabi, without finding *Khairat Oman* or anyone who even admitted to having seen her. It was a frustrating time. The UAE authorities seemed determined to hinder the Tanzanian efforts as much as possible. The police did admit that the dhow had been held, but said they had released the crew; they claimed there were only three tonnes of ivory on board – though the Tanzanians knew seventy tonnes had been loaded in Tanga; they refused to say where the dhow was being held; they wanted the Tanzanian documents translated into Arabic before they would even consider arranging any meetings . . . It was hopeless. Every day the trail grew colder. I was very conscious that the hours to the May deadline for the Appendix One proposal were ticking away while I ran around in circles here.

Khor Fakkan is a two-hour drive across the desert from Dubai. It was my last hope, one of the few potential mooring-spots for *Khairat Oman* that I had not yet visited. The road to the port climbs into the hills and sweeps round to the coast, on its way brushing the border with Oman. The sea stretches out from here to join the Indian Ocean, and the entire coastline is famous for its coves and its smuggling.

Just outside the smart modern town of Khor Fakkan is a small dhow cove which adjoins a Customs berth and a container port. I headed for the cove, but *Khairat Oman* wasn't there. Getting back into my car, I drove to the container port where I knew a European official worked. I'd met him on one of my other trips when I was posing as a photojournalist.

'Good morning. How are you?' I greeted him breezily. 'I'm passing through UAE, so I thought I'd come out and see you.'

He gave me a bemused look. Not many people pass through Khor Fakkan.

There seemed little point in beating about the bush. 'I'm following up a story on ivory,' I said. 'You haven't heard of a boat being arrested by the coastguard around here, have you?'

He hadn't.

'It was a long shot,' I conceded. 'Actually it was a good excuse to get out of Dubai for a bit. It's not my favourite place.'

That seemed to break the ice. He brewed some coffee, and over it we chatted about the shortcomings of Dubai and about the ivory trade. He was amazed to hear that UAE was the world's biggest entrepôt for poached ivory. Most people were.

'Come with me,' he said, putting his coffee down. 'I'll introduce you to a local person who might know something.' In another office, a small group of Arab men were drinking tea. I was ushered in and given a friendly welcome.

'Ivory?' One of them considered my query. 'There was a boat arrested a couple of years ago with ivory.' He scratched his chin thoughtfully. 'From Senegal, I think. Wait a moment. I will make a telephone call.'

Walking over to the telephone on the wall, he dialled a number and for almost a minute he spoke rapidly to someone in Arabic. I had no idea what he was saying or to whom he was talking, but when he came off the phone he was smiling.

'I would make a very good reporter,' he said. 'You see, I have the information for you.'

'Thank you. You are very kind. Perhaps I can find you a job!' I joked.

'*Khairat Oman* arrived here two weeks ago. She wasn't arrested; she just sailed into the Customs berth. It was twenty-four hours before the coastguard arrested her and handed her over to local police.'

By which time she only had three tonnes of ivory left on board, I thought grimly.

'What happened to her?'

'My friend said there was a lot of discussion for two or three days over what would happen to her. But in the end the ivory was handed over to someone. I'm not sure who. The dhow and the crew were freed. She sailed towards Dubai three days ago.'

Back in Dubai I telephoned Paul and told him what I had learned. We discussed the possibility of publicizing the ivory story to embarrass the United Arab Emirates, but Paul's superior felt it would be counter-productive and I saw no point in pursuing the idea further. What newspaper or television company would be interested in a story about a ship smuggling Tanzanian ivory when the ivory was missing, the ship had gone and the Tanzanians wouldn't talk?

To fill in the remaining couple of days before my flight to London, I decided, though with little hope, to visit my old friend at the Statistics Department. On my last visit I was sure he had been instructed not to co-operate with us, but it seemed I was mistaken. To my delight he at last produced the details for the last three months of 1988. I took the printout back to my hotel room and studied it eagerly. But it was disappointing. What I was looking for was evidence that Hong Kong or Singapore was still receiving ivory from Dubai. That would provoke the United States into action. But Poon had been too clever for us. Taiwan was the only country named as receiving ivory since August.

The day before I left Dubai I phoned a contact who knew the Poons. He told me that a third Poon brother ran one of the Ajman factories and George ran the other. 'Just like they did in Jebel Ali.'

'Who owns which?' I asked. Incidental facts like this completed the picture and reduced our chance of being caught out over details in debates.

'I think the units are all together,' he answered. 'I haven't been out there, but a colleague of mine has. He says it's a row of three or four units. It's called the Handicraft Factory.'

I pricked up my ears. The factories I'd seen in Ajman were called the Pearl Workshop and the Coral Workshop.

'Wait a minute. Is this near the Municipality Building in Ajman?'

He sounded puzzled. 'No, I don't think so. It's out near the Pakistani school.'

I took down directions and drove feverishly out to Ajman. Yet more factories! Where was this going to end?

The Ajman National Handicraft Factory was, as my

contact had said, a row of three units, each with its metal shutters firmly closed. I parked the car and got out. The tarmac was so hot it was melting underfoot.

'Hello! Fine work in there.'

Startled, I turned to find an Arab man standing behind me.

'In there?' I could hear drills buzzing away behind the shutters.

'Oh, yes,' he nodded.

'What are they making?'

He looked about him shiftily and wandered off down the street mumbling to himself.

I took some pictures of the outside of the factory and got back into the car. It would be stupid to try to go in on my own. I knew what was going on inside, and we already had pictures of the inside of the other Ajman factory.

All at once I felt very depressed. I had thought that maybe the growing worldwide anti-ivory campaign would be having some effect here, but it seemed I'd been wrong. New factories were springing up like mushrooms. Every day elephants were still being slaughtered to feed their demand. Even if we did get a ban, would it be in time?

I drove back via the other Ajman factory. I had been monitoring it regularly during the past two weeks, spending hours in the car outside watching the comings and goings. Ajman's main street has road bumps to slow the traffic down, and as I passed over the first bump a white BMW slowed alongside me. A Chinese man was driving, and beside him in the front passenger seat sat an elegant Chinese woman. My heart skipped a beat. George Poon was said to drive a white BMW. I stared straight ahead and let the BMW pull in front of me. As it reached the Ajman factory it drew in to the verge and the man got out.

I parked my car in the spot I'd used on the visit with Susie and turned the air-conditioner on. George Poon (for

I was sure now it was him) was supervising the hanging of a sign which read 'Pearl Workshop' over a unit which had been empty on my last visit.

It seemed his business, too, was expanding.

Before I left Dubai for London I took Paul Sarakikya out to dinner. He had spent much of his time here confined to his hotel, and I wanted to have a final talk before we left. We went to the Inter-Continental, which though reasonably priced was very luxurious. Eating out is popular in Dubai, and good food and entertainment are taken for granted. People from all around the Gulf flock there.

To Paul it was all a novelty. He looked around him shaking his head in disbelief at the sumptuous fittings, the elegant interior. 'Incredible – and all from oil,' he laughed. It must have seemed the ultimate in decadence to Paul, who admitted to being at his happiest in the bush away from all the trappings of civilization.

'Will you be glad to go home?'

'I can hardly wait,' he smiled. 'But we can't go yet. My superiors want to stay. They're determined to try to get some co-operation from the Dubai authorities.'

I felt pessimistic about their chances but said nothing.

'I've been disappointed by our reception here,' Paul admitted. 'The authorities have not been very helpful. I get the impression they have no wish to stop the trade.'

'Well, if Tanzania gets its proposal accepted by CITES, they'll have little choice. They won't be able to sell their poached ivory any more. Not to CITES countries anyway.'

'You must make sure that CITES does accept it, Dave. You've got to show people what happens here and in Hong Kong. If you can sway public opinion enough, then CITES will have to go along with it.'

It was a friendly and happy meal. Paul and I had become good friends in these few days, each of us appreciating the other's commitment to the elephants' cause.

As we left the table Paul put his hand on my arm. 'I would like you to come to my wedding in October, Dave.'

'Thank you, Paul,' I said. 'I'd love to. But I doubt if I can afford it. Anyway, I'll be in Switzerland that month fighting for the ivory ban at the CITES meeting.'

Paul looked chastened. 'Of course. How could I forget?' He considered for a moment. 'In that case I could get married in November.'

'I'm very honoured,' I said, touched. 'I would like that very much.'

14

APRIL 1989,
WASHINGTON DC, TANZANIA AND DUBAI

ALLAN

It was the day after I returned from Tanzania – a Sunday – and I had gone in to pick up my mail and messages at the EIA office. An unwelcome surprise awaited me. At the top of the two flights of stairs, pieces of wood were scattered around the hallway. It was evident where they had come from; the main entrance door was shattered into splinters of lumber, while the door frame itself was half ripped away from the wall.

In total about a hundred pounds in petty cash had been taken, together with a few small desk items, but we were more worried about our research work. The intruder, whoever he or she was, had rummaged through the office files, and papers were spilled everywhere. It was impossible to be certain that no documents were missing. Certainly it appeared to be the work of a petty thief. But supposing it wasn't?

There was no time to dwell on it. Dave had just returned from Dubai, and over the next few days Jenny brought us up to date with the developments at home while we'd been away. The publicity over elephant poaching was continuing. The 'Cook Report' on the ivory situation was due out on 15 May, and we wanted to get our film out before that. Dave talked again with ITN. After seeing the latest film they were keen to make a three-part 'special', to be broadcast as news items on successive nights. The broadcasts would coincide with the deadline date for submissions to CITES:

12 May. There was one slight snag. They wanted to shoot some pieces on location with their reporter and they wanted either Dave or me to go back to Dubai and Tanzania to help with that. Since we were almost out of funds again and ITN were paying us £7,500 for the first news rights, we could hardly refuse; but I was committed to go to Washington, so it would have to be Dave, who had just told me that after the latest trip he'd sworn never to visit Dubai again.

My American visit had two purposes: to pass on our latest discoveries to the United States Fish and Wildlife Department, and to meet some of the American wildlife groups, in particular WWF US. To my relief, Jorgen's Appendix One proposal was delivered to the Wildlife Conservation Society of Tanzania just before I left for Washington. It was an excellent document, well researched and authoritative. Provided Tanzania did not back out at the last minute, it looked as though we were all set to meet the 12 May deadline.

The American position on this Appendix One proposal was crucial. For the past year the EEC countries had been following the American lead in imposing new, more restrictive regulations on ivory imports. If the United States supported a ban, then almost certainly Europe would, too. Our new evidence might just be the swaying factor needed to move the Americans. It was worth a try anyway. I had been asked to brief two senior officials in the Fish and Wildlife Service, Marshall Jones and Art Lazarowitz, on EIA's research into the ivory trade. Christine Stevens came with me. It would be the first time she had heard a detailed account of what EIA had discovered with the aid of her group's funding.

It was hard to know where to begin, but our own starting point, *Fadhil Allah*, seemed as good a place as any. I outlined the activities of Al Redha, describing the routes taken by its smuggling boats as they ferried ivory between Kenya or Tanzania and Dubai. I also told them of the network of poachers and middlemen that had arisen in Tanzania during the nine-year term of Fred Lwezuela, and of the containerloads of ivory which were smuggled through Tanzania's ports and along Tanzania's roads to Burundi. I spoke about the loads of ivory being smuggled out of Africa by foreign diplomats as 'diplomatic baggage'.

'If the present annual level of the world ivory trade amounts to seven hundred or eight hundred tonnes, we estimate that a quarter of that originates in or passes through Tanzania each year,' I said. 'We have provided the Tanzanian cabinet with documentation to prove this, and it's that information which we believe will lead them to propose the Appendix One listing. Tanzania is not benefiting from the trade at all. It is a desperately poor country, yet the profits from ivory sales are almost all going to other countries. As far as Tanzania is concerned, there is no justification for the WWF argument that sales of ivory help the African economy.'

Marshall Jones and Art Lazarowitz listened intently, occasionally asking questions but for the most part silently taking notes.

Finally I passed on a personal message from Costa in his new capacity as Director of Wildlife in Tanzania, requesting the United States government's support for an Appendix One listing for African elephants. His message concluded: 'Tanzania intends to propose the Appendix One listing because it is the only way to save their remaining herds.'

'Well, thank you for that, Allan,' said Marshall. 'Please tell Costa Mlay that we would welcome a well thought out proposal from an African country and hope that one will be forthcoming. We will give it our fullest consideration.'

Typical diplomatic jargon meaning 'We're not going to commit ourselves', I thought.

'What have you found out about the ivory factories in UAE?' Marshall continued. 'Have they closed?'

'Far from it,' I said. I outlined Dave's discoveries in Ajman and Dubai, and told him of Burundi's continued exports to Dubai in 1988 even after its government's undertaking to ban trading. 'We also believe that ivory traders in Dubai are circumventing Hong Kong's new regulations which were introduced in August,' I said. 'No ivory is being sent there openly now, but instead there have suddenly been a lot of shipments described as "fashion jewellery" or "imitation fashion jewellery". Ten tonnes of it in 1988. A lot of it is going by way of European accommodation addresses. And we know those same addresses were receiving ivory before the August restrictions came in.'

I outlined what we knew of the Singapore ivory trade, describing how worked ivory was still being sent there openly from Dubai, and informed them of Dave and Susie's discovery that spare 'fragment permits' were being used to launder large quantities of poached ivory.

Surely, I thought, they must see now that the CITES controls are not working, can't ever work, when you have dealers who are so good at finding ways around the system.

They both continued to make notes for some time after I finished speaking. Then Marshall looked up.

'I hope Costa Mlay will attend the next meeting of the CITES elephant group in Botswana in July. It will be an extremely crucial meeting. It would be very helpful if he was there.'

They had made no promises. I had not really expected them to. But I left the Fish and Wildlife office with a distinct feeling of optimism.

* * *

I had agreed to give a talk on our work to the office staff at the Washington headquarters of Greenpeace USA. Preparing what I would say had reminded me of the fundamental principles which lay behind our campaign to save the elephants. It was easy to lose sight of those sometimes when we were caught up in the day-to-day frustrations of an investigation. After showing the group our 'box film' from Dubai and the video of the poached elephants in Tsavo national park, I addressed the meeting, which included a lot of old friends from my days at Greenpeace.

'One of the early philosophies of Greenpeace was adopted from the Quakers and is known as "bearing witness",' I reminded them. ' "Bearing witness" means simply that if you perceive or see an injustice, then you are responsible to address or resolve that injustice. In the early days of Greenpeace, that ethical responsibility of "bearing witness" caused us to drive our little inflatables in front of the harpoons of the whale catching ships and made us put our bodies on top of seal pups on the ice floes off Canada's east coast. Now the terrible slaughter of Africa's elephants – as many as a hundred thousand a year – needs people to bear witness again if we are to prevent their extinction.'

The response from my Greenpeace friends was warm and supportive, and I was still glowing when I arrived back at Christine's house. I saw at once that she was also bubbling over with excitement. 'I've just had an interesting phone call from Mr Lujan,' she said. Manuel Lujan was the Secretary for the Interior and in charge of policy for the Fish and Wildlife Service.

'What did he say?'

'He wanted to know more background and asked what opposition I thought there would be to a ban. He thinks the hunters might be opposed to it, and you know how important the hunting lobby is in the States. But I told him hunters won't be affected because tusks from elephants shot on safari aren't considered a commercial trade. So I think it looks hopeful they might support Appendix One.' Christine smiled at me exultantly. 'At last we've got them stirred up about elephants, Allan!'

WWF US had a new president, Kathryn Fuller, a former lawyer at the United States Department of Justice. Christine was very impressed with her and felt she was far more inclined to push for a ban than her predecessor, Bill Reilly, had been. She had fixed an appointment for me to meet her the following day at the WWF US headquarters, a modern opulent building on 24th Street.

Kathryn Fuller had the piercing analytical gaze you expect from a successful lawyer. I felt that here was a person who would see her way straight to the heart of a problem. In our meeting I stressed our concern that WWF did not seem to have a unified voice on the ivory issue. Conflicting messages were coming from different groups, and I told her I felt it was important for WWF to declare unequivocally where it stood as regards an ivory ban. Obviously my view was that they should support it, and I did my best to persuade Kathryn Fuller into my way of thinking. 'It would be a very negative image for WWF if they are not seen to be actively behind a ban on the ivory trade,' I said. 'It will look as if there is a split in the wildlife conservation movement, and that can only reflect poorly on WWF.'

Kathryn nodded. 'I agree. I have in fact lobbied the president of the Central African Republic to support the Appendix One proposal. The US group is behind a ban, but I do share your concern that WWF hasn't unified its position yet. We must do this soon.'

Before I left I gave Kathryn a brief résumé of our work in the United Arab Emirates and the Far East, explaining the loopholes that still remained in the ivory control system. I could only hope that, under the combined effect of a 'new broom' at the top and Jorgen's influence, common sense would now prevail to change WWF policy.

My flight for London left the following day. Just before I set off for the airport Christine arrived back at the house bursting with news. 'Somebody seems to have been listening to what we've been telling them at last,' she exclaimed. 'Mr Baker, the Secretary of State, called me up and asked for a meeting. I've just finished talking to him. He thinks the Bush administration will soon come out in support of a ban! There should be an announcement very soon.'

DAVE

The single-engine Cessna flew south, heading for the Selous game reserve. Our pilot, Gerald Bigarubi, was manager of the Selous project and involved in the anti-poaching operation there. Below us we could see the flooded Rufiji river, its banks burst by recent heavy rains. Gerald pointed. 'If you look carefully, you'll see some hippos.' Beside me Desmond Hamill, one of ITN's senior correspondents, craned to look. Desmond was already very involved with this story, and his personal interest in wildlife was apparent. From the plane, the hippos looked just like floating debris, but as they heard our engine one by one they came to life and dived beneath the surface in panic.

Also with us in the plane was Paul Sarakikya, my friend from Dubai, who was now the commander of the anti-poaching forces in eastern Tanzania. The fifth member of our party was Mohinder Dhillon, a freelance film cameraman hired by ITN. The aim of this flight was to get additional film to include in the first of our ITN specials. This was the one which would concentrate on the realities of poaching and the difficulties of combating it. Prior to the flight we had already recorded footage of Desmond in the ivory room in Dar es Salaam.

We landed first on the grass airstrip at Kinżupira, an anti-poaching station in the eastern sector of the Selous reserve. A group of rangers, forewarned of our arrival, came out to meet us and helped unload the equipment from the plane. They carried it over to a large prefabricated shelter which housed a motley collection of broken-down vehicles; Gerald Bigarubi told us that funds were in such short supply that many of these anti-poaching patrol vehicles remained out of action permanently simply for want of a spare part.

Desmond picked up on this. Tanzania's poverty-stricken economy was obviously a crucial factor in the story. He filmed an interview with Gerald standing beside his plane.

After elaborating on the shortage of vehicles Gerald added as an afterthought that the radio in his plane had been out of order for four months because they could not afford the spare parts. Apart from the danger of flying without radio contact, this meant it was impossible for him to contact rangers on the ground if he spotted poaching activity from the air. In every aspect of the battle with the poachers the rangers were handicapped. Any band of poachers who were half-competent could run rings around them. And were doing so. Costa had told us that the poaching was particularly bad at the moment. A band of about fifty poachers was known to be operating in a forested area in the south-west of Selous, but the anti-poaching unit was essentially powerless to do anything to stop them. The airstrip there was closed because of flooding and, in any case, to police forest areas would require vast numbers of foot patrols – for which no funds were available.

We were keen to get airborne again while the light still allowed filming and we crammed ourselves once more into the Cessna. Mohinder asked if Gerald would take the door off the plane to make filming easier. Gerald said he'd never flown with the door off before but intrepidly agreed to try. With the wind whistling into the cockpit we took off down the bumpy strip. 'We'll head west; there are usually elephant not far from here,' Gerald said.

In 1981 a census of the elephant population of the Selous had shown 100,000 elephants. By 1986 it had fallen to 50,000. Nobody knew how many were left now, but we hoped to be able to film at least a few hundred from the air. The Selous reserve is the size of Scotland; but the area we were flying over was open apart from occasional clumps of high grass and trees, so we were able to scan the park for miles around. We passed over several herds of impala, which dispersed in all directions at the noise of our engine, but we saw very few elephants.

At last Paul pointed to the horizon. 'There's a herd.' We flew over it. There were no more than thirty animals.

Mohinder and I both recorded the scene as the plane circled and passed over them.

'We'll head further into the centre of the reserve,' Paul suggested.

The scenery was breathtaking. Now and then we flew over forested hills – we were approaching the region where the poachers were known to be operating – but our search for a big elephant herd was fruitless. At one point Gerald pointed down towards a river bank where two piles of white bones were clearly visible. 'They must have been poached months ago,' he said.

Gerald was supposed to fly back to Dar es Salaam before nightfall to receive an injection – he had barely recovered from a bad bout of malaria – but he valiantly decided to forgo his medication so that we could spend the night at a lodge in the north-west of Selous. Once more we flew over glorious country, following the Rufiji river much of the time. While passing over a small lake we spotted a canoe with two men in it and a camp on the shore.

'Poachers,' said Paul. 'They're catching fish for their supper.'

We flew low over them a few times and watched them paddle frantically for the shore.

'They know that we'll tell the rangers where to find them,' Paul explained. However, without a radio it would be hours before anyone could get out here in a vehicle, by which time the camp would certainly be empty. The incident brought home to us the futility of much of the anti-poaching unit's efforts.

The lodge where we were to spend the night was closed for the wet season, but a few staff had remained to keep it ticking over and they rushed around trying to make us comfortable as we sat on the veranda enjoying the view over unspoilt wilderness. In the distance warthogs were playing frenzied evening games. One of the staff found a bottle of Johnnie Walker that had been secreted somewhere, and Des, Gerald, Mohinder, Paul and I sat contentedly until way past dark sipping Scotch and listening to the lions roaring into the night.

Next day the filming went very well. The previous week the anti-poaching unit had brought in sixteen poached tusks and a rifle, and Paul helped them reconstruct the discovery of the cache so that we could film the unit loading the tusks into a Land Rover. Desmond interviewed Paul, asking him what he thought should be done to stop the poaching. Conscious that millions of people might hear whatever he said, he considered his answer for some time before confidently addressing the camera. 'Surely I'll pray the international community to suppress all the ivory trade. Because as long as there is a trade somewhere – in Hong Kong or Dubai, or wherever it is – it will threaten our elephants. So if they can close the markets altogether that would be great for us. It will lessen our burden.'

On the flight back to Dar es Salaam I quizzed Paul on the outcome of his trip to Dubai. He smiled ruefully. 'I don't think that ivory was ever confiscated, whatever the authorities said. Did you know that we were able to speak to Abdullah Ali Bamakramah, the man who owns Al Redha General Trading?'

I hadn't known. 'What did he say?'

'He said he had sold the ivory from *Khairat Oman*, but he couldn't remember who to!'

But there was consolation for Paul, and for all of us, waiting back in Dar es Salaam. The news we had been hoping for had at last come through. The Appendix One proposal from Tanzania had just been delivered to the Swiss embassy to be forwarded to the CITES secretariat. Costa had sent a telex to CITES headquarters in Switzerland informing them formally that Tanzania had proposed an international ivory ban.

We were all exultant, and to celebrate ITN treated Liz, Neil and the rest of the 'elephant lobby' to dinner at a luxury beach hotel up the coast. We were all very high, and there was a real party atmosphere.

'It's up to you guys now,' Neil said to Desmond and me. 'Put together some good reports on the international ivory trade, alert the world to the decline in elephants, and campaign like mad!'

'Yes, OK. We'll do all that at the weekend,' I said. 'Don't forget, first I've got to show Desmond around Dubai.'

There was a wave of laughter. Everyone knew of my growing antipathy towards Dubai.

'The Poons will have missed you, Dave,' teased Neil. 'They haven't seen you for weeks!'

Desmond and I stood on the roof of the rather grand car we'd hired, courtesy of ITN, and peered over the wall at the back door of the Belhon Trading ivory factory in Dubai. It wasn't one of Poon's enterprises but, even so, it was a fair-sized operation.

'It looks as though we're in luck. It's the first time I've seen the shutters open,' I said.

'I think we should go in and have a look, don't you, old chap?' Des suggested. I was getting used to Des's extravagant public school manner by now. It was all part of the light-hearted approach to life which had seen him through various horrendous situations in his twenty-two-year career with ITN.

The film we hoped to obtain in Dubai was intended for cutting in with EIA's existing footage to illustrate the role of the United Arab Emirates as the intermediary in the ivory trade. This would be the second film in ITN's three 'specials'. Mohinder our cameraman had returned to Nairobi, and the filming in Dubai was going to be my responsibility. I slung the Video 8 camera over my shoulder as we pushed open the door of the factory. Inside, carvers sat hunched over their machines. On the floor nearby were buckets of ivory, apparently soaking in water. An Indian man approached us.

'Hello, we're looking for the health club,' I said. (There was a health club three doors away.)

'This is very interesting, though,' Des interrupted jovially. 'What are you doing?'

Accepting our claim that we were sightseers, the man explained the carving operation and let me shoot some videotape. 'Come through here.' He beckoned us through a corridor into another room. Piled up on shelves on three of the walls were hundreds of cut pieces of ivory. On the floor were packed boxes, sealed and ready for shipping. The man happily watched us film, seemingly unaware that he had anything to hide. Des held up the tiny microphone attached by wire to the camera and asked him a few questions as I filmed.

The Indian left the room for a moment, and Des suggested that we take advantage of his absence. 'I'll just walk into the workshop and talk us through the scene here. It'll have more impact than if we put a voice-over on afterwards.'

'It's worth a try,' I agreed. 'He doesn't seem too perturbed, although why he thinks we're filming all this if we're supposed to be just tourists, I can't imagine!'

Holding the tiny microphone, Des addressed the camera in a low voice. 'Well, this is in fact one of the elephant tusk factories that are not supposed to exist in Dubai. We're just going to go through here and see what we can find.' He started walking, and I followed him, continuing to film. 'We're going through the kitchen now,' he continued. 'In this room we've got sacks, and these sacks' – he paused beside one and opened it up – 'are full of chopped-up bits of ivory all ready to be worked in the next-door room.'

It was all going unbelievably well for us, and when I finished filming Des's commentary I decided to get my stills camera from the car. As I walked back towards the factory I noticed a Chinese man further down the street who seemed to be making for the factory. As he got closer I recognized him as the manager of Belhon Trading. I had seen him on several previous occasions as I sat outside in my car observing.

189

I rushed back into the factory. 'The manager is on his way back,' I warned Des. I was not a moment too soon.

The manager halted in his tracks when he saw us. 'What are you doing here?' His gaze took in my camera and the Video 8 in Desmond's hand.

'Oh, hello! We were actually looking for the health club,' said Des with an unconcerned smile, 'but this is so interesting.'

'We're tourists,' I added.

Amazingly the manager swallowed the story and invited us upstairs to see some whole tusks. His name, he told us, was Simon Li. 'Some of these tusks are in very bad condition,' he apologized. 'They have been damaged by sand and water because they have been buried in the African forest.' When we pressed him he admitted that some of it was poached.

'What do you actually do in this factory?' asked Des, holding the microphone up while I pointed the camera at him.

'We make the semi-finished products here. The final product will be finished in the other factory,' he volunteered, somewhat confusingly.

I knew what he meant. I just hoped that Des was able to translate it. But I needn't have worried.

'Where is that?' asked Des.

'Maybe in Hong Kong or Taiwan,' he replied.

It was just the incriminating admission we wanted. This should get the United States on to Hong Kong's back again.

Perhaps realizing the implications of his remark, Simon Li suddenly looked concerned. 'This is just for your own use?' he demanded.

I crossed my fingers behind my back. 'Don't worry. We're just tourists,' I assured him.

'Not a bad start to the day,' said Des as we ordered lunch in the Hilton. We had just viewed the footage I'd shot in the factory, and it was exciting.

'Well, it's your friend Poon this afternoon, then we can go home,' he said. 'I want to start cutting the Tanzanian story over the weekend so it can go out on air next week.' It was already the beginning of May, and the campaign was poised to swing into top gear.

I drove the hired car out to the Municipality Building in Ajman, not at all sure what we would find there. Although the scenes we had shot that morning would make good television, it would be the film from Jebel Ali and Ajman that would give the three specials continuity because the factories there were all part of the Poon empire. Our aim this afternoon was to get some film that would strengthen that Poon connection.

I pulled the car up where we could overlook the Pearl Workshop and its neighbouring factories. This time one of the metal shutters was partly raised, so we could see people moving about inside. Despite all our prying into their activities over the past year, it seemed the ivory factories were becoming less security-conscious than before.

Yet more units had been occupied since my last visit, and outside one of them a large container vehicle was parked.

'Looks like they're taking a delivery, Des, or maybe they're shipping more ivory out to Hong Kong. It might be a bit too brazen to film that. Let's go over to the other factories on the outskirts of Ajman and see what's happening there.'

But when we arrived, although the noise from inside told us that the Ajman National Handicraft Factory was operating, all the shutters were completely closed. There was no easy entry here.

'I think it will have to be the first one after all,' said Des. 'I don't see why we don't just go and ask for the man in charge.'

On returning to the Pearl Workshop we found quite a lot of activity going on outside. We sat in the car for about an hour, taking turns to film Chinese men moving boxes about.

'OK,' said Des finally, 'shall we go over and say hello?'

I switched the video-camera on and grinned at him. 'I'm right behind you.'

I had put black tape over the red operating-light on the video-camera so that the only giveaway that it was on was the lens turning as it focused automatically. Holding it down by my side, I climbed out of the car into the dry Ajman heat and headed with Des for the unit with the part-open shutter.

'See if you can get a shot under there of the carvers,' suggested Des quietly.

Without raising the camera I pointed it under the shutter. Within seconds a very agitated looking Chinese man came out and started babbling in Cantonese.

'We're looking for the owner of the factory,' said Des unperturbed.

'Owner?' repeated the Chinese man doubtfully.

'Yes,' Des nodded. 'The man in charge.'

'Mr Poon?'

Des smiled. 'Yes, that's right. Mr Poon.'

Seemingly reassured, the man led us across the road and down the row of units towards the one where Susie and I had filmed many weeks earlier. It was clear that the whole row was now occupied by the Poon operation.

'Wait,' the man ordered. He went into the unit.

A few moments later he emerged accompanied by the man I had seen driving the white BMW on my last visit. George Poon was in his thirties, rather overweight and dressed in expensive looking slacks and a blue T-shirt. He regarded us warily.

Des stepped forward. 'I'm from Independent Television News in London, and we understand you have ivory factories here, Mr Poon.'

George Poon stared at him appraisingly, obviously thinking hard.

'We would like to film inside a factory,' Des continued.

There was a brief pause. Then suddenly Poon started

to talk fast at us in Cantonese. We regarded him blankly. The torrent of words ceased for a moment, and a crafty look came over his face. 'No English. You speak Chinese?' he said.

'I would like to ask you about the ivory factories here,' Des repeated. Pointedly turning his back on us, Poon walked towards the factory with the part-open shutter. From our point of view this 'interview' was going perfectly. Poon's attitude would speak for itself when a television audience saw it. I looked down to check the video-camera. And looked again. I felt like exploding with frustration. The zoom was fixed on the most powerful setting, which meant that nothing I had filmed so far would come out. Cursing inwardly, I surreptitiously readjusted the lens to 'wide-angle', the only setting that would capture Poon on camera without me using the viewfinder. I pointed it at Poon's back, praying he would turn to face me again. Des was hurrying alongside Poon chattering away to him but meeting with no response.

Finally reaching the part-open shutter, Poon screamed in Cantonese at a man inside who immediately slammed the shutter closed. 'We understand you are dealing in ivory,' Des persisted. To my relief, Poon had now turned back towards the camera and was shrugging his shoulders and shaking his head with a very smug grin on his face. I was so close to him that I had to tilt the camera up to capture him. But it didn't matter. I'd got him. Des touched Poon's arm to try to get him to listen to his questions, but Poon just continued to shake his head and shrug his shoulders indifferently, his smug mask-like smile never altering.

We moved away, giving me a chance to get a full-length shot of George Poon in front of the new 'Pearl Workshop' sign. That would clearly link him with the other Ajman footage. He followed after us, chivvying us in the direction of our car, before going to join some of his workers who had congregated on the other side of the road, attracted by all the shouting.

'I'm going to film the container,' I announced to Des.

'Good idea,' he nodded. 'I think we've got all we can get really. He's not going to co-operate. He knows perfectly well what I'm saying.'

For the first time I raised the camera directly to my eye and shot a few seconds of the container on the truck. Behind us, about thirty feet away now, Poon stood complacently, perfectly calm, secure that he had foiled our attempts to enter his domain. I pointed the camera directly at him.

The reaction was dramatic. 'No film of me, no film!' he screamed – in English.

Des and I exchanged glances and resumed walking towards the car.

'Give me your film,' he yelled angrily and charged towards us. 'You can't do that. Give me your film!'

As we reached the car I turned back towards him. 'I've stopped filming,' I shouted at him, throwing the video-camera on to the back seat. Des got into the front passenger seat. Poon was still running towards me, and I jumped hastily into the car, but before I could close the door he had grabbed it and was holding it open.

'Give me that camera,' he screamed.

The back doors were locked, and the camera was now safely on the back seat. To get to it Poon would have to get past me, and to do that he would physically have to attack me. I fumbled with the keys and somehow got the right one into the ignition. The engine started obediently.

'You can't have that film of me. Give me that camera!' he repeated again, his face contorted in an uncontrollable rage. Suddenly he shouted something to one of the Chinese men who had been watching all this as though hypnotized. Immediately the man ran off into one of the units. For all we knew he was going to fetch a gun.

'Just put your foot down. We've got to get out of here,' said Des calmly. I didn't need telling twice.

As I accelerated away Poon leaped on to the car and clung on grimly to the open door. He seemed to be trying to break it off its hinges. Determinedly I changed gear. 'I want that camera!' Poon yelled in at us as the car continued to accelerate away from his workers.

'Just keep your foot down,' Des urged. 'If he's never been filmed before, he's not going to give up easily.'

The car lurched forward. Poon was reaching into the car now, trying to grab either the steering wheel or me – he didn't seem concerned which. I put my foot down harder, realizing that the street ended soon and I would have to slow down, giving Poon a chance really to attack me. His screaming was incomprehensible now, but his rage was crystal clear.

And then to my relief discretion prevailed, and with the speedometer approaching 50 kilometres per hour he finally baled out. I looked in the rear-view mirror and saw him pick himself up off the ground and shake his fist as he yelled after us. I could still hear his abuse as we turned the corner.

I cast my eyes towards Des in the passenger seat. He raised one eyebrow and gave me a faint unruffled smile . . .

So George Poon didn't like being recognized. I pulled out on to the main road and started a cautiously circuitous route back to Dubai. Well, he had better start getting used to it. This was only the beginning.

15

MAY 1989,
LONDON

DAVE

'The African elephant, the largest of all land mammals, has a life-cycle that closely resembles our own. They are intelligent, live contentedly in family groups, mate at around the age of thirty, and live into their sixties and seventies, when a male elephant's tusks could each weigh sixty kilos or more – or that's what used to happen . . .'

Desmond Hamill's commentary, relayed over the EIA film of live and dead elephants, introduced the first of the ITN specials, broadcast on 10 May 1989 – the day the Tanzanian government appealed to the world to support its call for a ban on the ivory trade 'before it is too late'. ITN had pulled out all the stops for this story. It was the main news item on the one o'clock news. The item lasted several minutes, and its summary of the threat to the African elephant pulled no punches. Even John Suchet, in the traditionally neutral newscaster's role, did not mince words in his lead-in to the piece. 'The African elephant is literally fighting for survival against the poachers who are shooting it into extinction to satisfy people's desire for ivory,' he declared.

The film included footage of Des in the ivory room in Dar es Salaam holding up six-inch tusks of baby elephants and comparing them with sixty-six-kilo tusks that used to be the ivory hunters' objective. Then followed the interview Allan and I had filmed with Costa in March; then Des's interviews with Gerald and Paul in the Selous park.

The film finished with the shot of the anti-poaching unit unloading the cache of small tusks from the back of the Land Rover while Des's voice reminded the viewer that 'The figure to remember perhaps is that, even now, one elephant family in every three consists of orphans. In six years' time even they'll be dead.'

The impact of the programme was immediate. I called Allan from the ITN studios as soon as the lunch-time transmission was over. He told me the EIA phones were already ringing with messages of support and press enquiries. 'Probably there'll be even more response when it goes out on the main news this evening,' he predicted.

I went back into the editing suite where Des and our editor Alex Barbour were working on the film for the next night. Des, too, was on the phone. 'I see. Yes, that would be fine,' he said to the caller. He put his hand over the mouthpiece. 'Dave,' he whispered, 'it's Ian McIntyre, the public relations officer for WWF. He wants to send me a fax about their efforts to protect elephants.'

So we'd stirred up WWF. Good, I thought.

'Ask him if they support Tanzania's call for a ban,' I suggested.

Des put my question to him.

'Well, what did he say?' I asked after he hung up.

Des grinned. 'He tried to avoid answering. He said they were raising money to protect the elephants, but that their position was "different".'

'He doesn't have to tell us that,' I said bitterly. What, I wondered, would it take to win WWF over to our way of thinking?

But there was cheering news that evening. Christine rang Allan to say that, as we had hoped, the United States was going to support Tanzania's Appendix One proposal. That was fantastic. The Americans had a lot of influence, and with the United States as a co-signatory proposing the ban the pressure on CITES would now be enormous.

The second 'Elephant Special' the following day was also

the first item on the one o'clock news, and was preceded by the announcement that not only the United States, but now Kenya, too, had joined Tanzania in proposing a ban. Today's film was about the role of the United Arab Emirates in laundering poached ivory. It included the footage I'd shot of George Poon in Ajman, intercut with a shot of his signature in the Dar es Salaam ivory room visitors' book. There was the film we had shot inside the Ajman factories during Chinese New Year, and then the *pièce de résistance* of all our camera work in the past year: Clive's shots from inside the cardboard box in shed 65A. The film culminated in Simon Li's incriminating admission that the semi-finished products stacked up behind him in his Dubai factory were bound for Hong Kong and Taiwan. I had shot a long pan across all the piles of ivory on the factory shelves, and this had been used as Des brought the item to a close. 'In four weeks this ivory will all have been used and replaced, which means another three hundred elephants will have died just to keep this little factory in business. Desmond Hamill, ITN, Dubai.'

The final special on the third day focused on Hong Kong and was put together almost entirely from EIA footage. It took us several hours in the editing room to come up with a satisfactory structure for this film. Starting with shots of the Burundi ivory we had found in Lee Chat's factory, we then moved on to Poon's Kowloon factory with its boxes of semi-carved ivory from Dubai, so linking it up with the previous day's item. The next shot was of finished carvings, to illustrate the end result of the killings, followed by the film of 'our' Americans enthusing in the souvenir shop. I promised to make them famous, I recalled as I watched them laughing and smiling on the monitor. During this scene Desmond pointed out that, though these souvenirs were sold with 'papers' to get them through Customs, the Tanzanian figures demonstrated that 94 per cent of such souvenirs had come from poached elephants. Finally, bringing the story round full circle, we went back to Dar es Salaam where Des had been filmed standing on the roof of the Kilimanjaro Hotel.

'So a great deal is going to depend on how this document is received in the months ahead.' He held up the Appendix One proposal to the camera. 'Pages of detailed information, in which the Tanzanian government argue that the only real way to stop the ivory poaching is to ban the sale of ivory worldwide and shut down the markets. That's what this document is asking the world to do.'

Archive film then showed the pathetic sight of a baby elephant, dead on its knees, staring blindly out of the screen. 'And, unless the world does act, this sort of killing will go on,' Des's voice warned. 'The big elephants have been shot out. Now even the baby elephants are targets . . . It's a long way from the smart jewellery stores, but this is where it all starts. In the killing-fields of Africa.'

'I think we've done it,' Allan said cautiously. 'I've never seen such extended coverage of a wildlife issue on the news before, not even in the heyday of *Rainbow Warrior*.'

'ITN did the elephant proud,' I agreed. Now we had to capitalize on the public reaction to get international support for the Appendix One proposal.

Two other television programmes about ivory were broadcast soon after ours which helped the cause considerably. The first, the 'Cook Report', came out on 15 May. It covered much of the same ground as our films. The commentary claimed that it was impossible to get into UAE factories. But of course the public had already seen inside them on ITN the previous week. This gave us some competitive amusement, as did the sight of Poon Tat Hong throwing an ashtray at Roger Cook in Hong Kong!

The following evening Granada screened 'A Place of Skulls' which showed the Zimbabwean army out hunting poachers. From being an issue that no-one seemed concerned about the elephants had suddenly become *the* wildlife priority as far as television was concerned. Even the cover of *TV Times* that week had an elephant on it.

The newspapers were equally enthusiastic about the story. Virtually every paper, from the tabloids to the heavies, gave it some coverage in the days that followed our 'specials'. Editorials called daily for a ban, and most newspaper editors criticized Britain for not supporting Tanzania, the United States and Kenya in their call for a ban, particularly since four other countries – Chad, Niger, Hungary and Austria – had now added their support to the proposal. So far Mrs Thatcher had resisted all the pressure. But now the press were demanding action. They pointed out that four African nations were now supporting the proposal. It was not a credible argument any longer to claim that Africans did not want a ban. Under the headline 'Ivory Scandal' in the *Sunday Mirror* that week, a leader commented: 'They [the British government] can – and should – ban all ivory imports into Hong Kong, where most of this illegal international trade is controlled. And there is something that the rest of us can do to help. STOP BUYING IVORY.'

Still there was no official reaction. But then a heaven-sent opportunity to embarrass the British authorities came our way. A contact told us that a shipment of ivory from Zaïre was being held at Heathrow because of falsified CITES permits. The ivory was destined for UAE. Now we could really set a cat among the pigeons. Allan issued a press statement to the effect that Britain was being used as a transit route for poached ivory, and the papers seized on it. When the Department of the Environment issued fresh permits so that the shipment could be released to continue its journey to Dubai there was a flurry of indignation in every paper from *Today* to *The Times*.

Whether this was the deciding factor we had no way of knowing, but on 23 May, eleven days after the last ITN special, Margaret Thatcher stood up in the House of Commons and announced: 'We believe the sale of new ivory should stop altogether.' She also declared her intention to seek a European Community ban at the next meeting of EEC environment ministers. It was a major volte-face. And not the only one. A day earlier WWF had made a public announcement that they now supported a ban. The tide, it seemed, was turning.

It was important that the story was kept in the public eye right up until the crucial CITES meeting, and we co-operated wherever possible with any newspaper wanting information. On occasion we were perhaps too co-operative. David Jones, a reporter from *Today*, had approached Allan wanting to go to UAE and get into the ivory factories. Allan supplied Jones with all our information on the factories: who owned them, where exactly they were . . . He even let him have twelve original slides that I had photographed inside the factory in Ajman. The understanding was that Jones and a photographer would try to photograph the factory themselves but would use the EIA slides if they were unsuccessful.

For some reason best known to themselves, instead of dropping the slides off at the *Today* picture desk, Jones and his photographer flew to Dubai with them. There they drove out to the Ajman National Handicraft Factory, where they started taking photographs; they were locked in by the workers, and arrested by the Ajman police. Their film was confiscated, as were our slides which unbelievably they had taken with them to the factory!

Released from gaol, the two men proceeded to use our directions to lead one of the Sheikh of Dubai's advisers to the Belhon Trading factory. Shortly afterwards *Today* proudly proclaimed that all factories in UAE had been closed down. If it was true, we were of course delighted, but we were far from delighted with the way the story was presented to the public. The report not only claimed *Today* had discovered the factories and 'tracked the traders down' but credited WWF with closing down trade in Dubai. The part played by EIA was not acknowledged at all.

We were beginning to realize that self-promotion would have to come higher on our list of priorities. Our work was already hampered by lack of funds, and we had hoped, perhaps naïvely, that all our co-operation with the press would result in our attracting more supporters. (At present our membership stood at just four hundred.) But in the general rush of support for the elephant's cause we were missing out badly. We had placed a few small advertisements in national newspapers but we could not compete with the professional fund-raising of organizations like WWF and the newly formed, catchily named, Elefriends.

The newspaper stories had probably profited WWF the most. The *Daily Mail*, in particular, had been waging a tremendous campaign, probably the most effective of any of the newspapers, and had consistently been putting WWF's name to the fore and encouraging its readers to support it. In the first week of the campaign the *Mail* reported that the WWF offices in Godalming, Surrey, had been 'inundated' with sixteen thousand letters. No wonder WWF had felt compelled to change its position regarding the ivory trade!

Elefriends was a lobbying organization which encouraged the public to become involved by collecting signatures in support of a ban, and buying stickers and badges. Such lobbying was vital to keep the pressure up, and we welcomed the formation of Elefriends and helped supply them with information; but the question remained: Where was the money for *our* investigative work on elephants to come from? We needed to go to Taiwan and maybe to South Africa to see what was happening there, and we also had to attend the African Elephant Working Group meeting in Gaborone, Botswana, in July. ITN's payment for our film was going to have to stretch a very long way.

On Tuesday 6 June, World Environment Day, Christine Stevens's prediction came about: President Bush announced that the United States would ban all imports and exports of ivory within a week. That was good enough news in itself, and we could hardly believe it when on the same day Dubai announced a similar ban. Then, on 9 June, the European Community did the same. A mere four weeks after the ITN–EIA bulletins, the countries which consumed half the world's ivory had banned its trade. It might not have gone away, but undoubtedly the shadow of extinction which had hung for so long over the African elephant had begun to lift.

16

JULY 1989,
GABORONE, BOTSWANA

ALLAN

'Every worthwhile action requires an element of sacrifice,' said Costa Mlay. 'Loss of profits alone does not constitute an argument against a ban. We are talking of the survival of a species that is important to mankind and to Africa. Every generation will be judged by its moral courage to protect species that are in danger of extinction.'

His audience listened in rapt silence. From the moment Costa had arrived at the African Elephant Working Group meeting of CITES in Gaborone, he had been sought out. Everyone wanted to speak to him and listen to what he had to say: the American delegation, the Japanese, the Europeans, the press, the conservationists . . . His determination and integrity shone out. For too long the CITES elephant meetings had been characterized by vacillating policies decided by weak and easily influenced men. The CITES secretary-general, Eugene Lapointe, had admitted to the press in May that the CITES Ivory Control Unit in Lausanne had received contributions of $200,000 from ivory dealers in Hong Kong and Japan. In those circumstances who could believe that CITES had ever had the elephant's best interests at heart? But now in Tanzania's Costa Mlay the elephants had found a new protector.

Costa ended his address to the Group by stressing the price of ivory in human terms. 'Ivory is not used to protect the health of humans or to produce medicines. But people in our country and in others are now losing their lives, not just their livelihoods, because of ivory. It is too big a sacrifice that our people should die so that a few people beyond our borders can make a living.'

The atmosphere was hushed for a few seconds after Costa finished speaking. Rarely before had there been such plain talking at one of these meetings.

I glanced around the conference room trying to identify the delegates. Most countries from central, eastern and southern Africa were represented, as were the traditional ivory consuming countries: the United States, Japan, Hong Kong, Britain, Germany, France, China, Belgium and Germany. But apart from Senegal there were no representatives from West African states. I mentioned this to Pierre Pfeiffer, a scientist from the French delegation. He nodded sagely.

'Perhaps it's because the West Africans are solidly in favour of a ban on the ivory trade,' he said. 'But all the southern African states which oppose a ban were invited: Zimbabwe, South Africa, Malawi, Mozambique, Botswana and Zambia. They're all here. Frankly, this secretariat is doing the work of the ivory traders for them.'

Professor Pfeiffer was a distinguished biologist who had spent thirty years in Africa studying elephants. Two years earlier he had been ousted as head of WWF in France because of his vociferous support for a ban on the ivory trade. Undeterred, he had launched the hugely successful 'Amnesty for Elephants' campaign in France. 'The secretariat even brought ten French journalists to their offices in Switzerland to give them a briefing against the ivory ban,' Pfeiffer informed me now.

I was only just beginning to appreciate what we were up against in the CITES secretariat. Of course, I'd realized commercial interests held a powerful sway with them, but not quite how powerful. For the first time I began to have serious qualms about our chances of victory against such adversaries.

The machinations of the CITES secretary-general and

some of his staff had coincided with a major public attack against the ivory ban by Zimbabwe and South Africa. They were protesting that they had plenty of elephants and that they exercised good control over them, so for them the ivory trade should continue. Hong Kong and Japan were joining in the counter-attack, pleading loss of jobs if the ivory trade was closed down. Botswana itself, host to the conference, was strongly pro-trading and had underlined this by staging a vast display of tusks and carvings in the entrance hall of the Gaborone Sun Hotel where the conference was being held. As I had walked into the hotel on the first morning of the conference I had spotted Doug Hykle, the new ivory control officer at the CITES secretariat.

Like me, Hykle was a Canadian, and when I had met him at the Nairobi CITES meeting he had struck me as a decent, if somewhat inexperienced, university graduate. Then he had been pleasant enough. His attitude now was less gracious. Striding towards me challengingly, he demanded: 'What are you doing here?'

I replied drily: 'Attending the meeting.'

'And do you have the chairman's permission to attend?'

'I certainly do.' I walked away from him, not anxious to get into a slanging match. Fortunately for me and the representatives of other wildlife groups, the chairman this week was Richard Leakey, Kenya's newly appointed Wildlife Director, whose attitude was very much to encourage the participation of all interested parties – a policy very different, it appeared, from that of the CITES secretariat.

Costa was having problems with the Zimbabwean delegation. Chris Huxley, the former CITES secretariat employee who had first introduced me to Ian Parker in London, was working with them, and they and Botswana were putting a lot of pressure on Tanzania. Zimbabwe had even offered a one-year moratorium on ivory trading if Tanzania withdrew the Appendix One proposal. Fortunately Costa was resolute. Nothing was going to change

Tanzania's decision now it had come this far; but the opposition was both well organized and strong in numbers, which was worrying. The Zimbabweans had a huge team of people, and even Botswana had ten representatives to plead its case (a case based largely on the loss of profit motive that Costa had so eloquently dismissed in his address).

In response to Costa's words both Zimbabwe and Botswana put forward the argument that their research showed their countries to be seriously overstocked with elephants, so that culling was essential. However, over the next few days, after speaking to several experts, I had serious doubts concerning the validity of their 'scientific' research. No-one I spoke to had seen their raw data. Zimbabwe refused to publish it, merely circulating the estimates they claimed to have derived from that data. The estimating of populations requires tremendous precision in sampling and extrapolation, and is a very skilled science. Publishing the raw data would have allowed outsiders to confirm Zimbabwe's estimates if they were correct. Their refusal to release the figures and their insistence that despite culling their elephant population continued to increase made me very suspicious. I was also unhappy about Botswana's complacency. I learned that a scientist working in Botswana had admitted to a colleague of Iain Douglas-Hamilton that Botswana had not done any long-term vegetation monitoring on the impact of elephants. That meant they had little scientific basis for saying there were too many.

In fact the only information published by either country were their own population estimates. Since the countries bordered on each other and elephants frequently migrated from one side of that border to the other, at least one scientist I spoke to believed that many elephants were counted twice and included in both countries' population estimates. If we could find evidence to support that theory, we would greatly undermine the strength of their arguments. I made a mental note to pursue it.

All sorts of handouts and documents were being circulated during the conference, and at the end of the first day I picked up a Hong Kong Department of Agriculture leaflet. As I glanced through it I noticed a familiar-looking photograph. It was one of EIA's pictures taken in Poon's Hong Kong factory, which showed a box of ivory that we had described as poached. The accompanying text claimed that EIA had lied in the ITN film. The box in the picture did not contain poached ivory as EIA claimed. The Hong Kong authorities had traced the shipment through the airline flight number on the box, and it came from Poon's factory in Singapore, not from Dubai. The rest of the leaflet deduced from this that all EIA's information was inaccurate and Hong Kong was not, as we had maintained, a centre for illegal ivory trading.

I tackled Richard Chan of the Hong Kong Department of Agriculture. 'Are you distributing this document here?'

'I think I will be distributing it tomorrow,' he answered cagily.

'Well,' I began, 'there are two things about it that I object to on behalf of EIA. One is that you have reproduced a photo from the EIA film without our permission. The second is that you are providing misleading information about our broadcast.'

'What do you mean?'

'I mean that you have ignored the fact that in the ITN piece we have an interview with Simon Li, the manager of an ivory factory in Dubai, saying he still sends his ivory to Hong Kong and that his factory buys poached ivory from Africa. That's not *our* claim. It's his admission. On top of that the fact that the box of ivory in the photo comes from Singapore doesn't weaken our argument at all. Poon's Singapore factory received twenty tonnes of carved ivory from Dubai last year. That ivory was then sent on to Hong Kong. This box in the picture had almost certainly come in by that same route.'

Richard Chan was silent.

So I concluded: 'I think you're making a very serious distortion of EIA information and are using a photo which belongs to EIA to promote this inaccurate claim. The Hong Kong authorities are in a dubious legal position if they release this document, and I can assure you that EIA will take legal action to protect our material and information.'

Chan looked taken aback. 'Well,' he said irresolutely, 'I hadn't decided finally if I was going to circulate this document tomorrow. I have to think about it. Maybe I won't release it.'

The document never did appear at the meeting. Instead Chan distributed a brief, carefully worded circular which outlined Hong Kong's 'rigorous enforcement of CITES regulations'.

Dave joined me in time for the opening sessions of the conference and the presentation of Ian Parker and Rowan Martin's reports on the ivory trade, which had finally been completed. Unfortunately these reports had only been posted to delegates the previous week, which meant that very few people had received them and no extra copies were available. This seemed suspiciously fortuitous for the anti-ban lobby, since the figures contained in both reports confirmed illegal trading.

Martin's report, completed six months before the meeting, dealt with the ivory trade in southern Africa. While I was in America I had met Craig Van Note of the Monitor Consortium, an affiliation of American wildlife groups, who claimed that South Africa was exporting 100 tonnes of poached ivory a year. Rowan Martin in his report disputed that figure, but admitted it might be as much as 40 tonnes, and also agreed that poaching was on the increase in Zimbabwe.

At the end of the first day Dave and I were walking

through the hotel's reception area when I paused to say hello to Anthony Hall-Martin from the South African delegation. He was the scientist who in the early eighties had told me that he hoped a hundred thousand elephants in Africa would be saved 'in the long term'. Now I reminded him of that prediction.

'Your plan seems to be right on schedule,' I said wryly.

'Why is South Africa opposed to a ban?' Dave asked him. 'Surely ivory is insignificant economically for a country as rich as yours?'

Hall-Martin shrugged. 'It's a matter of principle, and we have to show regional solidarity with Zimbabwe. Regional co-operation is important.'

It appeared that politics as well as economics was influencing this debate.

The report of the Ivory Trade Review Group, the independent body of scientists and conservationists which had been commissioned by CITES to investigate the current situation, had also been completed, but this group was far less cautious in its conclusions than Rowan Martin. Its findings confirmed the overall decline in elephant numbers on the African continent and sounded a loud note of warning about their future. It came as no great surprise that the countries which wanted to continue ivory trading found cause to criticize this report.

Rowan Martin, speaking on behalf of Zimbabwe, rather spoiled his case by overstating it. He claimed that Zimbabwe's elephants were reproducing themselves, if not exactly like rabbits, then at a startlingly rapid rate. 'Our female elephants conceive first at seven years of age and give birth at nine years of age,' he stated.

At this, derisive guffaws erupted from the scientists in the meeting room, who were all well aware that the female African elephant does not reach puberty until its teens; the male even later.

'As a biologist I congratulate Zimbabwe's elephants

on reproducing so young,' said Pierre Pfeiffer scathingly. 'Maybe they are born with their tusks!'

When the appreciative laughter had died down Pfeiffer continued: 'How long does Zimbabwe think it will continue to survive the devastation that has hit the rest of the continent?'

It was a valid point. Since it first became a problem, poaching of elephants had swept steadily down from the north of Africa through Sudan and Ethiopia to Kenya, Uganda, Zaïre, Tanzania, then into Zambia, Mozambique and Angola. There was no reason to suppose that Zimbabwe had special immunity. On the contrary, Martin's report had outlined serious poaching problems already faced by parts of Zimbabwe

Undeterred by the ridicule, Martin continued his attack on the Ivory Trade Review Group, claiming that Zimbabwe had not been consulted about the study. Steve Cobb, who had overseen the production of the report, stood up. 'That is not true. Martin was invited to take part in the population modelling part of the study. He refused. What he said exactly was' – Steve Cobb consulted his notes – ' "My heart is not big enough to bleed for all the elephants in Africa . . ." '

That quotation provoked considerable reaction among the conservationists present. It was just not possible to regard elephants in such a parochial way if the species was to survive.

Obviously stung by Steve Cobb's revelation, Martin turned his venom on Costa. 'We have here a crusader who has found a new religion: elephant conservation,' he taunted. 'The crusader from Tanzania has even found a bible, which is the Ivory Trade Review Group's report. And he is searching for the Holy Grail, which is a ban on the ivory trade . . .'

To my amusement, his words backfired on him. Costa took Martin's attack with equanimity, knowing enough about the man not to rise to the bait. But several other delegates felt Martin had gone too far and publicly rebuked him for stooping to personal abuse.

One of the problems that had always faced those fighting for the elephant's survival had been the defeatist attitude of many African countries. It was still being displayed even now. 'The extinction of elephants is inevitable in Africa,' said the delegate from the Congo. 'They will surely disappear one of these days.' It was an attitude that had been conditioned over the years, and one of its main proponents had always been Ian Parker. His argument was that Africa could not afford to have its elephants any longer; that a growing population of poverty-stricken people would erode and destroy the land that elephants needed to survive. According to Parker's reasoning, the Hong Kong ivory barons were not responsible for the decline in Africa's elephants. He painted them as a benign group of people who assisted the African economy by buying ivory.

But the smokescreen he had promoted for years was at last being blown away. As if in recognition of this, Richard Leakey now challenged the Congolese delegate. 'As chairman of this meeting I agreed to be neutral,' he said, 'but as an expert in evolution I have to make it clear that the extinction of the African elephant is no more inevitable than the extinction of human beings is inevitable.'

At his words I felt a bubble of optimism. There was no denying that the strength of the opposition was formidable, but every day in Gaborone new voices were being raised on behalf of the elephant, matching the ivory traders point by point and blow for blow. The prospects for the CITES meeting in October looked promising.

WWF were taking a lot of flak from the pro-ivory countries. Their about-turn on the ivory issue had generated a hostile reaction from South Africa and Zimbabwe in particular, and Jorgen and his colleagues were finding it hard to cope with the pressure. To my dismay I learned that they were talking of a compromise – a four-year moratorium rather than a total ban. 'You can't go back on your commitment now,' I protested.

'You've been keeping quiet for the whole meeting,' Jorgen retorted. 'When are *you* going to say something?'

Neither Dave nor I had seen any good reason to intervene so far, as the delegates themselves were making most of the relevant points in favour of an ivory ban. However, the possibility that WWF might back out of their commitment to the ban jolted me into action. When the meeting reconvened I raised my card and Leakey called on me to speak.

'The African elephant is in danger of extinction because of the international ivory trade,' I began. 'That extinction looms just over the horizon, visible within our lifetime. International public opinion is firmly on the side of saving Africa's elephants. Hundreds of millions of people want these beautiful and graceful creatures to survive for future generations.

'Those people and countries who want to continue ivory trading have had almost fourteen years to try to control this destructive trade. More than a million elephants have died during this period, and the so-called controls of CITES have been a terrible failure. It is not enough for scientists to come into this meeting and criticize the work of other scientists who have contributed to the Ivory Trade Review Group. If people make claims that elephants in their country start to breed at an earlier age than elephants in other areas of Africa, if they say that elephants reproduce at a faster rate than they do anywhere else, then they are obliged to provide scientific evidence to substantiate such claims.

'We challenge those countries who oppose a ban to tell us about the poaching and illegal trade in their countries. Poaching has swept down from the north to the south of the continent and is now licking at the edges of

Zimbabwe's borders in the same way that it first arrived in Kenya fifteen years ago.

'Mr Chairman,' I concluded, 'the world expects the people in this room to support an international ban on the ivory trade. International public opinion has just woken up to the tragedy of Africa's elephants. That concern is growing, and the momentum of public opinion will mean that representations will be made at the very highest political level to those countries opposing a trade ban. In the next three months leading up to the CITES meeting, public concern will increase further and will be directed at those who oppose a ban.

'If elephants are to survive, they need total protection. There can be no compromises. The compromises that have been made over the years have resulted in the increasing slaughter of Africa's elephants. International public opinion will accept no compromises.' I sat down.

There was a lot of support for the EIA viewpoint, but not all the pro-ban delegates envisaged a complete halt to ivory trading. To our surprise and dismay, the German delegate, Gerhardt Emonds, spoke in support of an amendment to one important resolution: Conference Resolution 5.11, which had been passed at a previous CITES meeting. This resolution stated that once a species was moved on to Appendix One *all* trade in its products had to stop, including trade in existing stocks. The amendment Emonds was suggesting would allow ivory bought up until the end of 1989 to continue to be legally traded after a ban. Dave and I tackled him after the session ended.

'It would be a disaster. There would be less control than there is now, because everyone could find a way to launder newly poached ivory on to the market,' Dave said.

'I realize that's possible,' Emonds conceded, 'but don't forget we have to obtain two-thirds of the votes at CITES in October. We have to make concessions to ivory trading

214

nations or we'll fail. There are too many of them. And if we lose we will lose everything.'

It was a real dilemma, and he was not alone in realizing that. One or two other delegates the next day started to make noises about compromising. But other nations such as the United States and most of the pro-ban countries were adamantly resisting the idea of the German amendment, convinced, as we were, that they had to maintain a strong position now to have a chance of a ban.

On the final day of the conference, with no consensus on the Appendix One proposal in sight, it was suggested that a country be nominated to undertake 'shuttle diplomacy' to see if it was possible to reach a compromise between the two opposing African positions. The delegate from Cameroon was elected to organize the mission.

All the closing statements had been made. Leakey the chairman had adjourned the meeting, and delegates were standing up and about to make their way out, when Jacques Berney, the deputy secretary-general of the CITES secretariat, announced that he had a few administrative announcements to make concerning hotel arrangements and transport to the airport and so on. Most people halted in the aisles to hear what he had to say.

'I want to note that there was a consensus of the meeting that Resolution 5.11 should be amended,' said Berney. 'Now,' he continued, 'as far as the payment for hotel rooms is concerned . . .'

I was stunned. Berney had just interpreted discussion on the crucial Resolution 5.11 to suggest there had been a decision that it should be amended. No such agreement had ever been reached. But by making the statement it could be entered into the minutes of the meeting, which would undermine the call for a total ban at the October CITES meeting.

I reached for my name-card and looked frantically around the room to see if anyone else appreciated the significance of what Berney had said. Just as I lifted my card to object Marshall Jones lifted the American delegation's card. 'Mr Chairman,' he said sternly, 'I wish to note that the USA does *not* agree that there is a consensus to amend the Resolution 5.11. We note there has been no such decision by this group to amend Resolution 5.11.'

To my relief, Leakey nodded. 'We stand corrected.'

Before we returned home Dave and I wanted to write a press release to fax back to Susie and Charmian in London for urgent distribution. We asked the hotel receptionist if we might use a typewriter and photocopier, and she directed us to a room in the hotel management office. As I copied Rowan Martin's report I noticed that the fax machine had an incoming message still attached which was written in Japanese characters. I picked it up. At the top were tiny letters which read 'CITES, Lausanne', followed by the secretariat's fax number. We were alone in the office. I walked quickly back to the photocopier, made a copy of the fax, then returned it to the fax machine.

'There may be something interesting here,' I said to Dave.

'Probably the holiday plans of the Japanese delegation,' he joked.

He was wrong to be sceptical, but we were back in London before we realized that.

'Does anyone know who Kaneko is?' asked Susie one day, walking into our room.

'Kaneko? It rings a bell. Why?' I said.

'I've had your fax translated. It was sent to a Mr Wada. Do you know who he is?'

'Wada was on the Japanese delegation in Gaborone, but I don't know any more about him than that,' Dave said.

'Wait a minute,' I interrupted. 'Kaneko is the Japanese staff member on the CITES secretariat.' I rummaged through my overflowing files and eventually I found what

I wanted. A translation of a press clipping from one of Japan's major newspapers. 'Here.' I held it out. 'Kaneko wrote this article opposing the ivory ban.'

'Oh my!' said Susie.

'What is it?' asked Dave.

'Well, this fax is from Kaneko to Wada and advises him of different points he feels the Japanese delegation should stress at the CITES meeting in Gaborone to oppose the ivory ban.'

Dave and I read the translation. 'I don't believe it. So now the secretariat is writing briefings for the Japanese ivory traders,' I said.

'I thought CITES was supposed to be neutral?' asked Susie.

'We'll have to put this in our final report on the ivory trade,' said Dave thoughtfully. 'Maybe people should start asking questions about whose side they're really on.'

17

AUGUST–OCTOBER 1989,
LONDON AND HONG KONG

ALLAN

The bulk of our on-site research was now complete. Or as complete as it could ever be. What remained was perhaps the most important part of the whole exercise: to compile a written and pictorial exposé of the ivory trade based on our two years of investigation, to be distributed to the delegates at the CITES meeting in Lausanne in October 1989.

The whole EIA office knuckled down to meet the challenge. Over the next few weeks as the pace of our work grew ever more frantic we all somehow found a last burst of energy. The office was busy until nine each night; and most of us, including Charmian, Susie and Ros, who had now joined us full-time, worked through weekends as well.

There was still a lot of background work to be done before we were ready to publish. We had to collate other people's research and statistics, and, most important, we had to find more evidence and cross-reference other people's statistics with our own to counter the arguments of our opponents. It was clear that there were three major groupings threatening to block the ivory ban. The first was made up of the Japanese and Hong Kong ivory traders; the second was Zimbabwe and South Africa; the third was the CITES secretariat.

The political power of the first group had already been seriously weakened by the EIA film report and by the ivory import bans imposed in America and Europe. The Japanese government had reacted positively to public pressure, and since 19 June ivory imports from non-members of CITES and from nations with no elephant populations had been banned. Imports of worked ivory were also banned. In Hong Kong the Agriculture and Fisheries Department had imposed an import ban on raw ivory from 16 June. In addition they were 'registering' the stocks currently held in Hong Kong. Recently, on EIA's behalf Clive and another investigator had paid a visit to Taiwan, and what they had found there – a clutch of carving factories receiving shipments of raw ivory from Africa – was so incriminating that we hoped it would put the final nail in the coffin of the Far Eastern ivory trade.

In fact the two other anti-ban pressure-groupings, the southern Africans and the CITES secretariat, were far more of a worry now. Disturbingly, in some quarters there were signs of a press backlash, and the pro-ivory factions were receiving a lot of newspaper publicity for their views. Rowan Martin's recent comments on the situation, made at a press conference, were distributed through a news agency and reported in newspapers and magazines worldwide. Even *The Times*, previously supportive of a ban, carried his words.

'Why should we be punished because of the mismanagement of East Africa?' he had demanded. 'They have a history of corruption a hundred miles long in those countries.' An article in the respected magazine *New Scientist*, obviously inspired by Rowan Martin's comments at the Gaborone meeting, accused Tanzania of 'getting religion' where the elephants were concerned. 'Their minds are closed to other philosophies,' the writer alleged. Page-long articles in the British and American press declared, 'Save an elephant. Buy ivory!' and promoted the Zimbabwean view that treating the elephant as a financial asset – almost as a crop to be harvested – was the best way to ensure its survival.

This backlash was worrying. No less worrying was the attitude of the CITES secretariat. A resolution passed in 1985 had stressed that, although the secretariat was allowed to make recommendations, it should assume a neutral role, but this tradition of neutrality was being blatantly ignored. Apart from the embarrassing fax we had discovered in Gaborone, Eugene Lapointe, the secretary-general of CITES, appeared on television, giving an interview in which he publicly opposed a ban on the ivory trade. Unfortunately, ivory traders had contributed $200,000 since 1986 towards running the CITES secretariat's Ivory Control Unit. That a secretary-general, occupant of a post historically bound to be neutral, should be so biased was just not acceptable. Not only had Lapointe made strenuous efforts to legalize the Burundi ivory, but he had also recently distributed a package of proposals to all 102 CITES signatories, outlining numerous alternatives to a ban. Why did no-one raise an eyebrow at what was going on? It had to be one of the areas our report looked at. We decided to employ an experienced television researcher, Maureen Plantagenet, to look into CITES and the workings of its Ivory Control Unit.

We also had to find out more about southern Africa. The role of Zimbabwe and South Africa in this debate was too important for us to ignore. The only way successfully to challenge and refute their arguments against an ivory ban would be to expose any flaws in those arguments. Ros was keen to follow up this angle, and I drew up a detailed brief for her research; she was to look at every aspect of Zimbabwe's elephant-management policy: population levels, scientific surveys of their numbers, details of illegal ivory trade and poaching, the cross-border migration of elephants from adjoining countries and so on. Together Ros and I would also look into the activities of South Africa.

As well as writing the report it was important to keep up the lobbying. In the course of a few days I wrote a 3,000-word leading article for the Greenpeace USA magazine, a detailed report for Greenpeace Germany and a reply to the *New Scientist* article. In between times Dave and I gave interviews to whoever wanted to write or broadcast about the ivory trade. That included Japanese television, two American television stations and several magazines and newspapers.

We had decided to set up a tiny office in Washington. Not only would it present us with a good opportunity to develop a higher profile in the United States and hopefully raise more funds for EIA – we had at last employed a fund-raiser – but also America's Freedom of Information Act meant we would have access to information unobtainable anywhere else. I had to spend a few days in Washington organizing administrative details for the new office, and while I was there I visited WWF headquarters. There Buff Bohlen told me that the Hong Kong authorities had recently toured Washington and Europe and had visited WWF USA trying to gain an exemption for their ivory trade from a possible ban.

'They didn't get a very sympathetic hearing from us,' Buff informed me with a smile. Buff's attitude towards both the ivory ban and EIA had changed dramatically since Jorgen had produced the Appendix One proposal. He now seemed committed to the idea of a total ban and also seemed to recognize that EIA was a force to be reckoned with.

With Jorgen's permission I was copying some of WWF's files of elephant reports when I suddenly saw something that made me sit up: a press release from the information service of UNEP, the United Nations Environment Programme, dated May 1986. It was a feature article praising the CITES ivory control system, but what interested me most was a quotation by Eugene Lapointe. He claimed to have brought the ivory trade under control and have the traders 'jumping through hoops'. 'We have even had important dealers in illegal ivory offer to pay us off if we legalize their ivory,' he admitted.

Notwithstanding the suspicions that might consequently arise, only a few months afterwards Ian Parker had gone to Burundi to legalize their poached stockpile. Shortly after that Chris Huxley had visited Singapore and legalized 270 tonnes of ivory.

Maureen Plantagenet, our new researcher, was already shedding light on the working of the CITES ivory control system. She had interviewed various ex-members of the secretariat and had discovered that Rowan Martin had been hired by them in 1985 to draw up the structure of the new ivory control system. Based on that, the CITES secretariat had drawn up a lengthy resolution which called on states to 'register' their stockpiles of poached ivory.

The original intention of this registration had been to ensure that the amount of stockpiled ivory was known to the authorities. But later the CITES secretariat had interpreted the word 'registration' to mean 'amnesty'. However, there was no record of the word 'amnesty' having been mentioned prior to 1986. The whole idea of legalizing the Burundi and Singapore stockpiles seemed to have occurred almost overnight. As far as we could see, no-one had been given any notice of the secretariat's intentions. Was it possible that a payoff had been involved? That there was a conflict of interests within the secretariat seemed obvious to us. While we could appreciate that the secretariat required funds to implement its policies, the legalization of stockpiles had served to entrench the position of the major illegal traders as well as bringing in funds to the secretariat. Now both beneficiaries of the amnesty were campaigning against a ban. Whichever way you looked at it, it didn't look good.

We approached the *Mail on Sunday* with our information, and they took a keen interest in the CITES secretariat angle. 'It's an absolute scandal,' said Iain Walker, the deputy editor. 'We're going to send Jo Revill our environment correspondent over to Switzerland to speak to Lapointe and then to Nairobi to interview Parker. If we can verify what you're saying, we'll do a major article on the CITES secretariat and on Parker just two weeks before the CITES meeting to cause maximum impact.' The *Mail on Sunday* was very dedicated to this elephant campaign. In the following weeks there would be a flurry of phone-calls and interviews with their reporters as they followed in our footsteps and verified our story.

'Are Zimbabwe's elephants on fertility drugs,' enquired Ros, 'or don't they know how to count in Zimbabwe?'

Her research had revealed that Zimbabwe claimed that its elephants had increased in number by seventeen thousand in the past two years. Rather oddly, about nine thousand of those 'new' elephants had been counted in Hwange Park on the border with Botswana. When we learned that the Zimbabwe Parks Department had created large numbers of artificial watering-points in Hwange Park the penny dropped. There had been a drought in Botswana for the past six years, and their elephants had been migrating over the border to find water.

'Zimbabwe counted elephants in September 1988 when the Botswana elephants were in the park. Four months later when the elephants had migrated back over the border Botswana did its count,' Ros exclaimed. 'Clever, eh?'

'And both countries can say how well managed their populations are when in fact something quite different is going on.' I spread out some recent cuttings from Zimbabwe publications. 'There are three separate sources here which confirm that there's a lot of poaching going on in Zimbabwe. We've also heard from our contacts that there are a thousand elephant carcasses in Gonarezhou park, on the border with Mozambique, which the Zimbabwean army occupies. The Ivory Trade Review Group report confirmed that. And Zimbabwe says poaching isn't a problem!'

*

Ros and I had been having a series of meetings with South African contacts. They had told us that the major South African ivory dealer was a Chinese man called Pong. He was said to have worked out a deal with the South African security agencies whereby he arranged sanction-busting imports. In return the security agencies turned a blind eye to Pong's ivory and rhino horn dealings.

A year earlier Craig Van Note, the respected American environmentalist, had testified to Congress about the involvement of South African Defence Force personnel in ivory and rhino horn smuggling. Ros had accumulated a file of articles written since then, all pursuing Craig's exposé. There seemed no doubt of the truth of his allegations. The information, much of it published in South African newspapers, exposed a major network of ivory smugglers working from South Africa, with the obvious connivance of the South African Defence Force. In the past twelve months, we learned, there had been many more seizures of illegal ivory. The most startling claim that Craig Van Note had made during his testimony was that when the South African Defence Force gave military aid – weapons, ammunition and so on – to the anti-government forces of Unita in Angola that aid was paid for in poached ivory. The civil war in Angola, and also in Mozambique, provided perfect cover for ivory smuggling. Zimbabwean troops were stationed in Mozambique and were also accused of being involved in dealing. There was no doubt that a lot of ivory was moving out of Mozambique into South Africa and out through its ports.

We received a mysterious phone call from a man calling himself simply 'Donald' which strengthened our impression that we were getting in over our heads. Donald claimed to work for an independent anti-poaching unit based in southern Africa and London which was funded by wealthy philanthropists intent on saving elephant and rhino. He said that most of the sixty or so members of this unit were former SAS members; real heavy-duty guys.

Initially I thought it an unlikely, if chilling story, but the information Donald gave us checked out. He visited us – he looked a pretty heavy-duty guy himself – and let us look through documents on illegal ivory and rhino horn traders in the whole of southern Africa, with details of their transactions, shipping agents and business contacts. Some of what he said, including the involvement of the security forces, simply reinforced what we had already discovered, but a lot of it gave fresh insights into the way ivory poaching related to southern African politics, and there were also fresh leads – more than we could possibly hope to follow up.

Amongst other things, Donald's unit had discovered a North Korean involvement in the rhino horn and poached ivory trade within southern Africa. Donald claimed that his discoveries had been passed on to the governments of all the southern African countries concerned but no action had been taken. The case against these countries was building up steadily. In the face of all our evidence how could they possibly continue to maintain that they were managing their elephant populations satisfactorily?

As the October meeting drew nearer Isabel McCrea, head of the Greenpeace UK Wildlife Unit, took the initiative of inviting all interested British wildlife groups to a press conference where we called on the British government's support for a total ban on the ivory trade, especially in Hong Kong. Mrs Thatcher was still holding back from committing herself totally. During the meeting I made a strong attack on South Africa and promised that our report, when it came out, would reveal several unsavoury details about its connections with the ivory trade.

My comments were widely reported and brought instant reaction from South Africa. Their official press agency carried numerous denunciations both of EIA and of me personally by prominent politicians. My allegations were dismissed as 'ludicrous'. The EIA phone was red-hot that week with calls from people with deep Afrikaner voices asking 'Are you Allan Thornton?' Although some of them were journalists, others were menacingly anonymous. Editorials in papers across South Africa condemned me.

But there was a spin-off from the controversy as I was interviewed widely by the South African press and as a result EIA arguments were read by a much larger readership in South Africa than they would otherwise have been.

It was all coming together. Stacks of documents, files, reports and press clippings were spread across my living room floor, completely obscuring the carpet. Over at Dave's house the situation was the same. There was a mountain of data. Collating it and presenting it as a coherent and watertight argument against ivory trading was a daunting task.

We divided the responsibility for the various sections: Dave was in charge of the pages on the United Arab Emirates, Singapore, Hong Kong, Taiwan and Japan, while I dealt with Africa and CITES. We worked at home, phoning each other a dozen times a day, clarifying bits of information, checking the sources of documents. Each piece of fresh information seemed to raise one more vital question that could only be answered by obtaining yet another document. It was becoming a race against time. Each of us was working till three or four in the morning, then falling into bed for a couple of hours before starting again. But gradually we were getting there.

The report would centre on the failure of the CITES ivory trade controls. It would reveal how the CITES system was set up, and present the dubious tale of the amnesties, before tracing the ivory trail from Africa across the Middle East to Asia. It would name names, both of individuals and of companies, and give the dates of transactions, naming our sources wherever possible without endangering them. It had to be presented as a well-reasoned report, not as a piece of popular journalism. If we were to be taken seriously, it had to be comparable with academic documents in terms of accuracy and cross-references. And it had to look professional – glossy and well printed – if it were not to be eclipsed by the other promotional material that would be circulating at CITES. Fortunately a generous supporter had offered to print five thousand copies free of charge for us.

Finally, on Friday 15 September the report was ready to send to the printers. On the same day we sent a copy of the manuscript to the *Sunday Times*.

We did not have to wait long for a reaction. On Tuesday 19 September, Brian Jackman, the *Sunday Times* writer on wildlife issues, came into our office carrying the manuscript. 'This is terrific stuff,' he enthused. 'We must publish it. I'm going to talk to our people immediately.' An hour later the deputy editor of the *Sunday Times* called us. 'We'd like to run a major piece based on your report the day before CITES opens.'

They offered £7,500 for exclusive access. Our precarious financial state meant we didn't take long to consider. 'That's fine,' I said. 'We agree to your proposal.'

Ivory prices on the world market were dropping steadily now and, as ivory traders began to feel the pinch, violence was erupting behind the scenes. A Burundi ivory trader, Ali Suleiman, was shot dead in Belgium; another ivory dealer connected to one of the big syndicates was found murdered in his car in South Africa.

'Things are hotting up,' said Dave. He was right. After we had reached agreement with Brian Jackman on the *Sunday Times* deal he came into our office to pick up some documents. While preparing to leave he glanced down at the street from our office window. 'I think you may be being watched,' he said quietly. By the time I walked over to the window whoever Brian had been looking at had disappeared, but I took his suspicions seriously. A couple of days earlier I had been sure that a car with two men in it was following me as I walked home to my flat.

Brian rang me the next day. 'I was right,' he said. 'A man followed me from your office when I left.'

'What did he look like?'

'Average height, brown hair and a beard. Oh, yes, and he wore a peculiar sort of shoes.' He chuckled drily. 'You're not going to believe this. They were those special shoes you can buy in South Africa for bush-trekking. A coincidence, do you think?' Brian dropped his light-hearted tone. 'Seriously, you should be careful. The *Sunday Times* people in South Africa told us that the security services there are very concerned about what EIA's report will reveal. The apartment of our Johannesburg correspondent was turned over very badly. Everything was smashed up. The paper's even arranged to have security guards for me and for my family. So watch out, OK?'

Not long afterwards Donald, our ex-SAS man, asked me to meet him in a pub. 'There's an alert on,' he warned. 'The South African security services are very upset by what you know. Be very careful in the next few days.'

I decided to play safe and called the EIA staff together. 'I want you all to be extra vigilant until the CITES meeting,' I cautioned. 'Watch out for anything unusual like strangers who linger near the office and let me know if you see something.' Just in case, Susie removed all copies of confidential documents and placed them with our master photos of Poon's ivory factories in our safe-deposit box.

Two weeks before the CITES meeting Dave returned to Hong Kong to attend a press conference called by the Hong Kong Agriculture and Fisheries Department (AFD) to discuss its 670-tonne ivory stockpile. It was too important an occasion to miss. We did not want to be caught out if this huge stockpile proved to be a crucial negotiating point in the CITES meeting.

*

The Hong Kong government's ban on raw ivory imports had been operating for nearly four months. It was supposedly to back this ban up that they were now 'registering' the ivory stocks currently held in Hong Kong. We had always been suspicious that they might expect this registration to be a preliminary to an amnesty. And we were right.

The AFD had called the press conference to defend their request for exemption from Conference Resolution 5.11. The CITES secretariat was supporting their application. It would mean that, even if the elephant gained Appendix One listing, the existing stocks of ivory could continue to be traded indefinitely in Hong Kong. Our argument against this was exactly the same as when it was first suggested in Gaborone. Who could tell how old any given tusk was? As long as there was ivory trading at all, fresh ivory could easily be laundered on to the Hong Kong market. The killing would continue.

Wildlife organizations were not invited to the press conference, so I telephoned Brian Jackman at the *Sunday Times* who supplied me with a letter asking for me to be given all assistance since I was reporting on the ivory trade for his paper. The conference was addressed by Dr Lawrence Lee, Director of Agriculture and Fisheries, who read a brief prepared speech defending Hong Kong's position. The gist of it was that Hong Kong had the elephant's welfare as much at heart as any other country but that practicalities demanded a pragmatic approach.

'At present there is a strong tide of emotionalism among overseas conservation groups, advocating a total ban on the ivory trade,' he declared. 'However, as a responsible and reasonable government, Hong Kong believes that an outright ban would give rise to considerable problems . . .'

He proceeded to outline those problems, which were

largely related to the financial difficulties that would face the ivory traders.

'To sum up,' Dr Lee concluded, 'Hong Kong genuinely supports the conservation of African elephants and is doing its best to set a good example. We are of the view that no new ivory should be permitted to be traded unless more effective control measures could be devised by the coming CITES conference. We believe that trading of the existing stocks of legally acquired and legally held ivory should be allowed to continue. Now' – he smiled benignly at the assembled press corps – 'I would welcome any questions from media friends. My colleagues and I will try our best to respond. Thank you.'

I couldn't let this sweeping description of the Hong Kong stockpile as being 'legally acquired' go unchallenged.

'Dr Lee, since the call for the ban has come because of the failure of the CITES permit system, how can you be so sure that the 670 tonnes of ivory in Hong Kong is legal? Especially when at least one Hong Kong trader in Dubai has admitted that he sends his illegal ivory to Hong Kong?'

Dr Lee smiled blandly. 'Just because traders *come* from Hong Kong it is not our fault that they trade illegally. The trader in question has companies in ten countries and may travel on a French passport.'

Obviously he was referring to George Poon. I persevered. 'You said that the ban has been called for by non-governmental organizations. Whereas you must know that the call for an Appendix One listing comes first from the Republic of Tanzania, and also from other countries, including the USA and Kenya. The Tanzanians say that 94 per cent of ivory on the market today is poached and that the pieces of paper called CITES certificates are worthless. What do you say to them?'

Dr Lee looked disconcerted. Understandably. This was supposed to be a press briefing, not an interrogation. 'Well

. . .' He hesitated. 'If the documents are not in order, we take the ivory away.'

Another reporter joined in the cross-examination. 'What is the British government's position on the Hong Kong stockpile?'

'We have explained to them what we want,' Dr Lee replied, more certain of his ground now. 'And they think that the UK's position is complicated by its membership of the European Community. The UK has to consult with the EC, but it is quite sympathetic to us.'

An Australian reporter intervened. 'Your answers seem contradictory, Dr Lee. On the one hand you say you support a ban, on the other hand you want to continue to sell ivory and would review your position if, say, Zimbabwe decided to sell ivory. Do you or do you not support a ban?'

By now Dr Lee's smile was looking rather forced. 'If sustainable yield is possible,' he replied carefully, 'we would find it unfair not to support trade. In the case of Zimbabwe we have been told by many governments and NGOs that Zimbabwe has a managed population of elephants. If they wanted to continue trade, we would have to review the situation.'

The Australian nodded. 'So you don't support a ban.' He wrote briefly in his notebook.

'Dr Lee,' I said, 'is it true that Hong Kong has drafted a resolution to amend CITES Conference Resolution 5.11 so that ivory stocks could continue to be sold indefinitely throughout the world and not only in Hong Kong?' (I had heard a rumour to this effect before I left London.)

Dr Lee looked taken aback. 'Well, yes,' he admitted, 'Hong Kong did draft an amendment, but when we presented it to the CITES secretariat they said there was no need for it. They already had one. You see, there was an international meeting in Botswana in July which asked the secretariat to draft such a resolution.'

I couldn't believe my ears! So, despite Marshall Jones's

firm opposition at the end of the Gaborone meeting, the crucial resolution was being challenged after all. I was furious. 'I must contest what you just said, Dr Lee,' I interrupted. 'I know of that meeting. It was the African Elephant Working Group meeting that you are referring to.'

Dr Lee nodded. 'That's right.'

'I was there,' I announced. Some of the other reporters turned around to look at me. 'In fact in the summing-up the secretariat tried to suggest that such a decision had been made, and some countries strongly objected to such an interpretation.'

Obviously Dr Lee did not attach as much importance to this interpretation by CITES as I did. He looked around the room for a question from someone else.

'Why would a ban be complicated?' another reporter asked tentatively.

Dr Lee shrugged. 'As long as there is a demand, there is a trade,' he said.

'Dr Lee,' I interrupted again, 'are you aware that in Africa, because of trade bans in Europe, the United States and Japan, the price of raw ivory has already been reduced by 60 per cent?'

'Well, I don't know,' he replied impatiently. 'The situation is very complicated. Unless you reduce the demand, the trade will continue. If you were a legal trader who had acquired stock legally, what would you do?' He answered his own question. 'Fight for the trade. And sell your ivory outside CITES if necessary.'

'What would you say to Richard Leakey of Kenya, who, when asked recently what should happen to Hong Kong's ivory, said it should be thrown into the sea?' I queried.

He smiled. 'If they're prepared to pay the money!'

The press officer looked around the room. 'Just one more question, please. We have to vacate this room at four.'

All eyes seemed to be fixed on me. No-one expected me to let Lee off the hook now, and I wasn't going to disappoint them.

'Didn't Hong Kong support Conference Resolution 5.11 in 1985 when it was first drawn up to limit trading in wildlife products to ninety days after any species was transferred to Appendix One?' I asked. Laughter rippled around the room. Acknowledging it with a grin, I said: 'I'm sorry to take the floor again, but the UK certainly backed this resolution. Why should you now support an amendment to have it changed? Isn't it a question of drastic measures for drastic circumstances?'

Dr Lee was openly hostile now. 'I'm afraid I don't know if the UK supported Resolution 5.11, but Hong Kong was not active in CITES at that time anyway.' He stood up. 'Thank you, gentlemen, for your time,' he said firmly.

As soon as Lee had left the room I was approached by Tony Clark, the principal assistant secretary for financial services in Hong Kong. 'You certainly seem to know a lot about all this,' he said curiously, fishing for some clue to my identity.

'I've been following the story for some time,' I replied noncommittally.

Just then a journalist from United Press International came over. 'I hear you're from an environmental group,' he said. Tony Clark flinched visibly.

'Yes, I am,' I admitted. 'But I'm reporting for the London *Sunday Times* today.'

'What's the name of your organization and your name and position?' asked the UPI man.

I was supposed to be here undercover, but what the hell.

'The Environmental Investigation Agency,' I replied. 'I'm Dave Currey, the executive director.' The chance of further publicity for our cause was too good to miss.

The start of the CITES conference was only four days away when I returned to London, and EIA's report, *A System of*

Extinction, subtitled *The African Elephant Disaster*, had just been published. If you counted its two pages of references it came to forty-six pages. The front cover showed one of my photographs of the poached Tsavo elephants taken a year earlier. Satirically, over the dead elephants we had superimposed an official-looking seal, reading 'Approved, CITES Secretariat'. Inside we had spread our evidence over thirteen sections, each relating to one specific aspect of the ivory trade. As well as covering the important countries like South Africa, the United Arab Emirates, Hong Kong and Japan, we had devoted an entire page to the activities of Ian Parker. Another five pages focused on the workings of the CITES secretariat. Our conclusion to this section pulled no punches: 'The secretary-general and a number of his staff are guilty of gross incompetence at the very least. They cannot be trusted to objectively implement the decisions of the Parties and have proven themselves untrustworthy and incompetent to carry out the responsibilities entrusted to them by the Parties.' Advance copies of the report had been sent out to the press. We were certain of only one thing. No-one was going to be able to ignore it.

The press was continuing to give the ivory issue maximum exposure. As promised, the *Mail on Sunday* had attacked the activities of the CITES secretariat in a three page spread. It was a major story, which had instantly awakened the interest of the other British papers. A week later, the *Mail on Sunday* published an exposé of Ian Parker's role in the secretariat's functioning. The secretariat was being very publicly undermined only days before CITES met.

We had just got wind of some disturbing news. The CITES secretariat controlled a fund which had been set up to assist delegates from poorer countries to attend the CITES meeting. Conservationists, governments and traders all contributed to this fund after Lapointe had earlier complained of conservationists who paid for the fares of some delegates, then pressured them to vote for certain measures. Most African delegates were therefore now financially assisted to fly to the meeting in Lausanne, but were routed through Amsterdam where they had a day or two stopover. The African delegates had been informed, when receiving their travel itineraries from the secretariat, that an informal meeting was being arranged there by the Malawi delegate, who was chair of the African regional caucus. However, none of the other African delegates appeared to have been consulted about such a meeting, and we feared that undue pressure might be brought on the delegates to oppose a total ivory ban.

Maureen Plantegenet and Allan flew to Amsterdam to investigate while I remained in London to explain to the press what all this meant. We agreed that I would delay joining the other seven members of the EIA team until the first day of the conference. On the coming Sunday, the *Sunday Times* was to publish a major article based on our report, *A System of Extinction*, and there might well be follow-up interviews to do.

It was heartening on Sunday morning to see the *Sunday Times* give exposure and support to our attack on the secretariat. They quoted a Western European delegate to the convention: 'There is a growing feeling that the CITES secretariat has gone too far. Organizing meetings such as the one in Amsterdam is not within their remit.' In fact I had just learned that the sudden descent of EIA and the press corps on to the secret assembly in Amsterdam had thrown the delegates there into confusion and the intended meeting had not taken place.

On the eve of my departure for Lausanne I was invited to the ITN studios to explain our demand for an investigation into the CITES secretariat. Eugene Lapointe, the secretary-general of CITES, was also interviewed in Lausanne and attempted to defend his position. That same evening *Ivory Wars*, Philip Cayford's beautiful and moving film about the elephant tragedy, to which Jorgen

Thompson had been technical adviser, was shown on BBC television. The following morning Allan was interviewed from Lausanne, again by BBC television. The ivory issue was being given maximum exposure. And, judging by their response to the programmes, the public was overwhelmingly in favour of the ban. If only it were the public who could vote on the issue.

We still had little idea how the conference itself would react to the Tanzanian proposal. Although undoubtedly many delegates were in favour of a ban, the southern African states, Hong Kong, Japan, and the CITES secretariat had all been lobbying hard and there was no telling what political strings may have been pulled.

A System of Extinction: The African Elephant Disaster was our contribution to the arguments. Our challenge now was to present the material it contained eloquently and convincingly to the other delegates. On Monday 9 October 1989 I flew to Switzerland to join my colleagues.

The stage was set.

18

OCTOBER 1989,
LAUSANNE

ALLAN

'These are going like hotcakes.' Charmian bent down to lift another armful of EIA reports from the pile of cardboard boxes on the floor, in the process nearly colliding with Susie who was intent on the same errand.

'You're not kidding,' Susie said. 'People are literally grabbing them out of my hands. Do we have enough?'

We had brought a thousand copies with us to Lausanne, but already I was wishing we had brought more. The report had aroused tremendous interest. All around the hall in Lausanne's Palais de Beaulieu, delegates and conservationists sat with their noses buried in *A System of Extinction* as they waited for the 1989 meeting of CITES to commence.

Representatives from other wildlife societies were gathering around to collect the report.

'So I finally get a copy,' teased Jorgen with a smile.

'Hey, this is some report.' Craig Van Note scanned rapidly through the pages. 'You've really nailed those South Africans!'

Steve Cobb nodded approval. 'It's marvellous work. It's the report I always wanted to write.' Coming from the man who had compiled the report for the Ivory Trade Review Group that was praise indeed.

Television camera teams and journalists from all over the world were milling around feverishly in the hall, asking anyone who wore a name badge what they thought of the prospects for Africa's elephants. The CITES meeting had other species to consider, but at the moment the elephant was the only one the press were interested in.

'BBC Radio here, Allan. Would it be possible to do an interview with you about the CITES secretariat?'

'Allan!' It was Peter Pueschel from Greenpeace Germany. 'German TV would like to interview you about the ivory shipments from Poon's factories that went through Frankfurt.'

'Hello, Allan. Mike McCarthy from *The Times*. Can I ask you EIA's opinion on the British government's attitude towards the Hong Kong ivory trade?'

'ITN here, Allan. We have a shot of the South African delegation reading the EIA report. They went straight to the section on the dealer Pong and South Africa. Could we get film of you talking to the South African delegation?'

I had spoken briefly to Dave on the phone and knew that he was similarly besieged by the press in London. The interest was everything we had hoped for. A vindication of everybody's hard work. I struggled to deal with each request, though after almost an hour of repeating the same arguments my coherence was beginning to suffer. I paused for breath to find Ros standing beside me. The last box of reports was nearly empty.

'Are you going to give EIA's report to Lapointe?' she wanted to know.

'At the right moment,' I replied thoughtfully. 'Don't give him one just yet.'

I was keenly aware of the growing tension in the hall; the world attention focused on this meeting had galvanized everyone – me included. I wondered if this was how an actor felt just before the curtain went up. I thought back to the last CITES meeting in Ottawa in 1987 when Dave and I had been powerless to stop the ivory lobby from dominating the discussions on elephants. Now, in contrast, we were at the forefront of the race to save them.

At the front of the hall was a slightly raised podium where

the chairman and main speakers were to sit. Shortly before the meeting started, Prince Bernhard of the Netherlands, the guest speaker, a former president of WWF, and well known for his commitment to conservation, walked swiftly to the podium. He seated himself between Ralph Morgenwyk, the American chairman of the CITES standing committee, and William Mansfield, the deputy executive director of UNEP, the United Nations Environment Programme. Also on the podium were the mayor of Lausanne and the French chairman of this opening plenary session. Finally Eugene Lapointe, secretary-general of the CITES secretariat, made his entrance, striding importantly towards the stage, shoulders back, chest out. Moments later the chairman declared the meeting open.

Making the opening address, Prince Bernhard summarized what he felt would be the main points for the delegates to consider in the days to come. We were delighted to hear him announce his allegiance to the elephant's cause.

'If doubts persist between trade and the conservation of elephants we must err on the side of conservation,' he declared. 'Equally, it is important that the secretariat maintains its objectivity and impartiality . . .' More funds, the Prince suggested, should be made available to CITES to avoid the need to raise 'outside funding'. There was little doubt that Prince Bernhard's speech had been influenced by EIA's criticisms of CITES.

The next speaker was Eugene Lapointe, responding to Prince Bernhard on behalf of the secretariat. Lapointe was a polished public speaker. He spoke confidently, in the coded language of the politician, glossing over the implied criticism of CITES. His voice, his very appearance, projected respectability, moderation and reason. Unbidden, a picture came into my head of the dead and rotting carcasses at Tsavo, their faces hacked off by machetes. In the past ten years, while men like Eugene Lapointe had been laying people's fears to rest with these same glib reassurances, half of Africa's elephants had been massacred.

Purposefully, while Lapointe carried on speaking, I stood up and picked up a handful of EIA reports. Then slowly, conscious of people's eyes on me, I walked to the front of the hall. Lapointe was making his address from the lectern. Carefully I placed a copy of the report in front of his vacant seat. I saw Lapointe's eyes flicker towards me. Steadily, as he continued his speech, I moved along the podium and handed reports to each of the seated luminaries. William Mansfield, who was in effect Lapointe's boss, scowled disapproval at me. Prince Bernhard, too, recoiled at this breach of etiquette. But etiquette did not concern me. The niceties were over now.

As I walked back towards my seat dozens of faces beamed approval. I sat down, conscious that my heart was pounding. Lapointe was still pontificating. A colleague sitting behind me leaned forward. 'Even Rowan Martin laughed at that,' he whispered.

The rest of the day was taken up with a series of welcoming speeches and administrative announcements. The conference proper was not due to start until the following day, by which time Dave would have arrived from London. I was impatient now. Our preparations were over. We were ready to do battle.

DAVE

The American delegate raised his card. 'Mr Chairman, the whole world is watching us. Although the US strongly supports the concept of sustainable management of wildlife, in the case of the African elephant forces beyond the control of any one nation are conspiring to make any regulation of the ivory trade impossible.'

I leaned over to Allan. 'Thank God the US is supporting Appendix One.' Allan nodded agreement. The American influence was enormous and had generated a flood of ancillary support from nations anxious to associate themselves with America. So far on this opening day things were looking good. But then there was an interruption in the pro-ban speeches from a direction we had not expected. Martin Holdgate, the director of the International Union for the Conservation of Nature and Natural Resources, stood up.

'A uniform pan-African solution is unlikely to be appropriate,' he said. 'The IUCN suggests that the African elephant should be listed on Appendix One in the greater part of Africa, but on Appendix Two in countries meeting objective criteria, and that those countries should have a voluntary moratorium perhaps until the next meeting of CITES.'

I couldn't believe what I was hearing. 'He's just sold out the ivory ban!' I said, dismayed.

'That's going to make our job very difficult over the next few days.' Allan looked grim.

The IUCN is a union of various governmental organizations and conservation groups. It has a scientific bias, is affiliated to WWF and has considerable influence. But Martin Holdgate's suggestion was quite unacceptable. A two-year moratorium would mean that in 1991 we would revert to the same situation as before. Even if only a few southern African states continued to export ivory officially, Hong Kong and Singapore could legitimately keep their trade operating; that would permit the poachers a market into which they could launder their ivory. To permit any trading at all would be to allow poaching to carry on as before. A two-year moratorium would make no difference whatsoever. Did Martin Holdgate suppose the elephant populations could recover in that time?

But the opposition was in full spate now. Rowan Martin, speaking for the Zimbabwean delegation, was playing down the impact of poaching in that country. 'Since 1984 we have been fighting a guerrilla war against rhino poachers and I am pleased to say that concerning poached elephants I doubt if they've even reached double figures yet,' he said.

I could almost see Allan's hackles rise. He raised his

card. 'Mr Chairman,' he protested angrily, 'the Zimbabwe delegate claims that poaching has not reached double figures yet, but his own report says that poaching is on the increase in many parts of Zimbabwe. EIA knows that one thousand elephant carcasses were found last month in the Gonarezhou park, and the Zimbabwean army is heavily involved in this poaching.'

Determined to score as many points against Zimbabwe as possible while he had the floor, Allan pressed on. 'We are also very concerned at the double counting that is occurring across the Botswana and Zimbabwean border. The evidence shows that Zimbabwe counts the elephants when they have migrated across the border, and Botswana counts them again when they return.'

Loud murmurs greeted this revelation. Obviously not every delegate had read our report. But now some of the consumer countries joined in the debate, protesting that the ivory trade provided a livelihood for many of their citizens. This was too much for Costa, who rose to his feet on behalf of Tanzania.

'Mr Chairman, I would like to thank Austria, Hungary and the United States for their far-sightedness and wisdom in supporting the Appendix One listing. It is difficult for us to listen to consumer countries talking about "livelihoods" when people are losing their lives in Tanzania and across Africa trying to protect our elephants.'

This point, that foreign ivory carvers and traders 'earned a living' at the expense of African lives, was a very important one, and other speakers took it up. It was convenient for the bureaucrats who talked in terms of businesses and markets and balance of trade to forget that vital fact. But for Costa and others in similar positions who had seen members of their anti-poaching units mown down by poachers' bullets it was impossible to ignore.

At the close of session it was hard to tell who had scored most points. I felt unsettled. It had been easy before the conference to get carried away by the public response to our films and to feel that the battle was as good as won, but it was becoming clear from their uninformed questions that many of these delegates were hearing the arguments for a ban for the first time; they knew nothing about the issues and would make their minds up solely on what they heard in these few days. Had we said the right things? Had we said enough?

In the main concourse, several booths had been set up with educational materials. Three of these booths – Christine's Animal Welfare Institute, Greenpeace and the Humane Society of the United States of America – were all carrying a display of EIA photographic and film materials. Video machines ran continually, showing the ITN 'Ivory Trail' exposé and extracts from EIA's earlier film *Let Them Live*. As Allan and I stood watching the displays, the Burundi delegate sidled up to us. 'Hello, my friends,' he said ingratiatingly.

It soon became apparent that his friendliness was designed to persuade us to compromise on the amendment to Conference Resolution 5.11 so that trading could continue.

'You know, all Burundi wants is to sell its ivory stock,' he wheedled. 'We are happy to support Appendix One but we must not be penalized.'

'Penalized?' said Allan. 'You must be joking! You don't have any elephants. The stockpile you have is all poached. How do you expect us to take you seriously?'

The Burundi delegate looked hurt. 'Our new government supports conservation. But you must understand that we have to sell our ivory.'

If he wanted sympathy, he was knocking on the wrong door. 'No one wants to buy your ivory any more, though, do they?' I said with satisfaction. Since the American and Japanese restrictions had been introduced, the demand for ivory had dropped dramatically. Whatever CITES decided at this meeting, the attitude of the European and American public towards the slaughter of elephants was already crystal clear. The Burundi delegate looked disconsolate. The plunging price of ivory was one thing he could not deny.

The BBC World Service wanted to interview the main participants in the elephant debate, and I found myself sharing a taxi to the studio with Costa, Rowan Martin and Jean Patric Le Duc. Le Duc was a former worker in the French conservation movement but he was now employed by the CITES secretariat as enforcement and press officer.

He was in bantering mood. 'How can you say I am corrupt?' he demanded as we waited in the studio for the presenter to arrive. 'I paid for the taxi and now you are corrupted, too.'

'EIA has never said that you are corrupt,' I objected. 'But we do think that there are a great number of questions that need to be answered regarding the secretariat's activities and ethics over the last few years.'

Neither Costa nor Rowan Martin joined in this exchange. Costa was staring out of the window looking depressed. He sensed the mood of the meeting was turning against Tanzania and had told Allan earlier that he had phoned his ministry to tell them: 'We might lose it.' His words had been greeted with incredulity by his staff. They had come so far, they protested. Surely they couldn't lose now. But Costa wasn't so sure.

Rowan Martin was pacing around the room chain-smoking. He certainly wasn't behaving like someone who thought he'd won the day. I guessed that the latest intervention by Victoria Chitepo, the Zimbabwean Natural Resources Minister, had thrown him somewhat. Mrs Chitepo, the widow of a famous freedom fighter, wielded considerable power in Zimbabwe, but she had just announced at a press conference that she categorically refused to support any moratorium on ivory trading in Zimbabwe. The proposal for a temporary one- or two-year moratorium, in exchange for allowing Zimbabwe and South Africa's elephants to remain on Appendix Two, had won many people over to Zimbabwe's side. It had given her a moderate image, that of a nation willing to compromise. Now Mrs Chitepo had undone all that and had left Rowan Martin with little room to manoeuvre. Maybe, after all, Costa's pessimism was premature.

Both Rowan Martin and Le Duc used the broadcast to defend their superiors' actions rather than to enter fresh debate with me or Costa. While Martin struggled to justify Mrs Chitepo's stance, Le Duc desperately tried to salvage the reputation of his secretary-general, Eugene Lapointe, who was now under fire from all quarters. The strain on both their spokesmen was, in my opinion, beginning to show.

'There's hardly any sympathy for Hong Kong.' Isabel McCrea from Greenpeace fell into step with me as we came out of the Asian regional group meeting which we had attended as observers.

'No, except from the British delegation,' I replied drily. 'They won't tell anyone what the British position is.'

Isabel pursed her lips reflectively. 'There's only one possible reason as far as I can see. They must be going to support or abstain on the vote to overturn Conference Resolution 5.11. If they do that, it'll mean Hong Kong can continue ivory trading.'

The British press had been using all their powers of persuasion to get Chris Follands, head of the British delegation, to declare the British position on Hong Kong, but his only response so far was an obdurate 'No comment'. The reporters here were becoming increasingly annoyed at his evasive replies. The British government had received a lot of favourable publicity over its decision to ban the ivory trade in Britain, and its stance on Hong Kong was seen as hypocritical. Earlier in the week *The Times* had carried the headline 'Britain in Row over Hong Kong Ivory', and many other papers had taken up the story.

But the criticism had made little impression on Follands,

who continued to fudge the issue. 'We shall listen to all the arguments and then we shall see what happens,' was his standard noncommittal response.

ALLAN

Elephants were not the only endangered species being discussed. Whispers from other meetings reached us from time to time. And some of them revealed more disturbing facts about the activities of the secretariat.

'What's this I hear about the secretariat deal with the Cayman lizard skins?' I asked of Jorgen.

He threw me a cautionary glance and motioned me into a nearby anteroom where he shut the door firmly behind us.

'The secretariat received a payment of eighty-thousand dollars from the sale of confiscated lizard skins in Guyana,' he said quietly. 'It was a species of lizard that doesn't occur in Guyana, so it's certain they were smuggled illegally from another country. Apparently the secretariat arranged to sell the skins to a dealer in Japan and to have the money paid into CITES' bank account. Of course an arrangement like that goes against the direct orders of the standing committee. Their directive is that the secretariat shouldn't receive money from the sale of confiscated specimens.'

'And what have they done with the money?' I asked.

'Well, that's the crucial part,' Jorgen smiled wryly. 'The secretariat haven't included the eighty-thousand-dollar payment in their budget report to this CITES meeting.'

I gave him a sideways look. 'Oh, haven't they, indeed? And is anyone going to do anything about that?'

'The US delegation are about to confront the secretariat with it in the budget committee.' Jorgen looked at me warningly, anticipating my intentions. 'You have to keep this quiet until that happens. OK?'

Obediently I waited until the budget committee was in session before going to Mike McCarthy from *The Times* and passing on Jorgen's bombshell. As I'd hoped, news of the illicit payment spread rapidly. By the time the budget meeting ended, a mob of journalists was waiting to question the secretariat and the American delegation about the deal. The secretariat had little option but to arrange a press conference for later that day to defend their position.

For most of the wildlife groups this latest revelation was the final straw. After consulting with various groups I drafted a letter to Mostafa Tolba, head of the United Nations Environment Programme, calling for Lapointe's resignation. Within two hours, twenty-four groups from all over the world had signed it. A day later the number of signatories had grown to thirty-eight.

To everyone's frustration Eugene Lapointe did not put in an appearance at the secretariat press conference. 'Why is Mr Lapointe not here?' demanded an angry pressman. Jacques Berney, representing Lapointe, did his best to defend the secretariat's actions, but his arguments were sounding more and more unconvincing and muddled. The open letter to Mostafa Tolba was distributed around the room.

'Do you have any response to a call by these organizations for the resignation of Mr Lapointe?' asked Mike McCarthy.

'I have no comment as I have not seen this,' Berney replied tight-lipped.

'Do you have any comment on the statement by the head of the US delegation that Eugene Lapointe has exceeded his authority and they intend to take the issue up with UNEP?'

But Berney refused to be drawn. 'The US is free to do as it wishes.'

McCarthy tried again. 'Can you tell us when Mr Lapointe will be available to talk to the press himself?'

Berney shrugged. 'Mr Lapointe is a very busy man. I do not know if he will be available.'

It was stalemate.

But there was some evidence that the discontent with his leadership was getting through to Lapointe. I was a guest at a reception hosted by the French delegation and was sipping champagne with the chief Japanese delegate as we discussed his country's policies and its changing attitude to the environment. As the Japanese delegate filled my glass with more champagne Eugene Lapointe walked into the room and headed immediately for the group of people standing behind me. Suddenly my elbow was jogged from behind and champagne spilled down the front of my suit.

'Oops!' said Lapointe innocently.

I swung around to face him. He regarded me warily. Somewhere I remembered reading that he helped with the coaching of his local hockey team back in his native Canada. 'I bet you're a hell of a hockey coach, Mr Lapointe,' I said levelly. Lapointe acknowledged my words with the ghost of a smile.

'I am, too!' he said.

DAVE

Lapointe continued to appear at various sessions, though we noticed that other members of the secretariat seemed to be carrying out most of his public tasks. If nothing else, our resignation call seemed to have made him reluctant to stick his head above the ramparts. But Lapointe was a secondary concern to us now.

An informer had told us that the Japanese delegation was divided. Half of them were in favour of a ban; the other half were against it. Disturbingly when I spoke to Mr Takimoto, a Japanese delegate, he quoted the IUCN position back at me. The IUCN suggestion of a two-year moratorium for South Africa, Botswana and Zimbabwe could be our undoing, as we had suspected when it was first mooted. All we could do was to repeat our reservations about such a split listing. And repeat them. And repeat them. 'It would allow continued trade which would give the illegal traders ample opportunities for smuggling,' I pleaded with Mr Takimoto. 'There are no ivory trade controls that can be trusted to work. History proves that.'

But Mr Takimoto kept returning relentlessly to the IUCN position. We suspected that the idea of a split listing was extremely attractive to delegates who really wanted to oppose the ban but did not want to be seen to be opposing it. To our consternation WWF were now also pushing for this option.

The EIA delegation had been keeping a count of the way countries intended to vote. We needed a two-thirds majority vote to push the Appendix One listing through. On the basis of declared intentions we were very close to that, but there were still ten or fifteen countries who were keeping their intentions to themselves and might still be sitting on the fence. We could not afford to let up the pressure for a moment.

Friday the 13th. Tension was mounting in the meeting of Committee One. This was the crucial phase. Committee One dealt with changes to Appendices. If the Appendix One proposal was passed here, then its adoption by the full plenary session should be a mere formality. There was a strong feeling amongst many delegates that delaying the Appendix One vote until after the weekend would damage our prospects. 'There are countries that want to discuss other endangered species,' Costa pointed out. 'They're becoming frustrated, and if we don't have the vote soon they'll be angry.'

The discussions continued fruitlessly throughout the afternoon. Nothing new was being said now. We were just going round in circles. Eventually the Austrian delegate protested. 'Mr Chairman, we are tired of all this filibustering. We call for a vote on the Appendix One listing right now!'

Under the rules of procedure a call for a vote meant it had to take place immediately; but Peter Dollinger, the Swiss delegate who was chairing the meeting, refused to call the vote. Dollinger had been making censorious comments whenever delegates expressed support of Appendix One. 'We will not proceed with the vote now,' Dollinger insisted.

There was a clamour of protest. 'We challenge the chairman's ruling,' complained one delegate. 'We wish to have a vote on it.'

Reluctantly succumbing to the pressure, Dollinger said: 'All those voting Yes, please raise your cards . . .' No-one knew what he meant. A handful of cards went up hesitantly, wavered and came down again. 'And all those against raise your cards.'

There was a confused murmur. 'Mr Chairman,' shouted a delegate, 'we don't know what we are voting for.' The vote was halted amid a wave of questions and exclamations from the delegates.

'I will explain the vote again,' said Dollinger, exasperated now. 'If you agree with my ruling, you vote No and if you support my ruling – I'm sorry – I mean if you oppose my ruling, you vote Yes.'

Even the English-speakers were confused by this time, while the non-English-speaking delegates looked totally bewildered. 'Mr Chairman! Mr Chairman!' Commotion erupted around the hall.

Dollinger glanced around, and his eyes alighted on Jacques Berney. 'The secretariat will now explain what you are voting for,' he said, passing the buck.

'Uh-oh,' Allan said. 'Here comes total confusion!'

Berney turned his microphone on.

'If you don't agree with the chairman's ruling, vote Yes; and, if you oppose the chairman's ruling, vote No.'

By now no-one had a clue what the chairman's ruling was. The frustration of the assembled delegates threatened to reduce the meeting to chaos.

Allan raised his eyebrows. 'And the future of the elephant has been in the hands of these people!'

Someone finally clarified the vote, and it was called.

Disappointingly, a majority of countries supported the chairman's ruling against allowing an immediate vote on the Appendix One listing and it was, after all, delayed over the weekend. But as the meeting broke up many of the non-English delegates were grumbling. 'Some of them still thought they were voting in favour of an immediate vote,' said Costa despairingly.

'I think we're losing it, Dave,' said Allan dejectedly after the Committee One meeting broke up. 'Unless we can get WWF and the IUCN to support a complete ban, the elephants have had it.'

I shared his gloom. 'What can we do?'

Allan looked suddenly purposeful. 'I'm going to talk to them.'

I nodded. 'OK. I'm going to the NGO meeting now. I'll see what I can do there.'

The non-governmental organizations met at the end of each session to discuss the issues that had been raised that day. Jeff Canin of Greenpeace International was chairing the meeting today. 'Dave wants to raise an important issue,' he announced when everyone was assembled. I stood up.

'EIA is finding that its lobbying is being undermined by both the IUCN and WWF. We are all fighting for a complete ivory ban, and it is my understanding that WWF has publicly stated that this is their goal also. At this moment they are meeting in a separate room, and I think we need to let them know just how we feel about them.'

'Dave's right,' said Christine Stevens from the back of the room. 'I say WWF should account for themselves, because the public believe they are lobbying for a ban.'

There was a general buzz of agreement around the room. A lot of frustration and anger was brewing now among the wildlife groups, who felt they had been betrayed.

'Maybe we should get together with WWF now and discuss this,' suggested Greenpeace Germany's Peter Pueschel.

'I think Allan's arranging a meeting with them at this very moment,' I said.

I was breaching etiquette again but I had no choice. If I didn't step in, the ivory ban was in danger of slipping out of reach. I knocked lightly on the door of the room where I knew the WWF/Traffic group was meeting, and walked in. Twenty heads turned in my direction.

'Excuse me for interrupting your meeting,' I apologized, 'but there are a lot of strong feelings with the other NGOs that the conservationists are divided in support for Appendix One and that we're going to lose very heavily as a result.'

Tom Milliken of Traffic, WWF's trade monitoring group, protested: 'Gee, Allan, we've been consistent right through the whole meeting. We said we'd accept that some southern African countries could be exempted from Appendix One as long as they stop ivory trading for two years.'

'That may be so, Tom, but a lot of delegates are confused. If you and the IUCN are saying that something less than a complete ivory ban is acceptable, then your view differs from that of other conservationists.'

Before any of them could respond I continued: 'The flaw in the WWF position is that it's going to be impossible to restrict exemptions to Zimbabwe, Botswana and South Africa. Now that the possibility of exemptions has been raised it is snowballing. More and more African countries are trying to exempt themselves from a ban. Nine countries so far; probably more by Monday. There were two new resolutions submitted today. If we don't do something to present a united position from the conservation groups, we are going to lose this,' I warned. 'And we are going to lose very badly.'

At least they were listening to me. I saw Jorgen conferring with his neighbours. Then he looked over to me. 'We should talk some more later, Allan. We have to work together on this Appendix One listing.'

'Could I suggest that a few people from your group

meet with a few people from the other NGOs so we can try to agree on a strategy? We could get together in the bar downstairs when you've finished your meeting.'

'Is that all right with the people here?' Jorgen asked. There was a murmur of consent. Jorgen gave a brief nod. 'OK, we'll see you downstairs after our meeting in an hour.'

We convened in the bar as arranged, but the 'few people' from each group had grown to thirty and the debate became so heated that it was unmanageable. After an hour and a half Dave and I suggested that we reconvene a smaller group out in the reception area. Eventually ten people sat down to continue the discussion. The group included Jorgen, Christine, Steve Cobb, Sue Lieberman and Tom Milliken as well as Dave and myself.

'We have to have a united position,' I repeated yet again. 'We know that WWF, Traffic and the IUCN want to allow some southern African states to keep their elephants on Appendix Two provided they ban ivory trading for two years. But Zimbabwe has just said they will not agree to a ban under any circumstances, so that strategy is dead. That being the case, can WWF and Traffic now support a total Appendix One listing?'

Jorgen attempted to explain WWF's motives for backing a split listing. 'The concern some people have is that once elephants are listed on Appendix One the existing regulations make it very difficult to move them back down to Appendix Two. We want to have the possibility that some countries can downlist if they can show a good management of their elephants and the ivory trade.'

Another whirlwind of discussion ensued. After twenty minutes Christine stood up. 'I have to go now, but I just wanted to say that this is the most important issue this convention has ever faced.' She glared at Jorgen. 'I want WWF to know one thing. I'm a bad loser. If we lose the ivory ban because of WWF, I will write to every one of your supporters to tell them that it happened because of your organization.' With that Christine swept out of the meeting.

Jorgen looked as though he'd been mugged. 'I don't need that kind of shit!' he exclaimed.

'That was very destructive,' Steve Cobb agreed.

One up for Christine, I thought. They hadn't expected an attack from that quarter. Christine was a much respected figure in Washington conservation circles, and her uncharacteristic outburst underlined the depth of her feeling on this issue. She wasn't going to let WWF sell out now. And nor were we.

But I had to recognize the WWF position. A split in the conservation movement was the last thing we needed. Was there a way we could get back on the same side? To a limited extent I understood Jorgen's argument. If countries with a lot of elephants felt that promotion to Appendix One was permanent, they were quite likely to be reluctant to support it.

'OK, look,' I said thoughtfully. 'Can WWF agree to support the Appendix One listing if it was agreed that special criteria would be established to allow certain countries to downlist in the future?'

Tom and Jorgen looked at each other. 'Well, yeah,' said Jorgen cautiously. 'We'd all go along with that.'

It was a major breakthrough. With an agreement in sight at last the impromptu meeting broke up. Jorgen came up to me as I headed out of the reception area. He still looked wary. 'I want your personal commitment that you're going to support this,' he demanded.

I nodded. 'Don't worry. You have it.'

The amendment I had suggested was one that had in fact already been put forward by the Somalia delegate on Friday but too late in the day to be read out. To the uninformed it might seem little different from the IUCN proposal for a moratorium, but in fact it was much more restrictive. Its big advantage over the moratorium was that the countries who wished to resume trading in two years' time would have to *prove* their case whereas with the IUCN proposal trading would resume automatically in 1991. The difference was crucial. Admittedly we would have another battle to fight in 1991 when the southern African countries were likely to try to downgrade their elephants back to Appendix Two; but the onus of proving good elephant management and control over the trade would be on them, and EIA for one would make certain they could not pull the wool over people's eyes as they had in the past.

On Sunday night the NGOs met again, and I explained EIA's backing of the new proposals. There was only minor dissension. By the end of the meeting all the wildlife groups were at last united behind the Appendix One listing. All we had to do now was to persuade everyone else to join us in backing the Somali amendment. It was not going to be easy. Because it had not been read out, most delegates were unaware of the existence of the Somali amendment. We had very little time now to bring it to their attention. In the few hours before the meeting started the eight-person EIA team lobbied like people possessed.

On Monday morning a paper was distributed at the resumed Committee One meeting showing the resolution for an Appendix One listing together with three amendments.

The first amendment, proposed by Zimbabwe, Botswana, Malawi and Mozambique, was designed to adjust the Appendix One listing to exclude their own elephant populations. They also wanted to exclude Namibia and Angola, although neither was a party to CITES! The second amendment was similar except that the countries applying for exclusion were Cameroon, Congo and Gabon. The third amendment was the Somali amendment.

Just before the vote was called, Simon Lyster, evidently influenced by Jorgen, spoke for the first time on behalf of WWF. Dramatically he appealed to the assembled delegates 'on my knees' to support the Somali amendment.

The Zimbabwe and Gabon proposals were to be voted on

first. If they failed to get the necessary two-thirds majority, the full Appendix One proposal – for a total ban – would be put to the vote. Only if that, too, failed to get a two-thirds majority would the Somali amendment be put before the delegates. If any of these resolutions was passed, it would then need to be confirmed in the full plenary session of CITES, but in this case that was considered a formality. Frequently Committee One meetings were attended by only a minority of delegates, but this Committee One meeting had attracted virtually a full complement of delegates, such was the interest in the elephant issue.

If all the resolutions failed to get adopted, the entire debate would have to be reopened.

'We will proceed with the proposal from Zimbabwe first,' said Dollinger after he had explained the voting arrangements.

Rowan Martin immediately raised Zimbabwe's card. 'Mr Chairman, Zimbabwe calls for a secret ballot on this vote.'

Dozens of cards shot into the air in protest. A secret ballot would be a disaster. Countries who had declared support for the elephants could renege on their commitment with impunity.

'Is there a seconder for this proposal?' asked Dollinger quickly. Gambia, Zambia and Botswana all raised their cards.

'Gambia has the floor,' Dollinger announced. But he had made the wrong choice.

'Gambia opposes the Zimbabwe proposal for a secret ballot, Mr Chairman.'

Dollinger looked vexed. 'We have a challenge from Gambia. That means I must put Zimbabwe's proposal to the vote,' he said. 'All those in favour of a secret ballot raise your delegate cards.'

A small flurry of red cards shot into the air. I scanned them with interest: Switzerland, China, Zimbabwe, Zambia, Botswana, Mozambique, Burundi, Botswana, South Africa, Venezuela, Sweden. Not many surprises there.

'All those opposing a secret ballot?' Dollinger asked. An ocean of red cards waved furiously.

'The motion by Zimbabwe for a secret ballot has been defeated,' said Dollinger. 'And now we start the vote with the Zimbabwean proposal which is identified in document 7.43.6.'

Dave, Ros and I exchanged glances. 'Here we go,' I said.

'Austria – No; Bangladesh – No; Belize – No; Benin – Yes; Bolivia – No; Botswana – Yes; Brazil – No; Burundi – Yes; Cameroon – Yes . . .'

'They've lost it,' said Dave well before the last of the ninety countries cast their votes.

Dollinger stood up. 'The vote is twenty in favour and seventy against, and therefore the motion fails.' He looked down at his notes. 'The next vote is on the Gabon proposal, which is document 7.43.7 in your papers.'

Even fewer countries supported the Gabon proposal. 'Eight in favour and eighty-three countries against,' Dollinger announced several minutes later. He cleared his throat.

'And now we come to the Appendix One proposal, the unamended version, as proposed by Austria, Gambia, Hungary, Kenya, Tanzania and the US . . .'

'Belize – Yes; Benin – No; Bolivia – Yes; Botswana – No; Brazil – No; Burundi – No; Cameroon – No; Canada – Yes; Central African Republic – Yes; Chad – Yes; Chile – Yes; China – No; Colombia – No; Congo – No.' It was going against us.

'This motion has failed to gain the necessary majority,' said Dollinger dispassionately. 'There were fifty-three votes in favour and thirty-six votes against.'

There was a ripple of reaction among the delegates as the closeness of the voting sank in.

'Only six votes in it,' breathed Ros.

'At least the UK voted yes,' I noted.

'This is it,' said Dave as Dollinger announced the Somalia proposal: the Appendix One listing with special criteria to allow downlisting of a country's population, if appropriate, at any future CITES meeting.

'China – No; Colombia – Yes; Congo – No; Costa Rica – Yes . . .'

As the votes were being cast, my mind was flooded with images from the past two years. I thought of Sidney risking his life to track the ivory dealers in Tanzania, of Daphne Sheldrick and her elephant orphans. I thought of the elderly man who had sent us a thousand pounds with the message 'I can't think of anything better to spend my money on than ensuring that elephants survive for future generations'. I thought of Paul Sarakikya's anti-poaching squad who risked their lives protecting elephants for ten pounds a month. So many people's hopes all hung on this moment.

'Rwanda – Yes; Saint Lucia – Yes; St Vincent – Yes; Senegal – Yes; Singapore – Yes; Somalia – Yes; South Africa – No . . .'

Dave and I looked at each other for a fraction of a second and then looked away. I could tell he sensed, as I did, that we were going to win. But neither of us dared to believe it. We had to wait for the official announcement.

'The result of the vote is as follows,' said Dollinger. 'There were four abstentions, eleven against, and seventy-six in favour. Therefore the motion is passed.'

For a brief moment the entire room was still. No-one uttered a word as the meaning of Dollinger's words sank in.

The ivory trade, which had existed since time immemorial, which had inexorably been pushing the earth's elephants towards extinction, was finally illegal.

Somewhere someone began to clap, and slowly a gentle applause started in the hall, building gradually like a growing wind. I turned to Dave and we hugged each other, and then we were exchanging hugs, kisses and handshakes with the rest of the EIA team. There were tears in everyone's eyes. Around us the applause grew and grew. People were standing up in their places, cheering and clapping.

In vain Dollinger attempted to regain control of the proceedings. 'This display is not . . .' he began. But he was drowned out by the noise of the ovation. In front of me on the other side of the aisle, Professor Pfeiffer who was sitting with the rest of the French delegation turned around, caught my eye and let out a piercing whistle of approbation.

It was too much for Dollinger. 'Get him out! Get him out!' he screamed, pointing at me. He thought I was the one who had whistled, when in fact it was one of the most respected delegates!

'Out!' Dollinger bellowed again, almost incoherent with rage now. 'Out! Secretariat! Get him out!' He jabbed his index finger repeatedly towards me. Hundreds of people turned their heads in my direction, then back to Dollinger. Jacques Berney stood up in his place and seemed about to stride towards me to do Dollinger's bidding when someone whispered something to them, at the same time gesturing towards Professor Pfeiffer. Dollinger's hand faltered in mid-air as he realized his error, and Berney sank back into his seat. Dollinger was covered in confusion. 'I would never have thought that a *delegate* would do such a thing,' he muttered in embarrassment, his microphone picking up every word.

The drama at an end, people started to stand up and walk out of the hall. 'It's over,' I thought numbly, then smiled as I looked over and saw Costa being congratulated by everyone around him. I gave a thumbs-up to a jubilant-looking Jorgen and then, as Dave and I turned to go, we found ourselves facing Christine, our fund-raiser, our mentor, our inspiration. Her eyes were bright with elation; her expression spoke for her. I gripped her hands in mine. 'Christine, thank you so much for everything you've done for the elephants.' Dave echoed me, nodding. 'Thank you, Christine.'

★

It had been a long haul, and even now the battle was not quite over. The following day the plenary session was to adopt the resolution in what should, as we knew, have been a mere formality; but we had a few heart-stopping hours when we learned that the agenda of the morning session had been rearranged and the plenary vote postponed.

It emerged that Zimbabwe and Botswana had said they would leave CITES unless they were allowed to submit a proposal to the plenary requesting exemption for their populations from the Appendix One listing. I was incensed. In my opinion, and Dave's, too, if the southern African delegations would not agree to be bound by a democratic vote, then they should be allowed to resign. Yet it appeared the bureau were submitting to the blackmail. And worse, much worse, WWF were yielding to it, too. Simon Lyster and Buff Bohlen had joined the bureau meeting to discuss whether the committee vote should be changed.

Furious at the possibility that backroom wheeling and dealing might yet stop a total ivory ban from being passed, I telephoned a senior staff contact at WWF International and asked for a personal message to be passed to Charles de Haes, the secretary-general: 'If WWF does anything to endorse or accept the overturning of the Appendix One vote, we will ensure that they are publicly denounced for selling out the ivory ban,' I promised. Surely we couldn't lose it now; it would be too cruel.

We didn't lose it. After spending the morning in suspense we learned that the bureau had been unable to reach agreement on the exemption plea. It was Zimbabwe who had blown it. If only Mrs Chitepo hadn't refused to allow a moratorium, a compromise would probably have been reached. But in taking that stand the Zimbabweans had effectively shot themselves in the foot. Jorgen and Steve Cobb had made use of the delay to draft a resolution which spelled out the strict criteria for allowing downlisting of elephants to Appendix Two in the future. The regulations they suggested were tough and uncompromising, and required absolute proof of good elephant management by any country applying to downlist. Stable populations and control over poaching, as well as effective trade controls, would all have to be proved to the satisfaction of a committee of experts appointed by CITES.

At two o'clock in the afternoon the plenary session was at last called to order. Camera lights lit up the hall as the chairman of the session came to the Appendix One listing. A Zimbabwe delegate interrupted the proceedings to make a statement on behalf of Zimbabwe, Botswana, South Africa and Malawi. They intended, he announced, to take out reservations to an Appendix One listing. Burundi endorsed this statement. 'Taking reservations' meant they were putting themselves out on a limb and refusing to be bound by a CITES decision, but it was a fairly futile gesture. Since all the consumer nations *had* agreed to be bound by the decision these countries would have great difficulty in finding a market for their ivory. In effect the victory was still ours. Moments later the French chairman of the plenary session confirmed it when he announced that the Committee One recommendation was accepted.

There were still other battles to be fought that afternoon, but we were riding on the crest of a wave now. With such universal acclaim of the CITES decision its critics stood no chance. Hong Kong's attempt to be exempted from the ban was firmly put down. So was its attempt to continue trading its existing stocks by overturning Conference Resolution 5.11. Efforts by Burundi supported by the CITES secretariat to get its ivory stockpile legalized were also defeated. We had won on almost every front.

As the proceedings were formally brought to a close, press and friends once more gathered round to share the celebrations.

Earlier the Burundi delegate had denounced EIA as 'enemies of the people'. However, now even he walked up with a smile to say 'Congratulations'.

Perhaps the most gratifying tribute came from Dr Ron

Orenstein, a Canadian conservationist who had defended us against that Burundi attack.

'EIA has achieved something that has been needed for years,' he declared. 'They have exposed the illegal ivory trade for what it really is and risked their lives to do so. We should all thank them for that.'

Outside the hall we were besieged as wellwishers descended on us from all sides. Our hands moved euphorically from person to person; acknowledging congratulations, sharing the achievement with delegates and NGOs. Today we had changed history. Between us we had eventually brought about what people had said was impossible.

The ivory war was not over. Perhaps it would never be completely over. There would be a great deal more work for EIA to do before the next CITES meeting in Japan in the spring of 1992. The traders would not give up their livelihood easily. But for the time being at least the elephants had a breathing-space. Hopefully, now too they had a future.

'I don't know about you, Dave,' I said, 'but I feel like a holiday.' With a smile I suggested: 'How about going to see some *live* elephants . . . ?'

EPILOGUE

NOVEMBER 1989,
TANZANIA

The clatter of tusks against tree-trunks echoed through the woods. Cautiously we drove round to the other side of the crater and stopped as we reached a clearing where a few dead trees lay on the ground. A dream-like scene met our eyes. As we watched, half a dozen huge elephants walked slowly and purposefully in Indian file into the clearing and began to browse on the branches of the fallen trees. The bright midday sun reflected off their wrinkled skin and their enormous curling tusks.

These were old elephants; the oldest we had ever seen; their tusks so long they curved right round until they touched each other. Against the odds they had survived the elephant holocaust in a natural haven: Tanzania's spectacular Ngorongoro Crater, an extinct volcano twenty kilometres across which had collapsed inwards ten thousand years ago. Protected for decades from the attention of poachers by the steep crater walls, these ancients presented us with a vision of the past; of how things used to be. Hopefully, it was now a vision of the future, too.

The elephants chewed meditatively at their food, taking no notice of the two people watching them. To them, humans had never been a cause for fear. A little later, having eaten their fill, they walked majestically back towards the protective shade of the forest and disappeared from view.

POSTSCRIPT

Since October 1989, when African elephants were placed on Appendix One of CITES, the demand for ivory products in Europe and America has declined dramatically. In reaction to the plummeting value of ivory on the international market, elephant poaching has slowed down across much of east, central and western Africa.

On the political front there have also been many changes in the past two years. Eugene Lapointe was removed from his position as secretary general of the CITES Secretariat following the widespread criticism of his leadership. There is hope that under the new secretary general, Izgrev Topkov, CITES will emphasize its responsibilities towards wildlife conservation.

The reprieve from ivory poaching has allowed many African nations to begin to implement new conservation plans to protect their elephants. But some southern African states have been undermining the CITES ban by filing reservations to it. Now, Zimbabwe, South Africa, Botswana, Malawi, Zambia and Namibia have signed an agreement to set up an ivory marketing centre, to be located in Botswana.

Zimbabwe and South Africa are spearheading efforts to overturn the Appendix One listing at the next meeting of CITES to be held in Kyoto, Japan in March, 1992. In response, the Environmental Investigation Agency resumed undercover operations to study the illegal ivory trade in these southern African states.

Contrary to the rest of Africa where elephant poaching is declining, many southern Africa nations are experiencing continued illegal ivory trading, and increased poaching. Poachers have been encouraged by Zimbabwean and South African attempts to overturn the ivory ban, and are concentrating their efforts in this region of Africa.

Our investigations have uncovered the most disturbing revelations of a terrifying and murderous cover up of illicit poaching and smuggling by the Zimbabwe army. A smuggling network operating there is linked through Mozambique, South Africa, Zambia, Malawi, and Namibia.

In January 1990, Captain Edwin Bhundani Nleya, an investigator with the Zimbabwe National Army (ZNA) was found hanged from a tree in Zimbabwe's Hwange National Park. Nleya had uncovered a major elephant and rhino poaching operation run by top commanders in the Zimbabwe army stationed in Mozambique. Nleya was followed by his assassins on a train from Harare to Hwange. Just before he was killed Nleya telephoned his wife to warn her that he was in imminent mortal danger.

The Zimbabwe army's poaching and smuggling activities are well known for their activities in the Gonarezhou Park and in Mozambique. Detailed allegations linking army activities with wildlife department officials have been reported to the Government by some of Zimbabwe's most loyal and courageous conservationists. But appeals for a government inquiry have been ignored by President Mugabe.

Efforts by Zimbabwe conservationists to counter the army's growing interest in elephant and rhino poaching have met with a brutal response, ranging from Nleya's murder to death threats and other forms of intense harassment.

In South Africa the illicit ivory trade continues to thrive despite concerted efforts by the Endangered Species Protection Unit. Ivory from Zaire, Zambia, Zimbabwe, Malawi and Mozambique continues to flow through South Africa on its way to Taiwan.

Ivory moves back and forth between South Africa and Mozambique, piggy backed onto a complex web of military skulduggery involving the Renamo armed insurgents, the Frelimo government and an entrenched network of poachers, smugglers and spies that has devastated Mozambique's wildlife.

Elephant poaching in Zambia remains intense. Security forces there are also involved in poaching and rent their weapons to poaching gangs. Malawi has become a collection centre for poached ivory being smuggled onwards to South Africa.

As the Zimbabwean and South African cover up becomes ever more disturbing, the pro-ivory trading arguments are pouring out of those nations. Their arguments never mention the poaching or illicit smuggling of ivory by their military bosses.

The fate of the world's elephants may rest on the misguided willingness of the world to accept claims by the southern African countries that they have effective control over illicit ivory trading and meaningful protection for their elephant populations.

Should the world risk the extinction of elephants in thirty African nations to allow a handful of states to trade ivory? Our investigations underline the need for a resounding 'NO' to that question.

EIA will be doing all it can to uphold and enforce the international ban on the trade in elephant products. In doing so, we would like to pay tribute to the dedicated and courageous conservationists, and enforcement agents in Africa who are striving – often at the risk of their lives or livelihoods – to save the elephants.

Dave Currey
Allan Thornton
October 1991

If you would like to support the Environmental Investigation Agency, you can become a supporting member for £12 a year.

Your help towards protecting elephants, dolphins, wild birds and other endangered species will be greatly appreciated.

You can contact EIA at:

208–209 Upper Street
London N1 1RL

INDEX